tasty

Get Great Food on the Table Every Day

Roy Finamore

Photographs by Tina Rupp

Houghton Mifflin Company
Boston New York 2006

Visit our Web site: www.houghtonmifflinbooks.com.

Library of Congress Cataloging-in-Publication Data

Finamore, Roy.
Tasty : get great food on the table every day / Roy Finamore ; photographs by Tina Rupp.
p. cm.
Includes index.
ISBN-10: 0-618-24033-0
ISBN-13: 978-0-618-24033-3
1. Cookery. I. Title.
TX714.F56 2006
641.5—dc22 2005030153

Book design by Marysarah Quinn

Printed in the United States of America

MP 10 9 8 7 6 5 4 3 2 1

This is for Mom and Dad

acknowledgments

Over the years that it's taken me to write *Tasty*, many supportive voices have urged me on and offered help in a variety of guises. A few words on a page can do little to eliminate my debt to these friends, but I'd be a fool not to let the world know who has helped me.

Molly Stevens, my partner on *One Potato, Two Potato,* remains my ultimate cooking companion, even though we live in different states. I have to tell you that a friend you can complain with, gossip with, cook with, and have a telephone-and-drinks date with is a special treat. And when that friend tests recipes and tells you how eager her husband is for your book to come out? Be jealous, world. And thank you too, Mark Smith.

Without Marian Young, there would be no *Tasty*. Marian has been the gently motivating presence behind the book, tasting, washing dishes, reading, and saying, sensibly, "Just finish the book." Tom Pearson was again a great help, and he and his mom, Sarah Ann Pearson, continue to educate me about good, simple Southern food.

Over many years working as an editor, I have been incredibly lucky with authors, and I have learned something from each one of them. More, some have become friends. How can I not thank Diana Kennedy for years of friendship and support and Scourgedom? Or Carole Walter, for the check-in phone calls and recipe advice and reality checks? Or Constance Snow, who continues to promise her *Bad Tasty* CD? Don't get me started on John Martin Taylor, who may have problems with the rubber gasket on a jar of cherry peppers, but who just shares and shares and shares his enthusiasm for and vast knowledge of food. And who introduced me to his partner, the wonderful Mikel Herrington. Or Susan Simon, either, the first of my authors when I was at Clarkson Potter. Thank you all.

And thank you to Ina Garten, and Tom Colicchio, and Martha Rose Shulman, and Karen De Masco, and Jim Fobel, and Jean Anderson, and Gale Gand, and Martha Stewart, and Georges Blanc, and Anne Willan, and Anna Tasca Lanza, and Nigel Slater. I must also acknowledge two very important influences, both sadly beyond the reach of these words. Lee Bailey had an ease and grace and style with food that we all should envy. And for generosity and integrity, no one can match Richard Sax.

Barbara Albright's e-mails never failed to cheer me and keep me going. And Kathie Finn Redden's reports on her results with my recipes were marvels of common sense. I'm indebted to you both.

I've learned too from writers I wasn't fortunate enough to publish, and I thank Marion Cunningham, Nick Malgieri, Judy Rodgers, Chris Schlesinger and Doc Willoughby, and Faith Willinger in particular.

In the land of friends, in and out of the food world, how can I thank Pat Adrian, Jo Ann Clevenger, David Black, Richard Baxt, Jo Fagan, James Lartin, Jessica Harris, Fran McCullough, Rick Moonen, Teresa Nicholas, Cherie Nutting, and Trudy and Jim Reswick enough? Thanks, too, Bryan Cronk for keeping my Web site fresh.

I count myself very fortunate to call Marysarah Quinn my friend, and more fortunate still to be able to thank her for the delightful design of these pages. I love you, baby. And I thank Dylan and Katie Rose for making you so happy.

Thank you to Tina Rupp (photographer), Toni Brogan (food stylist), and Teresa Horgan and Craig Thompson (assistants) for the tasty food photographs. And I thank Ben Fink for an author photo that continues to make me laugh.

Rux Martin started telling me how much her partner, Barry Estabrook, loved the food in this book long before she'll remember, and I thank them both for that encouragement. And I thank Rux for continuing to navigate the path of editing an editor with grace.

Deborah DeLosa is ever a delight. Mimi Assad is quick to reply. Anne Chalmers keeps the design running smoothly. Judith Sutton copyedits exactly as a copy editor should. Thank you.

Please go to your farmers' market and buy local produce. Even better, make friends with the farmers and talk to them about what they grow and what you'd like them to grow and how they cook what they grow. I go to several markets here in New York, but my favorite is at Tompkins Square, and there I count Zaid and Haifa Kurdieh of Norwich Meadows Farm, Martina Bartova and Jiri Pospisil of Toigo Orchards, and Kira Kinney of Evolutionary Organics as particularly savvy friends.

I've dedicated this book to my parents for countless reasons, and I have to say that they are the best promoters any author-son could hope for. When they found out that I had bookplates I could sign and send, no one in the extended family was safe. The Amisanos were special targets, and I thank them all, Barbara Amisano in particular, who sent her rib recipe to me through Mom. My sister, Marie, her partner, Donna, and their children, David and Hannah (in alphabetical order, children!)—well, I don't know where to begin to thank you. My nephews Michael and Patrick Young make me smile always. And when Rebecca Young called to ask me what I meant by saying "when the oil shimmers," she pretty much jarred my pickles. She was cooking! I love you all.

contents

introduction

There seems to be a dilemma about cooking, that there just isn't time enough. Well, I say baloney. Sharing food—whether it's a quick lunch, a big Sunday dinner, or a fast supper after work during the week—with family and friends is about the clearest and simplest way to express that you care. So how can there be no time for that?

This doesn't mean that we all need to spend hours every day at the stove. I certainly don't. But it does mean that we can make some time to cook, and when we do that, we can make that time count. You can always find a way to pull together a quick meal on a weeknight and to have a pleasant dinner. Part of the plan is to remember that you're cooking in your home, not in a restaurant. When you keep that in mind, bingo, a lot of the pressure is gone. Home cooking isn't some kind of sport, a show-offy competition event. Concentrate on making some simple good food, tasty dishes, and you'll be smiling when you sit down at the table.

Start by thinking about who you're cooking for and why. When it's the couple of friends you love playing cribbage with, think of a dinner that leaves you time for a few hands of cards. Here's a plan. You set the table and do all your prep for Sumac Chicken—which, with a bread salad loaded with cucumber and tomato, is pretty much a one-dish meal—and have it ready to go into the oven when your friends walk in the door. You sugar some berries or cut up some apricots and put them into dessert bowls and chill them, and you set out some nibbles. The chicken, seasoned with a tart Middle Eastern spice, goes into the oven and takes care of itself, filling the house with its aroma while you play cards. When the chicken's ready, all you need to do is cut it up, toss the bread salad with the cukes and tomatoes, and pour some wine. Dessert just needs a bit of cream for the berries or a splash of sparkling wine for the apricots. And you've had the time to enjoy yourself and your guests.

Of course there doesn't need to be a card game before dinner. Cooking can be a form of theater, and it can also be a group activity. If you're the type who can delegate, then delegate. Have everyone in the kitchen, and you can cook together. When you've planned a meal of food that's familiar, you can assign tasks with confidence. I'm not really that kind of supervisor, but I do enjoy cooking for an audience. I make sure I've got someone who's ready and willing to keep the wineglasses filled. That leaves me the freedom to prepare something for us all to nibble on while dinner cooks, make a salad dressing (greens should always be washed in private; it's not that entertaining an activity), or finish a last-minute dish.

None of these schemes may fit your personality. Fine. Know yourself and plan accordingly.

I started cooking when I was pretty young; certainly I was under ten. My father's mother was a very good cook. I grew up living first upstairs, then around the corner, from her, and it was in her kitchen that I learned to love food and learned to cook. My mother's mom knew how to do something my other grandmother didn't: she could bake wonderful cakes. Grandma Gorman was a mix of Irish and Swedish; Grandma Finamore, Italian. Their tastes could not have been more different, but they both encouraged me and taught me what they knew. And from the beginning, I've loved cooking. I like the aromas that pervade the kitchen and knowing that when I can smell the cake baking in the oven, it's about five minutes from being done. The sizzle that a piece of fish makes when I put it on a properly heated cast-iron griddle is very satisfying. And the constant process of learning about cooking is just plain gratifying. Here are some things I've learned.

Follow James Beard's example, from his *Theory and Practice of Good Cooking*, when you shop: have an idea in mind, but keep your eyes open for what looks good that day and adjust your plan accordingly. He called this "intelligent shopping"; I call it common sense. There's no point in making a peach pie when all the peaches look dry and woody and the nectarines look luscious.

Ask questions. If you've got a taste for Bluefish Dijonnaise but there's no bluefish at the market, check with the fish guy. Find out if there's a similar fish that's good. Or ask which of the fillets is at its prime and try the recipe with that.

Taste what you're cooking. Over the years, I've worked with a lot of great cooks, and every one of them has put a tasting spoon to use. Cook what you enjoy. If you don't like broccoli, your heart is just not going to be in it when you cook it—and that will come across in the finished dish.

Tomatoes taste best in the summer.

Making big batches makes sense. A meat loaf made with three pounds of meat is going to take just about the same amount of prep time as one with a pound and a half and only a little more time in the oven, and that bigger meat loaf will give you leftovers.

Figure out what basic foods you love and have them on hand. Me, I love beets, so I roast a few bunches once a week and keep them in the refrigerator to heat up in butter, or dress with olive oil and thyme, or cut up and add to a salad. I do the same with beans, both dried and shell, cooking them so they're around to make soup with, or puree as a side, or mash and have on some toasted Italian bread as a nibble.

Cooking is about looking and smelling and listening. All those cues are much more important than the timing in any recipe.

Keep your knives sharp.

Good, simple food is meant to be shared and enjoyed. **Cook often.**

notes for the cook

ABOUT MEASURING

How you measure can make a difference in the final results. There are times when the result is significant—like when you're baking a cake—and other times when it doesn't matter so much. Cooking all boils down to taste, and since you're the one who's going to be cooking, it's your taste. So I think you should be left to your own to season with salt and pepper, say, or to figure out how much oil to drizzle with. Keep tasting, and you'll be fine.

Unless otherwise noted, the vegetables and fruits called for in ingredient lists are medium ones. Variations in size aren't going to make a big difference, though. Maybe you really like the flavor of onions and want to add more. Or the big Spanish onions were the ones that looked best when you went shopping. Go ahead. This is one of those things that make cooking fun.

That said, let me share some information.

Measuring flour

My editor obsesses about measuring flour. I don't. I scoop and swipe. First I stir up the flour in the canister, aerating it. Then I scoop the measuring cup into the flour, filling it to overflowing, and swipe off the excess with the knife or a spatula. Use dry measuring cups when measuring dry ingredients. Spooning flour into a glass measure is a pain, and it's not accurate.

Measuring herbs

When I cook for myself, I just chop up herbs and add as much as looks right at the time.

In developing and testing these recipes, though, I packed the herbs into measuring spoons or dry measuring cups. Follow your instincts; you can always use more or less. And you're going to be tasting as you go along, right?

Measuring grated cheese

I pack grated or shredded cheeses into dry measuring cups too.

ABOUT COOKING TIMES

Here's what I think about cooking times: they can only, and always, be just a reference. I say to cook something at medium heat, but is your understanding of medium the same as mine? Maybe, and maybe not. Trust yourself while you're cooking, and follow all your senses.

Medium heat is a gentle kind of cooking, so listen to what's happening. Are things popping in the skillet or making a lot of noise? If they are, chances are your heat's too high.

Use your nose too. Say you're adding garlic to a skillet. Cook it until it's fragrant. It may take 30 seconds or a minute or 2 minutes—no matter what the recipe says. A lot will depend on the freshness of the ingredients, and what the growing season has been like. If it's a year when tomatoes are watery, it will take longer for them to come together into a sauce, right?

Your nose is a great tool when you're baking. Very fresh nuts will toast more quickly than older ones, so keep sniffing and checking. And cakes will start filling the kitchen with their aroma about 5 minutes before they're done.

Taste what you're cooking, and not just for seasoning. Taste to find out if something's cooked enough. You may notice that I don't give even approximate times for cooking pasta. Different brands have very different cooking times for the same cut of pasta, so giving a time wouldn't be very helpful. Tasting is really the only way to tell if pasta is cooked al dente.

Don't forget you have backup tools too. An instant-read thermometer is invaluable for meat. Even more important is a timer. There's nothing like the ring of a timer to bring a wandering mind back to the task at hand, which is getting dinner on the table.

HEATING THE OVEN

I turn the oven on at least 20 minutes before I plan on putting something into it.

ABOUT INGREDIENTS

Anchovies

Just because you don't want anchovies on your pizza doesn't mean you shouldn't cook with them. One or two anchovy fillets are going to add depth to what you're cooking, a little bit of richness.

The best anchovies are preserved in salt, but they're difficult to find and you have to go through the rinse-and-fillet-them-yourself process, so I usually buy fillets in jars, since it's easy to take out just a few. Whether you buy them in jars or tins, look for anchovies packed in extra-virgin olive oil. Shun those packed in soy or canola oil.

Sautéed Spinach: Heat some olive oil and 1 or 2 chopped anchovy fillets in a large skillet. The anchovies will melt as you stir and as the oil heats. Peel a garlic clove and stick it onto a fork. When the oil is hot and spitting and the anchovies are melted, add 1½ pounds of spinach (some water clinging to the leaves is fine). Cook over high heat, stirring constantly with the fork that has the garlic on it, until the spinach is tender and the liquid the spinach has released has evaporated. Season with pepper and a few drops of vinegar or lemon juice.

Bread Crumbs

You can be frugal and grate dried bread on a box grater to make your own crumbs, or you can do what I do and get them from a bakery that makes them out of unsold bread. If you must get the grocery-store stuff, please buy plain, not the kind that's seasoned with all those dried herbs and preservatives. Whichever you choose, store them in the freezer.

I make fresh bread crumbs with close-textured bread, something like Pepperidge Farm. It's easy enough to do. Tear a few slices into pieces and whir them in the food processor until they're finely ground and fluffy. You'll get about ½ cup of crumbs from a slice of bread. Use them right away.

Butter

Unsalted butter tastes better.

"Softened" butter means just softened. Take it out of the refrigerator about 20 minutes before you need to use it—less if the kitchen's hot. Softened butter should still feel cool to the touch; when you press down on it, you'll make a slight impression.

"Room-temperature" butter should be soft enough to spread on very soft bread without tearing it; it may even have started to slump. If it's starting to look oily, though, put it back in the refrigerator for a few minutes to firm slightly.

Buttery Croutons for Soup: Cut the crusts off 4 slices of good commercial white bread (I use Pepperidge Farm or Arnold's) and cut the bread into ⅓-inch cubes. Melt 2 tablespoons of unsalted butter in a large skillet over medium heat. Add the bread once the butter stops sizzling, and stir right away. Cook the bread cubes, flipping them with a spatula as best you can (some cubes will insist on being browned on one side only), until they are golden brown.

Crostini

These little toasts are always better when you make them at home, even when all you can buy is mediocre bread. Heat the oven to 350 degrees, and cut a baguette into ⅓-inch-thick slices. If you want more surface area, cut the bread on an angle. Spread the slices on baking sheets and bake for 15 to 20 minutes, turning them over about halfway through. Some may brown a little, but what you're really doing is drying the bread out. Cool completely, and store in an airtight container. If you've really dried the bread, the crostini will keep for weeks.

Garlic

The garlic I really love is the kind with the woody stems, and I get it from Keith's Organic Market in the Union Square Greenmarket. It has great flavor, and it also has nice fat cloves. So when I call for a garlic clove, it means a garlic clove that looks like something—not, I'm sorry to say, like those puny things that too many grocery stores sell. Try to buy garlic from a farmer who grows it.

Look for heads with fat cloves—you'll be able to see them. And squeeze; the garlic should feel hard. If the head is missing cloves, or feels spongy, pass it by. If all you can find are heads with little cloves, use more. Garlic is good for you. And if the garlic looks withered and beige when you peel it, throw it out. Garlic that old will give you *agita*.

To peel a garlic clove, cut off the root end (where it was attached), then put the garlic on a cutting board and give it a smack with the flat side of a heavy chef's knife. Or give the garlic a solid hit with the heel of your hand. Either way, the skin should release. Cut the clove lengthwise in half. If you see a green sprout, the germ, nudge it out with the tip of your knife. It's bitter. Then you can slice or mince or smash.

Most times, I puree garlic with a knife. After it's peeled, I put it on a cutting board, rest the side of my chef's knife on it, and hit pretty hard with the heel of my hand. I sprinkle the garlic with a pinch of salt to create some traction, and chop for a bit. Then I use the flat of the knife to smear the garlic on the board. Chop, smear, chop, and in moments the garlic is reduced to fine paste.

Herbs

I like my herbs fresh, and I like chopping and adding them at the last minute whenever possible. I keep them in plastic bags in the crisper. Here are some favorites.

Basil Leaves only. Watch out for basil that's gone to seed; the leaves won't be as sweet. When you find bush basil, with its tight head of tiny leaves, and Thai basil, with its stems stained purple, buy it. The Thai has a particularly strong flavor, so go easy at first.

Bay There's nothing that compares to the flavor of fresh bay leaves, and there are few fresh herbs more difficult to find. For dried, go with the Turkish leaves.

Cilantro Small stems are fine. No need to obsess.

Dill Chop it with a knife. Life's too short to be snipping dill with scissors. And if you find dill with flower heads, snap it up and make yourself some Dilly Beans (page 383).

Mint The sharp taste of peppermint is my first choice, but I don't say no to the more flowery spearmint. The stems are very tough, so use only the leaves.

Oregano Oregano was meant to be dried. You'll be happier if you use oregano from Mexico or the Mediterranean. Avoid any oregano that doesn't declare its origin.

Parsley For the best flavor and texture, I always look for flat-leaf, which some folks call "Italian," but if it's looking yellow or slimy or over-the-hill, I'll pick up a bunch of curly. I don't mind small stems when they're chopped, and the big stems are good to tie up and add to stocks.

Rosemary Strip the needles from the woody stems, and be thorough when you chop the needles. No one wants a big bit of rosemary stuck in his teeth.

Oil

Inexpensive extra-virgin olive oil is what I use for most cooking, including for some frying, like String Beans Fritto (page 362). Look around for an oil that has a flavor you like and that won't break the bank. The expensive ones are good to have on hand, but just use them to drizzle.

As the most stable, peanut is the oil of choice for deep-frying, though I'll use corn oil too. Corn oil's good when you want to make an unassertive dressing. I think soybean oil tastes fishy.

Dried Orange Zest

I keep a jar of this in the spice cabinet to add to stews and brines. Sometimes I'll pulverize a strip in a spice grinder and use the orange dust in piecrust or sprinkle it over berries.

Scrub a couple of navel oranges and dry them. Use a vegetable peeler to remove long strips of the zest (avoid the pith, please). Or scrub some tangerines or clementines, peel them, and tear the peels into three or four pieces. Thread a big needle with heavy thread or thin kitchen string and stitch through the zest or peels. Hang them someplace in the kitchen (I tape them to the side of a cabinet) away from the light, and let them dry for about a week. Then slip them off the string and keep them in a covered jar out of the sun. They last for months.

Frozen Peas

They belong in every freezer, preferably in bags. They're the best of all frozen vegetables, and you can use the bag as an ice pack in an emergency. The ones left over when you don't use the entire bag should go into a zippered plastic bag.

Pecorino

This sheep's milk cheese is the one I grew up with, and it's the preferred grating cheese in southern Italy. I love that it's sharp and peppery and salty.

Pepper

I've got two pepper mills on the counter, one for black and one for white pepper. I wouldn't keep a tin of the preground or "cracked" stuff in the house if it came with a box of tea. Please grind your own.

Tellicherry is my black pepper of choice, but there are times when I'll substitute the flowery and fragrant grains of paradise—which is a seed from West Africa—for pepper. I've also got a jar of pink peppercorns in the cabinet, but I have to admit that I've never used them.

Cracking pepper: Use a mortar and pestle if you have one. If not, put the peppercorns on the counter or a cutting board and crack them with the bottom of a small heavy saucepan. Hold the handle and opposite rim of the pan and rock it back and forth, applying as much pressure as you can.

Hot Peppers

Grocery stores and little markets carry fresh ones, but I find the most interesting ones in farmers' markets. Commercial peppers seem to have all the flavor and heat bred out of them. So look around and taste as many as you can find. Try to find hot peppers (or chilies, as some people call them) that have flavor as well as heat. My favorites are the tiny Thai bird peppers, which do pack a wallop in the heat category, but they're small and flavorful so they don't overwhelm a recipe.

Little peppers freeze very well. I keep them in a zippered plastic bag.

Hot Peppers in Sherry: Check your farmers' market for the smallest hot peppers you can find. I use just about anything but habanero or Scotch bonnets for this. Wash and dry the peppers and pack them in impeccably clean jars. Cover with dry sherry and refrigerate. They will be ready to use in 2 weeks, and they'll keep for a year.

Drizzle the sherry over cooked greens. Chop the peppers and use them as if they were fresh. And one of these peppers dropped into gin and vermouth will make a very tasty Martini.

Salt

I've got a bowl of coarse kosher salt on the stove, and that's what I use for cooking. I pinch and sprinkle salt, and a shower of kosher salt is easy to control. It tastes good. You can put it where you want to, for instance, when you're salting meat, and you don't have the clogs or eruptions that you get from a shaker filled with overprocessed and basically repellent "table salt." When you're salting meat or poultry, fill a separate little bowl with salt so you don't have to worry about washing and drying your chickeny fingers before you reach for it, then toss out what's left.

Coarse sea salt has a flavor and crunch that works so well to finish a dish. I admit it: I'm something of a salt junkie, so I've got sea salt from the Ile de Ré, Camargue, Wales, and the Bay of Bengal in my cabinet—all different degrees of saltiness and coarseness. I use fine sea salt or kosher salt for desserts.

Herbed Salt: Sprinkle this on a piece of flounder before breading or frying. Or use it to season vegetables you are going to grill or roast. Rub some into lamb chops before grilling. Put a pinch or two into your burgers. Are you getting the idea that you can have fun with this? And it lasts for months. But be sure you use the best and freshest dried herbs.

Measure 3 tablespoons coarse sea salt, 2 teaspoons dried basil or mint, 1 teaspoon dried thyme, ½ teaspoon dried sage or oregano, and ¼ teaspoon crushed red pepper (or a bit more) into a spice grinder. Crumble up a bay leaf and add that as well. Process for about a minute. There should be no visible pieces of any herb and the salt should be fine.

Store in a glass jar out of the light. This makes about 5 tablespoons.

Seeds

When you want to release flavor from things like fennel and caraway seeds, it's a good idea to crush them. The easiest way to do it is with a mortar and pestle. Just crack the seeds; you're not looking to make a powder. If your kitchen is mortar challenged, you can put the seeds on a cutting board, dampen them with some water to keep them from flying all over the kitchen, and chop them with a heavy knife.

Stock

Having stock in the freezer is like money in the bank. Sure, I'll use canned stock in an emergency, but nothing compares to the flavor of homemade. I usually make double batches and freeze it in smaller containers—a few 1-cup, some 2-cup, and maybe a quart. That way I can defrost it easily for specific recipes. And I don't put salt in stock; it's easier to control when I salt the dish I'm using it in.

The simplest way to get the fat off the surface of a stock is to chill it. The fat will solidify on the surface, making it a cinch to scrape off and discard. Decant the stock into smaller containers for freezing or refrigerate and use within 2 or 3 days.

Chicken Stock: When I'm lucky, I can find chicken feet at my local grocery or at the farmers' market, and I buy them for delicious stock that will really jell. Otherwise, I look for bags of backs and necks. Failing that, I make stock with legs and thighs.

Rinse 1½ to 2 pounds of chicken parts and put them into a stockpot. Turn the heat on to medium and cook the chicken for about 5 minutes. Quarter 2 large onions (no need to peel; just pull off the loose paper) and add to the pot. Cover and cook, stirring every once in a while, until the chicken has started to steam and gotten very juicy. This should take about 10 minutes—don't let the chicken brown. Toss in a bay leaf and pour in 8 cups of water.

Bring slowly to a simmer, skimming occasionally to get rid of the goop that rises to the surface, and cook at a very gentle simmer for 2½ to 3 hours. Add a handful of parsley sprigs after about the first hour. Be careful never to let the stock boil or even simmer too vigorously as it cooks—you'll end up with cloudy, greasy-tasting stock. Strain and cool. This makes about 1½ quarts.

Beef Stock: Begin by heating the oven to 350 degrees.

Put 3 pounds of meaty soup bones (beef shank), 2 quartered onions (no need to peel, just pull off the loose paper), 3 garlic cloves (don't peel them), and 3 chunked carrots (scrubbed, not peeled) into a roasting pan. Drizzle with a tablespoon of olive oil and season with salt. Roast for 1 hour, stirring once or twice, until the bones are nicely browned.

Transfer the bones and vegetables to a stockpot, along with any juices in the pan. Put the roasting pan on high heat and add 2 tablespoons tomato paste. Cook the paste, stirring constantly, for 1 to 2 minutes, until it turns brick red. Deglaze the pan with 1 cup of water—making sure you dissolve all those tasty browned bits in the bottom—and pour into the stockpot. Add 6 cups of water and 5 or 6 parsley sprigs to the pot and bring to a boil over high heat, skimming any gunk that rises to the surface. Reduce to a simmer, cover the pot partway, and simmer gently for 2 1/2 hours.

Meanwhile, mince 2 celery stalks, 2 carrots, and 1 onion. Add to the pot with 2 sprigs of thyme and simmer for another 30 minutes.

Strain the stock, let it cool to room temperature, and then refrigerate it overnight—no need to cover. Next day, remove the fat that will have risen to the surface and freeze the stock in batches for later use. This makes about 1 1/2 quarts.

Vegetable Stock: This stock comes together much more quickly than chicken or beef, and it has a lighter taste.

The thrifty will have saved lots of vegetable trimmings in the freezer. I'm not that thrifty. But vegetable stock is forgiving, and it's not really worth a trip to the grocery to buy a turnip. Substitute what you have on hand. You've got some leeks? Use them instead of the onions. No fennel? Add more celery. Fresh mushrooms instead of dried are fine; parsnip instead of turnip—or neither. And if you've got tomato seeds and juice in the freezer, bless you. Add them to the pot.

Take out the stockpot and toss in 2 large onions, sliced; 2 large carrots, sliced (just scrub them first); 2 celery stalks, sliced; the tops and fronds from 1 fennel stalk (or the bulb itself), chopped; 1 turnip, peeled and chopped; a handful of dried mushrooms, rinsed; a bunch of flat-leaf parsley; 1 or 2 garlic cloves, cut in half (don't peel them); 1 bay leaf; 1 teaspoon peppercorns; and a few sprigs of thyme. Bring to a simmer over medium heat. This will take 30 to 40 minutes. Cover the pot partway, lower the heat, and leave the stock to simmer for 30 minutes.

Strain it now for the lightest stock, or leave it to infuse off the heat for an hour or two for something stronger. Use it within 3 days, or freeze it in small batches. This makes about 2 quarts.

Tomatoes

Every pantry needs to be stocked with canned tomatoes. The best are canned plum tomatoes from San Marzano in Italy. If finding these daunts you, try the organic ones from Muir Glen.

Now, about fresh tomatoes: I see those piles of imposters in the grocery, and I have to stop myself from asking the lady in line in front of me why on earth she's buying them. They have usually been grown in greenhouses, sometimes gassed to give them the illusion of ripeness or redness, and are bred so they can be shipped thousands of miles from where they were born. Even those deceptively pretty ones on the vine from Holland have no flavor. Their only possible use is as a stand-in when you have a taste for fried green tomatoes.

A case can be made for eating some out-of-season fruits and vegetables, but I draw the line at tomatoes. If they're not vine-ripened—in the sun—and sold by a local farmer, I won't touch them.

Tomato Paste

I buy this in tubes. It has a real taste of tomatoes and the advantage of coming in its own storage container: no opening a can and then trying to find a little container for leftovers.

Vanilla Extract

Yes, yes, you can buy extract, but it's fun to make it yourself. Get a nice bottle, and add as many vanilla beans as you dare. Snip them in half so they're not overly long. Then cover them with vodka or brandy by an inch or so. Let infuse for a month, and replenish with more vodka or brandy as you use it up. A bottle of vanilla that you've made is a very generous gift.

Vanilla Sugar

Simple as can be. All you do is bury a vanilla bean in a jar of sugar and let it sit for a few days. You can keep replenishing this with more sugar and with beans you've scraped for ice cream or pudding. Just shake it up when you add the new sugar.

Vinegar

Vinegar's not only for making dressings and sauces. A little hit of sour can brighten something bland. So think about adding a shot of it when you might add a squeeze of lemon, when the dish you're cooking tastes a little flat.

Good vinegar needn't be expensive, and it shouldn't be so puckeringly sour that it turns your face into a prune when you taste it. I stock up on red, white, and sherry vinegars for most of my cooking, and champagne vinegar when I'm looking for something crisp and light. I've got cider and distilled white vinegar in the pantry for pickling. Rice vinegar has a clean taste that's welcome too, particularly with cucumbers. You don't need the seasoned stuff, though; it's just got sugar in it.

Cucumber Salad: Cut a couple of cucumbers into thin slices (peel them if the skin has been waxed) and put them in a mixing bowl with some thinly sliced red onion. Season with salt and pepper, a little bit of sugar, and a lot of chopped dill and toss. Transfer to a bowl that's just large enough to hold the salad, and pour in rice vinegar to cover. Cover the bowl with plastic and refrigerate for at least 2 hours before serving.

White Wine and Dry Vermouth

If you're going to be pouring yourself a glass of white wine to sip on while you cook, go right ahead, and use that wine for cooking. Otherwise, I don't much see the point of opening a bottle of wine if all I'm going to use is a few tablespoons. That's when I turn to dry vermouth. This fortified wine keeps for weeks in the refrigerator, and I like the herby, woodsy accents it adds to food. Besides, even the best vermouth will be less expensive than decent white wine. That said, go for the best: Noilly Pratt or Martini & Rossi.

breakfast

breakfast

I think of breakfast not as a way of starting fresh but as continuing what happened the night before.

So when I pad into the kitchen in the morning, I'll toast an English muffin and eat it with a slice or two of leftover flank steak, some pickles, and, yes, I admit it, ketchup. Or I'll poke around for that last piece of chicken. Maybe I'll poach an egg to have on leftover salmon.

Oh, I can't lie. Breakfast for me is usually coffee. Lots of coffee.

However, when there are other people around, I do make breakfast. And I will start by raiding the refrigerator for leftovers, since I subscribe to the notion of savory for breakfast. I will slice up that leftover steak and serve it with Cream Biscuits. Or I'll plan in advance and make English Muffins—nothing better than a homemade English muffin. And with those as centerpiece, pretty much anything is possible. Some scrambled eggs, maybe. Chicken Hash, if there's leftover chicken. Some bacon and sliced summer tomatoes. Or just butter.

For all of you who like hot breakfast cereal and making magic, try the Overnight Oatmeal. No standing over the stove, stirring and waiting. The oatmeal goes into the oven before you go to bed; what waits for you in the morning is oatmeal for the gods: creamy and soft, almost a pudding.

You can also assemble a very impressive breakfast with a minimum of effort. Start with a basket of warm muffins or biscuits. While they bake, make a few platters. Be as extravagant as you want.

- ✧ Oranges and grapefruit, cut into wedges
- ✧ Melon, cut into cubes and tossed with berries
- ✧ The ripest figs possible
- ✧ Dried sausages, sliced very thin
- ✧ Smoked or cured fish

- Smoked chicken or turkey, sliced thin
- Fresh goat cheese (top it with a few spoons of Stonewall Kitchen's Roasted Garlic and Onion Jam)
- Plain yogurt, with honey and granola to stir in
- Sliced crusty bread, or fresh croissants or scones if you have time to run to the bakery
- Softened sweet butter
- Softened cream cheese
- All the jams, jellies, and marmalades you have in the house

And that's a nice way to end the day.

buttermilk pancakes with hazelnut butter

MAKES ABOUT 14 PANCAKES

They're light, they're fluffy, and the butter gives these classic pancakes a nutty goodness. It's true: there are no eggs in the batter.

The photo is on page 65.

FOR THE BUTTER

2 ounces (about 1/2 cup) hazelnuts

8 tablespoons (1 stick) unsalted butter

1/2 teaspoon vanilla extract

FOR THE PANCAKES

3 cups all-purpose flour

1/4 cup sugar

1 tablespoon baking soda

1/2 teaspoon coarse salt

4 tablespoons (1/2 stick) unsalted butter, melted

2 3/4 cups buttermilk

Vegetable oil

FOR SERVING (OPTIONAL)

Maple syrup

Strawberry Rhubarb Syrup (page 455)

FOR THE BUTTER

Heat the oven to 350 degrees.

Put the hazelnuts on a small baking sheet or in a pie pan and toast them in the oven until fragrant, 10 to 15 minutes. Shake the pan a few times while the nuts are toasting, and be alert: very fresh nuts will toast very quickly. Dump them out onto a kitchen towel and fold the towel over, so they will steam. Let cool for 15 minutes or so, then rub them with vigor in the towel to release as much of the skin as possible.

Put the nuts into a food processor and pulse until they are chopped fine. Cut the butter into a few pieces and add it to the processor, along with the vanilla. Process until smooth.

Scrape the butter into a small bowl and refrigerate until you're ready to use it.

FOR THE PANCAKES

Whisk the flour, sugar, baking soda, and salt together in a mixing bowl. Pour in the melted butter and the buttermilk and stir until combined. A few lumps are fine.

Heat a cast-iron griddle or skillet over medium-high heat. Brush it lightly with oil. When the skillet is good and hot, ladle out about $\frac{1}{4}$ cup batter for each pancake, using the back of the ladle to spread the batter out a bit. Cook the pancakes until they look dry around the edges and have bubbles rising and popping over the surface. Flip, and cook until the pancakes have risen and the other side is browned (yes, peek).

I put some hazelnut butter on these right away, stack them on a platter, and keep them warm in a 200-degree oven until all the pancakes are cooked. You could also serve them as you cook them. Pass some syrup if you want it.

ricotta pancakes with melted raspberries

MAKES ABOUT 16 PANCAKES

The surprise of these pancakes is that they're custardy rather than cakey. If you're making a full-scale breakfast, bring out the Canadian bacon—or even a ham steak.

When the only ricotta I can find is the watery grocery-store variety, I spoon it out into a strainer lined with dampened cheesecloth and let it drain over a bowl in the refrigerator overnight.

FOR THE PANCAKES

2 cups ricotta

2 large eggs

2 tablespoons unsalted butter, melted

1 tablespoon sugar

1 1/4 cups milk

2 cups all-purpose flour

1 tablespoon baking powder

1/2 teaspoon coarse salt

Vegetable oil

FOR THE MELTED RASPBERRIES

3 tablespoons unsalted butter

1 (6-ounce) basket raspberries

1/2 cup maple syrup

FOR THE PANCAKES

Whisk the ricotta, eggs, butter, sugar, and milk together in a medium bowl.

Whisk the flour, baking powder, and salt in another bowl, then stir the dry ingredients into the wet. Don't obsess: some lumps are fine. The batter can sit on the counter for an hour or so.

FOR THE MELTED RASPBERRIES

Melt the butter in a small saucepan over medium heat. Add the raspberries and cook, stirring once in a while, until they are bubbling and falling apart. Pour in the syrup and let it heat through. Keep warm.

Heat a cast-iron griddle or skillet over medium-high heat. When the skillet is good and hot, brush it lightly with oil. Ladle out about 1/4 cup batter for each pancake, using the back of the ladle to spread the batter out a bit. Cook the pancakes until they look dry around the edges and have bubbles rising and popping over the surface. Flip, and cook until the pancakes have risen and the other side is browned (peek).

If you want, you can keep the pancakes on a platter in a preheated 200-degree oven until you've made them all.

Pour the melted raspberries into a bowl and serve warm with a small ladle.

is the griddle hot enough?

Sure, pancakes will cook on a griddle that hasn't been properly heated, but they will be an even, insipid tan—not beautifully browned.

You could hold your hand a couple of inches over the griddle to feel the heat, but there's a much easier way to find out if the griddle is hot enough. Flick a few drops of water onto it. If the water boils where it lands, the griddle's not ready yet. If the drops dance across the surface, you've got the right heat. If the water disappears immediately, you've gone too far and the griddle's too hot.

overnight oatmeal SERVES 4 TO 6

There should be no debate about this: steel-cut oats make the best oatmeal. But while I'll stand over a pot for forty minutes to make polenta, I'm just not up for that kind of cooking first thing in the morning.

Slip the oatmeal into a low oven and let it bake gently overnight, though, and you will be rewarded with lusciously creamy oatmeal—creamier than any stovetop method will give you—right when you want it.

4 cups water
1 cup steel-cut oats
Coarse salt

Heat the oven to 200 degrees.

Pour the water into a deep heavy casserole and stir in the oats. Add a good pinch of salt, maybe as much as a teaspoon. Cover the casserole, slide it into the oven, and bake for 8 hours.

serving oatmeal

I like oatmeal with just butter and milk. Well, maybe some coarse sea salt too, for crunch. But you might want to have cream or buttermilk, brown sugar, maple syrup, and even some jam for those in need.

proper scrambled eggs SERVES 4

"Proper" sounds so English, doesn't it? But these eggs are very French and so very good.

I'm giving you a recipe that will serve 4, but you can scramble any number of eggs this way. The formula is 1 tablespoon of butter to each egg, and you hold back some butter to stir in at the end when you scramble a lot of eggs. For example, for a dozen, I reserve 4 tablespoons of butter for the end. If you want to cheat and add less butter, go ahead, but please don't cheat too much. The eggs won't be proper if you do. And you can always cheat the other way and add more.

About the pan: I like the width of a skillet because it makes largish curds. You could scramble in a saucepan too, and stir almost constantly; you'll end up with smaller curds and even creamier eggs. I don't like nonstick for scrambled eggs, nor aluminum or cast iron. It's heavy stainless steel for me, and a wooden spatula that I can use to scrape the bottom of the pot. Without scraping, you'll end up with a big film of egg in the pan and not moist scramble on your plate.

8 tablespoons (1 stick) unsalted butter
8 large eggs
2 tablespoons water
Coarse salt and freshly ground black pepper

Heat 6 tablespoons butter in a heavy skillet over medium heat. Beat the eggs with a fork in a bowl until smooth. You don't want them frothy, and you don't want globs of white left either. Beat in the water.

When the butter has melted, pour in the eggs. Season with salt and pepper and stir. Let the eggs start to set a bit, then stir with a big wooden spatula, making sure you scrape the bottom of the skillet.

Keep on cooking, stirring and scraping the bottom of the skillet frequently, until the eggs are almost set but still runny. Cut the remaining 2 tablespoons butter into bits and stir it in. The eggs should still be slightly undercooked. Turn off the heat.

Scrape the eggs onto a platter or onto breakfast plates and serve right away. The eggs will finish cooking and be beautifully creamy by the time you get them to the table. Scrambled eggs are like pasta: they are not meant to wait.

variations

Soft herbs are a terrific addition. Add 1/3 cup of chopped chives or parsley or a combination of the two with the butter. Use less, say 1 to 2 tablespoons, of more strongly flavored herbs like marjoram or summer savory or tarragon.

I make scrambled eggs for New Year's Day breakfast, and there's usually some leftover caviar in the house then. I top each serving of eggs with a generous teaspoon. The point is eggs and eggs—any good caviar is great on scrambled eggs.

chicken hash SERVES 4

Leftover chicken is a great way to start the day, and when you cook it in cream and serve it over English muffins, that is the promise of a good day. For the utmost in extravagance, top with a poached egg.

Cut the chicken into big chunks, say about 1 inch square.

2 tablespoons unsalted butter

1 onion, chopped

2 celery stalks, chopped

Coarse salt

2 tablespoons all-purpose flour

2 cups heavy cream, heated

3 cups cubed cooked chicken

Freshly grated nutmeg

Freshly ground white pepper

1 tablespoon dry sherry

4 English muffins, store-bought or homemade (page 38), split and toasted

Melt the butter in a saucepan over medium heat. Add the onion, celery, and a pinch of salt, and sweat the vegetables until they're translucent, 10 to 12 minutes. Sprinkle in the flour and cook, stirring, for 2 minutes. Don't let the flour brown. Pour in about half of the cream and stir, scraping out to the edges of the pan to dissolve the roux, then pour in the rest of the cream. Cook, stirring often, until the sauce comes to a boil.

Add the chicken and season with salt, nutmeg, and white pepper. Cook just long enough to heat the chicken through. Stir in the sherry and serve over the toasted English muffins.

fennel-orange gravlax with bagel chips SERVES 6

Baby fennel, which I get at the farmers' market, has very thin stalks and lots of fronds, and it's perfect for this recipe. If you can't find baby fennel, smash the thick tops of mature fennel, then chop them. You could also add other fresh herbs to the salmon cure: chives, dill, bronze fennel, and basil are all possibilities.

Ask for the head end of the salmon fillet. Or get a full side of salmon and double the ingredients for the cure so you'll have plenty of gravlax for other meals.

The photo is on page 71.

1½ pounds wild salmon fillet (see headnote)
⅔ cup coarse salt
⅔ cup sugar
Grated zest of 1 large orange
2 teaspoons fennel seeds, crushed
2 cups chopped fennel tops and fronds

FOR SERVING

6 bagels, each cut crosswise into 3 slices
2 ripe tomatoes, sliced
1 red onion, sliced very thin
Cream cheese, at room temperature
Capers, rinsed and drained

Take out your tweezers or needle-nose pliers and remove the pinbones from the salmon.

Combine the salt, sugar, zest, and fennel seeds in a mixing bowl and whisk to distribute the zest. Add the chopped fennel and toss with your hands.

Rip off a long piece of plastic wrap—about 2 feet long—and lay it on the counter. Make a bed with half the cure in the center of the plastic and set the salmon, skin down, on top of it. Pack the rest of the cure on top of the salmon. Wrap the fish tightly in the plastic, set it on a plate, and refrigerate for 36 hours.

Scrape the cure off the fish and refrigerate the fish on a rack for about 1 hour to dry it out.

FOR SERVING

Heat the oven to 350 degrees.

Lay the bagel slices out on baking sheets and toast them in the oven, turning after about 5 minutes. You can make the bagel chips well in advance.

Cut the salmon at an angle into very thin slices, cutting down to—but not through—the skin. Arrange the slices on a platter. Make up another platter with the bagel chips, tomatoes, and onion. Put the cream cheese and capers in bowls, and serve.

Store leftover gravlax wrapped tightly in plastic in the refrigerator.

gravlax for dinner

Cool cured salmon is a great dinner for a hot summer night. Serve it with boiled creamer potatoes rolled in butter and sprinkled with coarse sea salt; sliced tomatoes; capers; and a green salad. Have sharp grainy mustard on the side.

english muffins MAKES 10 MUFFINS

Chewy and delicious, these have the kind of dense crumb you expect from an English muffin but without the sweetness of the commercial ones. You start the day before to allow for a gentle overnight rise.

They freeze beautifully.

1 teaspoon active dry yeast

1½ cups warm water

1 pound (3½ cups) all-purpose flour

1 teaspoon coarse salt

Solid vegetable shortening

Cornmeal

Dissolve the yeast in ½ cup warm water and let it sit for a few minutes, until it's frothy.

Put the flour in a mixing bowl and stir in the salt. Add the yeast and the remaining 1 cup warm water, and stir with a sturdy wooden spoon to make a stiff dough. Empty the bowl onto a floured work surface and knead until the dough is smooth and elastic. Expect this to take anywhere from 5 to 10 minutes, depending on how vigorously you knead. Clean out your bowl and grease it with some vegetable shortening. Form the dough into a ball, drop it in the bowl, cover tightly with plastic wrap, and refrigerate overnight.

Next morning, grease a baking sheet with shortening and coat it with cornmeal. Scrape the dough out onto your counter, punch it down, and cut it into 10 pieces. Roll each piece into a ball, then flatten it between your palms to make a disk about 3 inches across. Place the muffins on the baking sheet, at least an inch apart. Cover lightly with plastic, and let the muffins rise in a warm spot in the kitchen for 1½ to 2 hours. They'll be much lighter and about half again their original size.

Heat a cast-iron griddle over medium heat. When it's hot, brush it with a little shortening. Slide a spatula under the muffins and place them on the griddle, cornmeal side down. You'll hear a sizzle when the muffins hit the griddle. Turn the heat down to medium-low and cook for 8 minutes. Lift the muffins up to peek once in a while; you want them to get a deep even brown, but you don't want them to burn. So monitor the heat, lowering it if necessary, and move the muffins around on the griddle to avoid hot spots. Turn the muffins over, press down on them with the back of the spatula to flatten, and cook for another 8 minutes, or until nicely browned. They'll feel like a very firm pillow when you press on them.

Cool the muffins completely on a rack. You can freeze them now, or split them open with a fork, toast, and slather with butter. Or butter and peanut butter.

They'll keep for a few days in a zippered plastic bag in the fridge.

raspberry muffins MAKES 12 MUFFINS

Tender, not too sweet, these are ideal breakfast muffins.
I've adapted this recipe from one by the baking king Nick Malgieri.

FOR THE TOPPING

1 cup all-purpose flour

1/3 cup sugar

3/4 teaspoon ground cardamom

Coarse salt

8 tablespoons (1 stick) unsalted butter, softened

FOR THE BATTER

2 cups all-purpose flour

1 1/2 teaspoons baking soda

1/2 teaspoon coarse salt

8 tablespoons (1 stick) unsalted butter, softened

1 cup sugar

2 large eggs

Grated zest of 1 orange (optional)

1/2 cup buttermilk

2 (6-ounce) baskets raspberries

Heat the oven to 375 degrees. Butter the top of a muffin tin and drop in 12 paper baking cups.

FOR THE TOPPING

Whisk the flour, sugar, cardamom, and a pinch of salt in a small bowl. Cut the butter into pieces and add it to the flour. Work the butter and dry ingredients together with your fingers, pinching and rubbing until the butter is completely incorporated and the topping holds together when you squeeze a handful. Set the crumbs out of the way while you make the batter.

FOR THE BATTER

Whisk the flour, baking soda, and salt in a small bowl.

Beat the butter with an electric mixer in a large bowl (or use the paddle with a standing mixer) for about a minute, then pour in the sugar in a steady stream, still beating. Beat the butter and sugar until light. Beat in the eggs one at a time, scraping the sides of the bowl after adding each egg. Beat in the orange zest, if using.

Add the dry ingredients alternately with the buttermilk—3 additions of dry and 2 of buttermilk—mixing just until combined. Fold in the raspberries. You don't need to be that gentle; it's nice if some of the raspberries end up crushed in the batter.

Divide the batter among the 12 muffin cups; you'll fill them pretty much to the top. Crumble the crumbs over the muffins, piling them on so you use all of the crumb mix.

Slide the tin into the oven and bake until the muffins are risen and the crumbs are a rich brown, about 30 minutes. Cool on a rack. Store leftovers wrapped in wax paper on the counter for a day or two.

variation

Nick makes these with blueberries, and you can too. You might want to substitute cinnamon for the cardamom in the topping, and skip the orange zest.

cream biscuits MAKES ABOUT 10 BISCUITS

This is the place to start if you've never made biscuits, since you don't have to cut in any fat (the cream takes care of that) and you don't need a particularly light hand to get tender results.

2 cups all-purpose flour

2 teaspoons baking powder

$^{1}/_{2}$ teaspoon coarse salt

1 tablespoon sugar

$1^{1}/_{3}$ cups heavy cream, plus more if needed

Heat the oven to 375 degrees.

Put the flour, baking powder, salt, and sugar in a mixing bowl and whisk to combine. Pour in the cream and stir with a fork or your hand; you may need to add a tablespoon or two more. When there's enough cream in it, the dough should come together and clean the sides of the bowl. For those of you who know buttermilk biscuits, this dough will be tighter.

Dump the dough out onto a floured counter and knead it 12 to 15 times, just until it's smooth. Pat the dough $^{1}/_{2}$ inch thick and pat in the edges so they're not ragged. Cut out biscuits with a $2^{1}/_{2}$-inch cutter and put them on an ungreased baking sheet. Gather the scraps together, pat out again, and cut out a few more biscuits. Gather the last scraps into one or two balls and flatten them out. Brush the tops with cream.

Bake for 18 to 20 minutes, until risen and golden. Serve steaming hot.

fresh bloody mary mix

A master mixologist and author of *The Joy of Mixology,* Gary Regan doesn't like tomato juice. ("Too bloody thick for a cocktail, mate.") Well, that's because he doesn't make his own, which is the work of a moment in a blender and perfect for a summer cocktail. But you will make this only with the ripest summer tomatoes, won't you? Beefsteaks that still smell of the sun. Or heirlooms if you feel particularly generous.

The photo is on page 71.

Start by halving 1¼ pounds of ripe tomatoes and seeding them over a strainer set in a bowl. Cut up the flesh and drop it into a blender. Do the same with ½ pound plum tomatoes. Then push on the seeds with a wooden spoon and stir them around to get all the juice out. Pour the juice into the blender and toss out the seeds. Pull one of the tender stalks out from the center of a head of celery—a stalk with leaves—and chop it. Add to the blender.

Now add ½ cup of water, the grated zest and juice of a lemon, at least 1 tablespoon of grated horseradish (more if you're the spicy sort), 4 or 5 shots of Tabasco sauce (again, let your tongue be your guide), and a pinch of celery seeds. Season with salt and pepper. Then whir it all up until completely smooth.

You can make cocktails in the kitchen, right out of the blender, or pour the mix into a pitcher and set it on a drinks table. You may want to keep a long spoon handy, because the mix will separate fairly quickly; a stir sets it right again.

What you use for stirrers is up to you. Celery is the traditional, but pickle spears and Dilly Beans (page 383) and pickled okra also beg for consideration. So maybe you'll break with tradition.

And maybe you'll continue breaking with tradition and make your Bloody Mary with gin instead of vodka. Go on, try.

lunch

lunch

My mother has a line about lunch.

She tells my father that she "married him for better or for worse, but not for lunch." How did I come to love this meal? Truth to tell, it came later in life, when I had friends with weekend houses. Then there was more of a reason to make something of lunch, or to make something *for* lunch. Left to my own devices, I'll have a sandwich and a piece of fruit.

So sandwiches play a pretty big part here. You probably don't need a recipe for grilled cheese, but what I really want to do is get you to break out of whatever box you're in with grilled cheese and try new versions.

Making any sandwich is cooking, you know, and the same kind of rules apply. Good ingredients make good sandwiches. We've all got tastes and guilty pleasures. Mine is white bread, and I can't imagine an onion and tomato sandwich without it. But more important is the tomato, which must be sun-ripe. Please don't put those awful grocery-store things, purchased in the dead of winter, into a sandwich. If you need something juicy, then get some roasted peppers or slice up some pickles. Or make some Burst Cherry Tomatoes, which you'll find on page 50, and at least have a little flavor.

I've got a bone to pick about lettuce too. It's good and flavorful and really pretty inexpensive. So I don't understand the sandwich made with the postage-stamp piece. Be extravagant. Pile lettuce on your sandwich. Consider it the sign of an overflowing heart.

Lunch is a great platform for leftovers. That piece of salmon sitting in the refrigerator could, and should, be a salad. Some minced celery, chopped herbs, a squirt of lemon—all sounds familiar. Instead chop up some sun-dried tomatoes (the ones in oil) and scallion. Rinse some capers, and sauté some spinach and chop it up. Toss it all with the flaked salmon, dress with olive oil, a squirt of lemon, and maybe a tablespoon of mayo to help bind it, and pile it into tomatoes that you've hollowed out.

Eggs are another thing that call out "lunch." If you've never made a frittata, now's the time to start. These Italian dishes are easiest to compare to omelets, but put your mind at ease: frittatas are much easier to make. You cook something in a skillet, maybe an onion, in olive oil. When it's tender, you add eggs that you've beaten with milk and grated cheese. Cook the eggs, scraping toward the center and letting the uncooked eggs run to the edge, until the frittata is almost set and has a shape, then top with chopped tomatoes and herbs. Pop into a 350-degree oven until browned and puffed up, which takes 20 minutes, and you've got a frittata. Serve it hot, serve it warm, serve it cool.

You can also make magic for lunch with some great bread, some great cheese, and pickles. If you've got a pork chop left over in the fridge, or a piece of steak, you could slice it up. Put out some butter and mustard, if you want. You're guaranteed magic with pickles you've made yourself. Be good to yourself and your dining companions, and bring out the beer. And imagine yourselves in a pub with your ploughman's lunch.

grilled cheese for grown-ups

Grilled cheese sandwiches can be a great treat for lunch, and an even bigger treat when paired with a cup of soup. You can make one for yourself, pretty quickly, or make a big batch for a crowd. And who says they have to be for lunch only? A big platter of sandwiches, a kettle of soup, a salad, and beer—it sounds like the makings of a real nice party to me.

Let's start by agreeing that those sandwiches made with processed cheese on spongy white bread are best left to children with problem appetites. Beyond that, it's obvious: good cheese and good bread. Spices and herbs and peppers and quick sauces and salads will give your sandwiches some zing. Here's your chance to find a use for those jars of red pepper pesto or tapenade that have been gathering dust in the pantry.

If you have the time, go to a cheese shop for your cheeses and a bakery for the bread. Otherwise, poke around the dairy case in your grocery for something out of the ordinary.

Making Grilled Cheese Sandwiches The best grilled cheese sandwiches are made on a cast-iron griddle. You've got a nice flat surface with even heat, and no pan sides to get in the way when you're ready to flip the sandwich, and you can make big batches quickly when you want to. You can also set a heavy baking sheet on the sandwiches; this works almost like a lid (but with air escaping at the sides, so the sandwiches don't steam) and it gives you just the right amount of weight to press the sandwiches without squeezing out the filling. (If all you have is one of those light cookie sheets, set a couple cans of tuna on top of it for added weight.)

Or pull out your George Foreman grill, if you've got one. It makes a fine grilled cheese.

Start by buttering the bread (soft butter is best so you don't tear the bread or end up with clumps of butter) or brushing it with olive oil. One slice of bread goes on the work surface, butter down. Cover with a layer of thinly sliced cheese. Fillings or flavorings come next, then another layer of cheese. Top with the second slice of bread, butter up. Do your prep early in the day if you've got a crowd coming. Lay the sandwiches on a baking sheet, with wax paper or parchment or plastic wrap between the layers if you've made a lot, cover with plastic, and refrigerate until you're ready to grill.

Heat the griddle over medium heat; you'll want the cheese to melt before the bread burns, so moderation is the rule. Set the sandwiches on the griddle and set the baking sheet on top. Grill the sandwiches until the first side is nicely golden and the cheese has started to melt. Flip the sandwiches, replace the baking sheet, and grill until the second side is golden and the cheese is creamy and soft. Set the sandwiches on a cutting board, slice them, pile on a platter, and serve.

You'll see from the list of possible combinations that I lean to the savory for grilled cheese. No reason for you to, though. You can slip thinly sliced apples or pears into your sandwiches. Or chopped dried apricots (with Gorgonzola, on oatmeal bread).

✧ Pumpernickel, Muenster (from the grocery), and cumin seeds. Sliced tomatoes, if you like. Butter the bread.

✧ Farm bread, Taleggio, and Burst Cherry Tomatoes (recipe follows). Brush the bread with oil.

✧ White country bread, Cheshire, sliced ripe tomatoes, minced sage, and a pinch of sea salt. Butter the bread.

✧ Black bread, Neal's Yard Kirkham Lancashire or Montgomery cheddar, and sliced ripe tomatoes. Butter the bread.

✧ Brioche, Emmenthal, French ham, and a dab of Dijon mustard. Butter the bread.

✧ Italian bread, Italian Fontina, and minced Hot Peppers in Sherry (page 19). Brush the bread with oil.

✧ Farm bread, smoked cheddar, Black Forest ham or prosciutto, and prepared tapenade. Brush the bread with oil.

✧ Farm bread or slices of Italian bread, mozzarella and shredded Asiago, and Fried Peppers (recipe follows). Brush the bread with oil.

✧ Seeded rye, cheddar, and Tuna-Melt Tuna (recipe follows). Butter the bread.

✧ Seeded rye and Gouda. Butter the bread.

Burst Cherry Tomatoes Heat 2 tablespoons olive oil and 1 minced garlic clove in a small skillet over medium-high heat. When the garlic is sizzling, add 1 minced hot pepper or a pinch of crushed red pepper and 1 cup of ripe cherry tomatoes. Season well with salt. Sauté for about 5 minutes, shaking the skillet often or stirring, until the tomatoes burst and the juices start to thicken. If you make this with out-of-season tomatoes, you may need to help the tomatoes along—once they've warmed through, crush them with a potato masher or the back of a big spoon. This is enough for about 4 sandwiches.

Tuna-Melt Tuna Drain 1 can of solid white tuna and break the tuna up into tiny flakes with a fork. Stir in 1 tablespoon India relish or sweet pepper relish, 2 tablespoons minced onion, 3 tablespoons mayonnaise, and some salt and pepper. This is enough for about 4 sandwiches.

Fried Peppers Slice 2 red or yellow bell peppers into thin strips. Heat 1 generous tablespoon olive oil in a skillet over medium heat until the oil moves easily across the pan. Add the peppers and a good pinch of salt. Cook, stirring often, until the peppers are limp and starting to brown. This is enough for about 4 sandwiches.

sweet onion and tomato sandwich SERVES 2

Make this with tomatoes that are still warm from the sun. It could be summer's best sandwich.

1 sweet onion (Vidalia or Walla Walla)
1 large ripe tomato
4 slices close-textured white bread (like Pepperidge Farm)
Mayonnaise
Coarse sea salt

Peel the onion and slice very thin. Core the tomato and cut it into slabs. Smear the bread with mayo and add a layer of onion and a layer of tomato to 2 of the slices. Sprinkle with salt (you'll get a nice crunch from the sea salt when you eat the sandwich) and top with the other 2 slices of bread.

Cut the sandwiches on the diagonal. And have napkins handy. These sandwiches are addictively messy.

pancetta and lettuce sandwich SERVES 2

Ask for thick-sliced pancetta when you buy it, or substitute a thick-cut bacon. As for lettuce, French Crisp from a farmer is great, but really, iceberg is all you need—or want—for its great crunch.

The photo is on page 276.

1/2 pound pancetta, sliced about 1/8 inch thick

1 tablespoon olive oil

4 slices brioche or close-textured white bread (like Pepperidge Farm), toasted

Aïoli (recipe follows) or mayonnaise

Lettuce

Coarse salt and freshly ground black pepper

Make a little cut into the edge of each slice of pancetta to help stop it from curling while it cooks.

Heat the oil in a large skillet over medium heat. When the oil slides easily across the skillet, add the pancetta—keep it in rounds. Fry until it's crisp, then drain it on paper towels.

Slather the bread with aïoli and divide the pancetta between 2 slices. Top with a lot of lettuce—if you're using iceberg, cut slabs rather than separating leaves—sprinkle with salt, and give the lettuce a few good grinds of pepper. Top with the other slices of toast, cut the sandwiches in half, and serve.

aïoli MAKES ABOUT 3/4 CUP

If you've never made this lush, garlicky, creamy sauce, now's the time to start. It will take you just about five minutes.

Extra-virgin olive oil is essential here. I find that it turns bitter if whirred furiously in a food processor or blender, so I use a big mortar and pestle, or a wooden bowl and a rice paddle. If you can't stop yourself from using something electric, you'll need a small processor (from one of those blender/processor appliances), and you should substitute pure olive oil. You won't get the flavor, but at least the oil won't turn bitter.

4 garlic cloves

Coarse salt

1 large egg yolk

3/4 cup extra-virgin olive oil

1 tablespoon fresh lemon juice, plus more if needed

Start by smashing the garlic on a cutting board. Scrape it into a large mortar. Add a big pinch of salt and work the garlic into a very smooth and juicy paste with the pestle. (If you're making the aïoli in a wooden bowl, make the garlic paste on the cutting board, using a large chef's knife to chop, then scrape the garlic and salt with the side of the knife, and chop again until smooth.)

Add the yolk to the garlic and stir with the pestle until it's well combined and lighter in color. Drizzle in a few drops of oil and stir with vigor, scraping the pestle on the bottom of the mortar as you stir. Continue drizzling and stirring. As you go, the sauce will thicken and you can begin adding the oil in a steady stream. If you find the oil pooling, stop adding it and stir vigorously with the pestle until the sauce comes back together. When you've put in all the oil, add in the lemon juice. Stir. Taste for salt and lemon juice.

You can serve this right away or keep it covered in the refrigerator for a day or so. The garlic will intensify as the sauce sits.

the mortar and pestle

I think it's worth getting this piece of equipment, if only for making aïoli. But it's great to have around for cracking peppercorns or crushing fennel seeds or turning garlic into a paste in an instant. And pesto can also be in your future. Besides, a mortar and pestle looks great in any kitchen, from a country one to the most modern and sleek.

Mortars are made in all sorts of materials: marble, porcelain, ceramic, stoneware, granite, lava (for the Mexican molcajete), wood, and a variety of metals. The most practical are the marble and porcelain, since they're so easy to clean and they retain the least amount of odor and moisture. The big ones are the most useful. Mine's 9 inches across the top, which is bigger than any I've seen in a kitchen supply store. But there are flea markets, and medical supply stores, and eBay (which is where I found mine).

tuna salad, italian-style

MAKES ABOUT 2 CUPS (ENOUGH FOR 3 SANDWICHES)

Tuna salad, when I grew up, meant solid white tuna with Hellmann's mayonnaise. Don't expect that from this recipe. Nor is it like that dense deli salad that holds its shape when you scoop up with an ice cream scoop. This has olives and capers and parsley and onion, with a bit of celery for crunch. It makes a gloriously messy sandwich, bursting with flavor. When you've got great Italian tuna (I'm particularly fond of Flott, which comes in cans and in jars), you can make a great salad. Use Oil-Poached Tuna (page 190) here, and your salad will be even better (you'll need about 3/4 cup). As for bread, go for something crusty.

1 (6-ounce) can Italian tuna packed in olive oil, drained

1 small onion or 2 shallots, minced

1/2 celery stalk, minced

2 teaspoons capers (rinse and chop salted capers)

10 or so pitted and chopped black oil-cured olives

2 Pickled Cherry Peppers (page 390 or store-bought), sliced (optional)

2 tablespoons chopped fresh flat-leaf parsley

2 tablespoons mayonnaise

2 tablespoons fruity olive oil

Freshly ground black pepper

Bread, for sandwiches

Put the tuna in a mixing bowl and break it up with a fork into fine flakes. Add the rest of the ingredients, giving the salad a nice hit of pepper, and mix well. The salad should barely hold together.

Make sandwiches.

curried chicken salad

MAKES ABOUT 3 CUPS (ENOUGH FOR 4 SANDWICHES)

Leftover chicken's what you want for this. It could be My Roast Chicken (page 176) or Alice's Picnic Chicken (page 180). You could also poach chicken breasts just for this salad. Cut the chicken into big chunks so you'll have something to bite into.

2/3 cup mayonnaise

1 1/2–2 teaspoons curry powder

Coarse salt and freshly ground black pepper

2 cups chunked cooked chicken (see headnote)

1 small onion, minced

1 celery stalk, minced

1 tart apple (like a Granny Smith), peeled, cored, and chopped

1/2 cup sliced almonds

Bread, for sandwiches (whole wheat could be nice); optional

Whisk the mayo together with the curry powder and salt and pepper to taste in a mixing bowl. Add the rest of the ingredients and stir well.

Make sandwiches. Or do the diner thing and serve a scoop of chicken salad on a big bed of lettuce with some sliced fruit and grapes on the side.

egg salad MAKES ABOUT 2 CUPS (ENOUGH FOR 2 SANDWICHES)

The key is to make egg salad chunky. At my house, a wire French-fry cutter that I found in a flea market does the job, leaving big pieces of white and yolk. If you don't have one of these handy tools—which don't do a good job cutting potatoes for fries, by the way—you can come close by slicing an egg lengthwise in half and putting it in an egg slicer.

Lettuce is mandatory, and not just one lone leaf of it. Add a few anchovy fillets, and the sandwich is sublime.

3 large eggs, hard-cooked and chopped
Coarse salt and freshly ground black pepper
About 1/4 cup mayonnaise

Bread, for sandwiches

Put the eggs in a mixing bowl. Season with salt and plenty of pepper. Fold in enough mayonnaise to make a lush, creamy salad, at least 1/4 cup. (You're folding so you don't break up those chunks of yolks.) And that's it.

Make sandwiches.

hard-cooked eggs

Whites that are tender, yolks that are bright yellow (or orange, if you're lucky enough to buy eggs from a farmer who feeds the hens well) but still moist in the center—this is what you want in a hard-cooked egg. How you get there is the trick.

Here's my method, with a couple of pointers.

First, make only what you need. I'm not a big fan of hard-cooked eggs that have been sitting in the refrigerator.

Second, don't crowd the eggs in the pot. A single layer is best, and not a tight layer. Give them room so they cook evenly. If you want to cook a lot of eggs, use several pans.

Put the eggs into a saucepan and cover them generously with lukewarm water. Bring the water just to a boil over medium to medium-high heat. Once the water starts to bubble, turn the heat to the lowest possible setting and set the timer for 8 minutes.

When the timer rings, turn off the heat and drain the water from the pot. Give the pot a few good shakes to crack all the shells and release any noxious fumes (you've smelled sulfur when you've peeled an egg, haven't you?). This step also ensures you won't have that telltale green ring round the yolk. Cover the eggs with cold water, drain, and cover them again with cold water. Let the eggs cool completely in the water before you peel them.

three frittatas

More often than not, when I'm in Virginia, my friend Marian will ask for a frittata for lunch. These Italian omelets (for want of a better word) are pretty easy to make. What's even more attractive about them is that you can serve them hot, warm, or at room temperature, cut into wedges or packed into a sandwich. Frittatas are great picnic food, and they're also pretty nice cut into bite-sized pieces and served with drinks before dinner.

Salad is the frittata's favorite companion. Have one ready to put on the plate, or between slices of Italian bread when you're making a frittata sandwich.

asparagus and mint frittata SERVES 4

1 pound asparagus

1/4 cup olive oil

Coarse salt and freshly ground black pepper

6 large eggs

1/2 cup milk

1/3 cup freshly grated Parmesan

1 garlic clove, minced (optional)

2 tablespoons chopped fresh mint

Heat the oven to 350 degrees.

Snap the tough ends off the asparagus and discard them. Cut the stalks at a sharp angle, about 1/3 inch thick.

Heat the oil in an ovenproof skillet over medium-high heat until it shimmers. Add the asparagus, season with salt and pepper, and cook, stirring often, until the asparagus is tender and starting to brown, 4 to 5 minutes.

Meanwhile, whisk the eggs, milk, and cheese together in a bowl. You want this well blended, but not light and frothy.

Add the garlic to the asparagus if you want to and cook until it's fragrant, about 30 seconds. Pour in the eggs and season them with salt and pepper. As the eggs begin to set, scrape them with a spatula toward the center of the pan, allowing the uncooked eggs to run down to the bottom of the pan. Continue cooking and scraping until the eggs have pretty much set, about 4 minutes; the frittata will look a bit raw on top, but it will have a shape.

Scatter the mint over the top of the frittata, pushing it in some with the back of your spatula. Slide the skillet into the upper third of the oven and bake for 20 minutes, or until the frittata is golden and very puffy. Let it cool for a few minutes, then serve it right from the skillet.

green tomato frittata SERVES 4

1 small onion, minced

1/4 cup olive oil

1 large green tomato, seeded and chopped

Coarse salt and freshly ground black pepper

2 tablespoons all-purpose flour

6 large eggs

1/2 cup milk

1/3 cup freshly grated Pecorino

1/4 cup chopped fresh flat-leaf parsley

Heat the oven to 350 degrees.

Put the onion and oil in an ovenproof skillet over medium heat and cook, stirring once in a while, until the onion is turning gold at the edges.

Meanwhile, season the tomato with salt and pepper and toss it with the flour.

Turn the heat up to medium-high and add the tomato to the skillet. Cook until the tomato bits are starting to brown, about 3 minutes.

Meanwhile, whisk the eggs, milk, and cheese together in a bowl. You want this well blended, but not light and frothy.

Pour the eggs into the skillet and season them with salt and pepper. As the eggs begin to set, scrape them with a spatula toward the center of the pan, allowing the uncooked eggs to run down to the bottom of the pan. Continue cooking and scraping until the eggs have pretty much set, about 4 minutes; the frittata will look a bit raw on top, but it will have a shape.

Slide the skillet into the upper third of the oven and bake for 20 minutes, or until the frittata is golden and very puffy. Let it cool for a few minutes, then strew with the parsley and serve it right from the skillet.

bell pepper frittata SERVES 4

3 tablespoons olive oil

2 large red bell peppers, cut into 1/3-inch-wide strips, strips halved crosswise

Coarse salt

6 large eggs

1/2 cup milk

1/2 cup freshly grated Pecorino

1 garlic clove, minced

Freshly ground black pepper

Chopped fresh flat-leaf parsley, for garnish (optional)

Heat the oven to 350 degrees.

Heat the oil in an ovenproof skillet over medium heat until it shimmers. Add the bell pepper strips, season with salt, and cook, stirring often, until they are tender and starting to brown. This will take 15 minutes or so. If the peppers are browning quickly, turn down the heat.

Meanwhile, whisk the eggs, milk, and cheese together in a bowl. You want this well blended, but not light and frothy.

Turn the heat to medium-high, add the garlic to the peppers, and cook for 30 seconds, or until it's fragrant. Pour in the eggs and season them with salt and pepper. As the eggs begin to set, scrape them with a spatula toward the center of the pan, allowing the uncooked eggs to run down to the bottom of the pan. Continue cooking and scraping until the eggs have pretty much set, about 4 minutes; the frittata will look a bit raw on top, but it will have a shape.

Slide the skillet into the upper third of the oven and bake for 20 minutes, or until the frittata is golden and very puffy. Let it cool for a few minutes, scatter some chopped parsley over the top if you care to, and then serve it right from the skillet.

asparagus and poached eggs SERVES 4

This is one of those perfect spring and early summer meals, when fresh local asparagus is plentiful. You can poach the asparagus or give it a quick roast.

1 pound asparagus

1 tablespoon sherry vinegar

1 small shallot, minced

Coarse salt and freshly ground black pepper

2 tablespoons olive oil, plus more if roasting the asparagus

4 poached eggs (see page 73)

Break the tough ends off the asparagus. Peel the lower third of the spears if they're thick.

To poach the asparagus, spread the spears out in a large skillet and barely cover with cool water. Bring to a boil over high heat, cover the skillet, reduce the heat to medium-high, and cook until the asparagus is just tender. This will take about 5 minutes for pinkie-thick spears. Drain—hold the lid on the skillet, offset a bit—refresh with cold water, and drain again. Lift the asparagus out onto a kitchen towel and pat dry.

To roast the asparagus, heat the oven to 350 degrees.

Toss the asparagus with a little olive oil and spread it out on a baking sheet. Roast until just tender, about 10 minutes.

Make a little vinaigrette while you're cooking the asparagus. Spoon the vinegar into a small bowl. Add the shallot and salt and pepper to taste. Whisk to dissolve the salt. Continue whisking as you pour in the 2 tablespoons olive oil and make an emulsion.

Divide the asparagus among four plates. Spoon on the vinaigrette, top each with a poached egg, and serve. Make sure you have salt and pepper on the table for the eggs.

buttermilk pancakes
with hazelnut butter (page 28)

pickled cherry peppers (page 390)

linguine with burst tomato sauce
and fried eggs (page 166)

homemade ricotta (page 352)

rosemary focaccia (page 366) and
olives with rosemary and thyme (page 364)

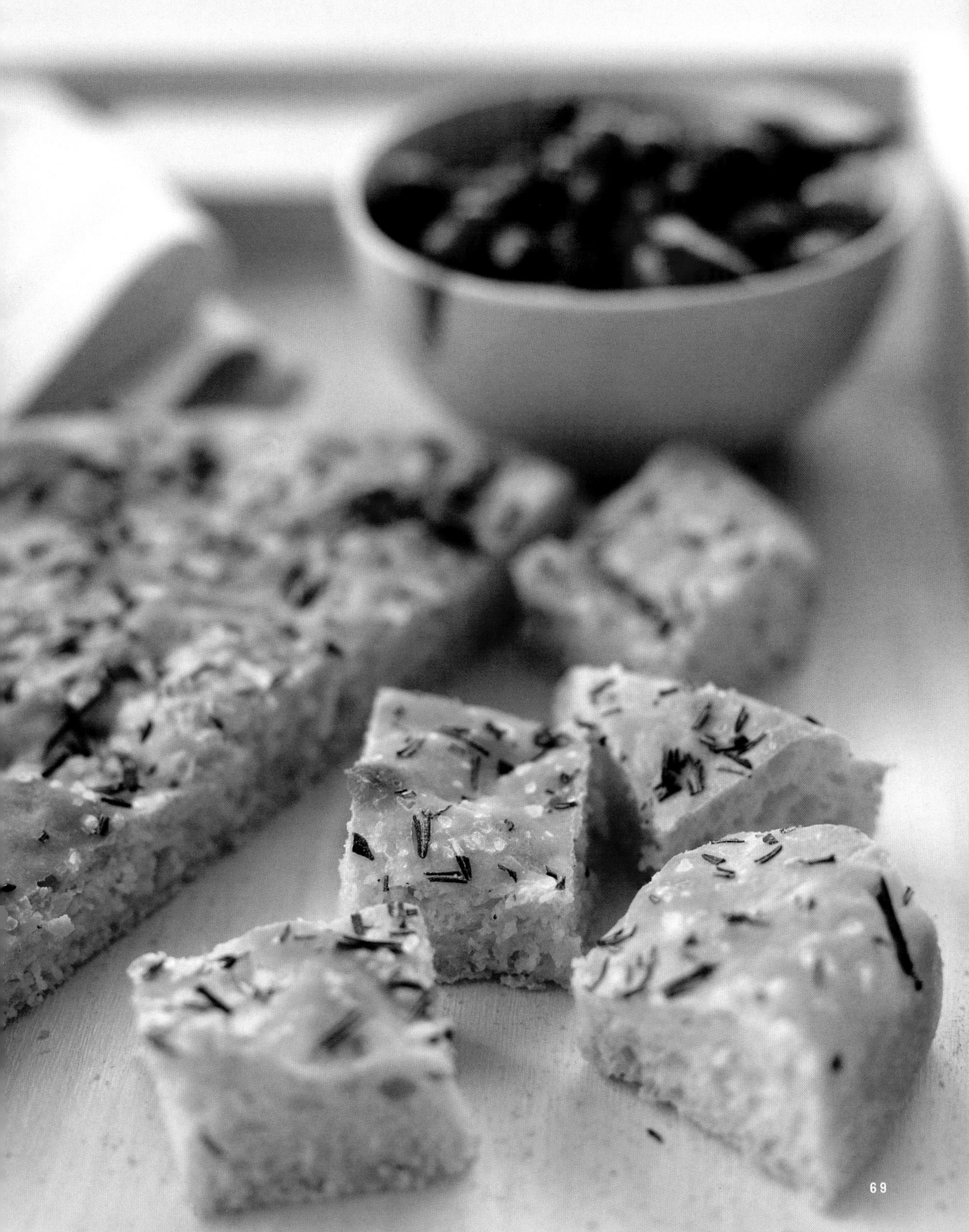

tomatoes and lemon (page 325)

fennel-orange gravlax with bagel chips (page 36) and a bloody mary (page 43)

tomato pie (page 80)

celery salad with ricotta fritters (page 342)

fried eggplant (page 270)

beets, tomatoes, and peaches (page 328)

poached eggs

The real key to pretty poached eggs—ones that are as fluffy as a new down pillow—is getting truly fresh eggs. As eggs sit in your refrigerator (or in the case at the supermarket), the whites get thinner and runnier and the yolks get flatter. If you can, buy fresh-laid eggs for poaching.

Heat about 3 inches of water in a deep skillet or wide saucepan. Add a good splash (a tablespoon or two) of white vinegar (this helps the white cling to the yolk), and bring the water to a simmer over medium-high heat. Crack the eggs into individual coffee cups.

When the water is just simmering, stir it several times so it is swirling, then slip each egg from its cup into the water so that the eggs are next to each other but not touching. You should be able to fit 4 to 6 eggs in a 10-inch skillet. Lower the heat so that the water is just barely bubbling—if it boils or even simmers too vigorously, the eggs will become tough and may break apart.

When the whites are set and opaque but the yolks are still soft, about 4 minutes, lift the eggs, one by one, from the water with a slotted spoon and slide them onto a cloth or paper towel to drain for a few seconds. If you are fussy about presentation, you may want to trim off any runaway bits of egg white with a small knife. Carefully slide the eggs off the towel and onto plates to serve.

If you must poach eggs ahead or for a crowd, you can hold them in a bowl of cold water for several hours in the refrigerator. Just slide them back into a bath of simmering water for a few seconds to reheat to serve. But they're never as good as just-made.

eggs in purgatory SERVES 2

Purgatory, here, is a buttery tomato sauce with a little crushed red pepper for heat. It's a great foil for the eggs you scramble into it. Don't make the sauce hellishly hot.

3 tablespoons unsalted butter
1 onion, chopped
Coarse salt
1 garlic clove, minced
1 (14.5-ounce) can plum tomatoes
Freshly ground black pepper
Crushed red pepper
4 large eggs
Farm bread or semolina bread, for serving

Melt the butter in a medium skillet over medium heat. Add the onion and a pinch of salt and cook until the onion is translucent and the edges are turning golden, about 8 minutes. Add the garlic and cook for a minute or so, until fragrant. Chop or crush the tomatoes and add them, with their juice, to the skillet. Season with salt, pepper, and a pinch of crushed red pepper. Bring to a boil, reduce the heat to maintain an active simmer, and cook for 15 to 20 minutes, until thickened.

Turn the heat back up to medium and crack the eggs into the tomato sauce, spacing them evenly. Season with salt and pepper. As the whites set, nudge them with a wooden spoon, letting the uncooked whites run into the sauce. Leave the yolks alone for now. Once the whites pillow up in the sauce, give everything a stir, to scramble the yolks in lightly.

Slice the bread. Toast it if you care to, and put a slice or two each on two plates. Spoon the eggs and sauce over the bread and serve immediately.

welsh rabbit SERVES 4

It's time to bring this simple dish back for lunch. In case you've never had it, think grilled cheese without the grilling. You melt cheese in a little beer and spoon it over toast. So good.

Brick cheddar doesn't cut it for this dish; buy a well-aged cheese, preferably from Vermont. The crème fraîche adds a welcome tang.

1/2 cup beer (I like ale for this)

1 teaspoon dry mustard

2 teaspoons Worcestershire sauce

1/2 teaspoon dried sage, crumbled

Pinch of cayenne

1 pound aged sharp cheddar, shredded

1/4 pound Gorgonzola dolce or other soft blue cheese, cubed

2 tablespoons crème fraîche (optional)

4 good slices country bread, lightly toasted

Broiled Tomatoes (page 293), as an optional accompaniment

Pour the beer into a saucepan. Whisk or stir in the mustard, Worcestershire, sage, and cayenne and warm the beer over medium heat, but don't bring it to a simmer. When it's steaming, reduce the heat to low and add about a third of the cheddar, stirring until it's incorporated and about half melted. Add another third of the cheddar, let it start to melt, and then add the rest of the cheddar. Add the blue cheese and let that melt, stirring and scraping the bottom of the pan to make sure everything is smooth. Stir in the crème fraîche if you're using it.

Cut the toast in half and put 2 pieces each on four plates. Pour the rabbit over the toast, dividing it evenly. Serve immediately, with the broiled tomatoes if you like, and a beer.

sicilian spinach pie MAKES 1 LARGE OR 6 SMALL PIES

One of the great pleasures of editing cookbooks is discovering recipes that are so good and so adaptable—and sometimes so obvious—that they immediately become part of my kitchen life. Cookbook author Martha Rose Shulman taught me this incredible pastry, which just might be the easiest I've ever worked with. Use a very fruity olive oil if you have one.

This tart is perfect to pack for lunch or a picnic. At home, serve it with a big salad or some grilled sausages, or both.

If there are other savory pies you'd like to make, try them with this pastry. Just be sure to roll the pastry thin; it does rise.

The photo is on page 277.

FOR THE PASTRY

1 packet active dry yeast

1/2 cup warm water

1 large egg

1/3 cup extra-virgin olive oil

2 cups all-purpose flour

Coarse salt

FOR THE FILLING

Coarse salt

2 pounds spinach, stemmed and washed

1 red onion, chopped

1/4 cup olive oil

1 garlic clove, minced

1 tablespoon tomato paste

Freshly ground black pepper

Crushed red pepper (optional)

$^{1}/_{3}$ cup raisins

$^{1}/_{4}$ cup pine nuts

1 large egg, beaten with 1 tablespoon water for an egg wash

FOR THE PASTRY

Combine the yeast and water in a large bowl and let it sit for about 5 minutes, until creamy. Add the egg and oil and whisk until smooth. Add the flour and a big pinch of salt and stir with a wooden spoon. Once the dough comes together, turn it out onto a floured counter and knead it until smooth. This will be a matter of moments. Clean out the bowl, oil it, and drop in the pastry. Cover with plastic wrap and leave it in a warm place until doubled, about 1 hour.

MEANWHILE, MAKE THE FILLING

Bring a few inches of water to a boil in a large pot. Add some salt and the spinach and cook until the spinach is tender, 2 to 3 minutes. Drain, refresh in a bowl of cold water, and drain again. Squeeze the spinach, getting out most of the water, and chop it.

Put the onion and oil in a large skillet over medium heat. Add a pinch of salt and cook until the onion is translucent and starting to go gold at the edges. Add the garlic and tomato paste and cook, stirring, for about a minute, until the paste turns brick red.

Add the spinach, a good amount of black pepper, and a pinch or two of crushed red pepper, if you want. Cook, stirring some, for 2 to 3 minutes, to get the flavors to combine. Stir in the raisins and pine nuts, taste for salt and pepper, and let the filling cool.

Heat the oven to 375 degrees. Line a baking sheet with parchment (you'll need two baking sheets for small pies).

Punch down the pastry.

FOR ONE LARGE PIE

Divide the pastry in half. Roll one half out on a floured counter to an 11-by-14-inch rectangle. Transfer it to the baking sheet and spread on the filling, leaving a 1-inch border. You'll find that it's easiest just to push the spinach around with your fingers. Roll out the other half of pastry the same size as the first and lay it on top. Trim to even the edges, then make a border by rolling the pastry in on itself 2 times. Press to seal, and make a decorative edge by pushing down on the folds with the back of a knife.

FOR SMALL PIES

Divide the dough into 12 equal pieces and roll into balls. Roll each ball into a 6-inch circle. Lay 3 rounds on each baking sheet. Add the spinach—leaving a 1-inch border—and top with the remaining pastry. (Don't form the pies on the counter; they will be impossible to move.) Make a border by turning the pastry in on itself 2 times, seal, and make a decorative edge with the back of a knife.

Brush the pie(s) with the egg wash. Bake for 30 minutes, until golden brown and risen. These are equally good hot and at room temperature.

gorgonzola and greens

This may have been my favorite lunch growing up and walking around the corner to visit my grandmother. You could start by making a batch of greens just for lunch, or use leftovers, as I do.

Reheat the greens, if necessary, in the juices you've saved with them, until they're very hot.

Meanwhile, slice up some good crusty bread, maybe pane de casa or farm bread, and slather the bread with Gorgonzola dolce. Grandma would have used the more assertive naturale, but she liked things sharp. Pretty much any blue cheese will be fine.

Put the bread and cheese into a soup plate and cover it with the hot greens. Spoon in enough of the juices to soak the bread, and drizzle with extra-virgin olive oil.

tomato pie MAKES ONE 10-INCH PIE

I first ate tomato pie like this in the eighties—at a tea shop in Connecticut. Salisbury, if you're interested. I couldn't imagine it when I saw it on the menu, and that's usually a trigger for my ordering something. What a good thing this turned out to be to eat in the middle of the afternoon. A big biscuit-crust pie filled with sliced ripe tomatoes—real tomatoes—with a little tang of cheese. But creamy too. The creamy secret is mayo.

This is one of those times when I ease up on my tomato stance. It's sublime when you make it with ripe tomatoes that you've gotten from the farmer who grew them and they're still warm with the sun. But, you know, this tastes fine with the best plum tomatoes you can find in the winter.

The photo is on page 71.

FOR THE PASTRY

2 cups all-purpose flour

2 teaspoons baking powder

Coarse salt

8 tablespoons (1 stick) unsalted butter, cut into pieces and chilled

2/3 cup milk

FOR THE FILLING

3 pounds ripe tomatoes, peeled, seeded, and sliced thick

2 tablespoons chopped fresh chives

3 tablespoons chopped fresh basil

1/4 pound best white cheddar, shredded

Coarse salt

2/3 cup mayonnaise

Heat the oven to 400 degrees.

FOR THE PASTRY

Put the flour, baking powder, and about ½ teaspoon salt in a bowl and stir with a fork. Drop in the butter and cut it into the flour until the butter pieces are about the size of small peas. Do this with a pastry blender, two knives, or your fingers. Pour in the milk and stir until you have a dough that hasn't quite come together. Dump it on the counter and knead it a few times to work in the dry flour.

Divide the dough in half. Roll one half out until it is large enough to line a 10-inch pie plate. The other half can sit unless the kitchen is hot. If it is, refrigerate the dough (or work fast).

FOR THE FILLING

Mix the tomatoes with the herbs, half the cheddar, and some salt. Pat this out evenly in the pastry. Spread the tomatoes with the mayo and scatter the rest of the cheese on top.

Roll out the rest of the biscuit dough, and top the pie. Trim the top and bottom crusts back to the rim of the pie plate, leaving no overhang. You can seal the crusts with either a fork or your fingers.

Bake the pie until it's golden, 20 to 25 minutes. Let it cool for a while before serving. It wants to be warm, not hot.

You can reheat slices in the microwave. Or in the oven, fellow Luddites.

To make this lunch, serve the pie with the simplest salad possible. Get a bag of mesclun in the grocery and toss it with extra-virgin olive oil, then add good salt and a few drops of the best wine vinegar you have—no pepper. Or, if you're making this when it's cold outside, use the inside leaves of a head of escarole and dress the salad (use more vinegar) when you put the pie into the oven.

savory cheesecake MAKES ONE 10-INCH CAKE

Let me tell you something: this cheesecake makes you friends at picnics. It's also a great lunch to eat outside, with a salad and a glass or two of wine, under a tree.

If you're getting your ricotta at the grocery, not at an Italian market or cheese shop, chances are it's watery. So, scrape it out into a colander lined with cheesecloth, set it over a bowl, and leave it in the fridge overnight to drain.

3 slices close-textured white bread (like Pepperidge Farm)
1/2 cup walnuts
4 tablespoons (1/2 stick) unsalted butter, softened
1 pound cream cheese, at room temperature
1 cup ricotta
5 large eggs
3/4 pound aged Asiago, shredded
1/4 cup chopped oil-cured olives (about 12)
1/2 teaspoon dried oregano, crumbled
Pinch of cayenne
Coarse salt and freshly ground black pepper

Heat the oven to 350 degrees.

Toast the bread on a shelf in the oven while it heats, until lightly browned. Rip it into pieces and put it in a food processor, along with the walnuts. Process until you have fine crumbs, then add the butter. Process until you've mixed the butter in completely.

Pour the crumbs into a 10-inch springform pan and tamp them down with your fingers to make a bottom crust.

Cut the cream cheese into the bowl of a standing mixer fitted with the paddle and beat at medium-high speed until smooth; or beat with a handheld mixer in a large bowl. Add the ricotta and beat to combine. Beat in the eggs one by one, taking your time while you do this so you beat in air, and scraping the bowl after you've beaten in each egg. Beat in the Asiago. Add the olives and oregano, season with the cayenne and salt and black pepper, and mix well.

Scrape the batter into the springform and jiggle the pan to even it out. Slide it into the oven and bake for about 1 hour, until the cheesecake is puffed in the center and golden. Let it rest on a rack for 30 minutes.

Run a knife around the edges of the pan before releasing the springform sides. Just leave the cheesecake on the springform bottom, and transfer it to a flat platter. You can serve this now or later. Refrigerate any leftovers, but take them out of the fridge for a while before you serve, to take the chill off.

soup

So, who doesn't like soup?

Doesn't it, in the end, bring us back into the high chair, the spoon circling, getting ready to land in the hangar that was our mouth?

For me, soup begins with stock. I'm lucky: I'm home most days, working in my dining room–library–office, so it's really easy to have a pot of stock simmering. But I usually make stock when I've got other things going on in the kitchen, or when I'm doing laundry. I'm moving around, passing the stove, and so I remember to skim. Yes, skimming is one of those things that you read about in just about every cookbook, and my friend Molly Stevens loves nothing more than standing over a big pot of stock and skimming, skimming, skimming. If I'm not in the kitchen, I'll forget to skim. Does this mean I've got stock that's ruined? Well, no. It will be murky. And maybe not as clean tasting as I want. So I'll give it a second strain, this time lining the colander with damp cheesecloth, and that gets rid of most of the undesirables floating around. Then I'll chill the stock, waiting until the fat rises and sets completely on top. Skimming molten fat is more than any of us has time for.

I know, though, that for most of you reading this, making stock will be something you'll do the day after never. Go ahead, use canned. Just make soup. Yes, you can use stock right out of the can, but you might like it better if you take a few minutes to doctor it up. Onions work miracles, and so do shallots. Pour the stock into a pan, add a cut-up onion or a shallot or two and a little bit of butter, a teaspoon or two. That bit of fat carries flavor. A sprig of thyme or a bay leaf will help even more, if you've got it. Bring to a simmer and then simmer for 15 or 20 minutes. You could prep the ingredients for a soup while you simmer the canned stock.

The fastest soup I know is one I learned from Jacques Pépin, and it has the attraction, aside from its simple comfort, of being the kind of soup you invent from your refrigerator. I'll give just the barest instructions here; reinvent the soup for yourself. Put some water up to boil, at least 5 cups for 4 people. While the water boils, shred vegetables on a box grater: an onion, of course, then carrots, zucchini, potato, tomato (over a bowl, so you capture all the juices), mushrooms—it all depends on what you have on hand. Be generous, and if your vegetables don't shred (cauliflower won't, for example), chop them fine. Mince some scallions or chives and cut a few handfuls of lettuce into thin strips. If you have tender herbs, pull off some. When the water boils, salt it and add all the vegetables and herbs. Boil for 2 to 3 minutes, then add a few tablespoons of Cream of Wheat or angel hair pasta broken into very short lengths. Cook for another 2 to 3 minutes. Serve with a pat of butter in each bowl and grated cheese on top. Add pepper if you want. And you did read this right: this is soup in about 15 minutes.

You could also play with fruit soups. Puree a cantaloupe, then season with a few drops of sherry vinegar and some salt and pepper. Garnish with crabmeat, and you've got a first course (tiny servings, of course). "Melt" some berries—raspberries, blueberries, sliced strawberries—in a saucepan with some red wine, or Sour Cherry Ratafia (page 396), if you have it. Puree in the processor or blender, push through a strainer, and add some more berries. Garnish with sour cream and pepper for a first course or whipped cream or a scoop of ice cream for dessert.

Just make soup.

summer minestrone

MAKES ABOUT 4½ QUARTS; SERVES 8, WITH LEFTOVERS

It's summer's bounty we're cooking with here, so the soup cooks in just a bit less than an hour. That's enough time for the flavors to meld, but each vegetable will still taste like itself.

This soup doesn't like being made with canned tomatoes, or plum tomatoes, or anything other than the ripest of summer tomatoes. You might splurge and use a big, meaty red heirloom, but certainly nothing less than a beefsteak. And when you seed the tomato, do it through a strainer set over that big bowl so you can capture the juices and add them to the pot.

This makes a vat, so see if you can't enlist help prepping the vegetables and serve it to a crowd. But it's so versatile, you can serve it hot or at room temperature. The leftovers can be warmed gently, or turned into ribollita (see below).

4 onions (about 1 pound), sliced painfully thin

¼ cup olive oil

3 pounds ripe summer tomatoes, peeled, seeded, and chopped (see headnote)

3 ears corn, kernels cut from the cobs

1 pound small zucchini (or avocado squash, if you can find it), cut into very thin half-moons

½ pound summer squash, scrubbed and cut into very thin half-moons

1 pound green beans (a mix of green and wax beans is nice), trimmed and cut into ¾-inch lengths

1 bunch Swiss chard (about ¾ pound), stemmed and leaves cut into very fine strips

2 pounds shell beans (cannellini, Jacob's Ladder), shelled, or one (19-ounce) can cannellini beans, rinsed well and drained

½ cup chopped fresh flat-leaf parsley

½ cup chopped fresh basil

8 cups cool water

Coarse salt and freshly ground black pepper

1 cup Arborio rice

Extra-virgin olive oil and freshly grated Pecorino, for the table

Take out your biggest soup pot, add the onions and oil, and place over medium heat. Cook until the onions start to soften and are becoming translucent. Add all the vegetables and herbs, pour in the water, and bring to a boil. Then reduce the heat, cover the pot, and cook the soup at a lively simmer for 30 minutes.

Add salt—don't be stingy—and some pepper and stir in the rice. Cook for another 15 to 18 minutes, until the rice is tender. Taste the soup again and make sure you've salted it well. You can serve it now or leave it on the stove for a few hours.

Have a cruet of extra-virgin olive oil on the table so each serving can get a healthy drizzle. And pass the Pecorino.

LEFTOVERS

As I said, you can reheat this soup gently to whatever heat you want. Since there is rice in the soup, it will thicken more, so add a little water if you need it.

You can also go the Tuscan route, following Faith Willinger's method for making ribollita. The name means "reboiled," and it's traditional with bean soups. You'll need about 6 slices of real country bread—the packaged stuff won't work—sliced about ½ inch thick. Dry the bread out in a 300-degree oven for about 20 minutes; you want it dry but not browned. Heat 5 cups leftover minestrone to boiling (adding a bit of water if you need it), then remove about 1 cup of the solids with a slotted spoon; set aside. Poke the bread into the pot of soup and turn off the heat. When the bread has softened completely, puree the soup in a food processor or with an immersion blender. Stir in the reserved vegetables and bring the ribollita back to a boil. If it is seriously thick, add some water. You want the consistency of hot cereal, or a bit looser.

This too wants a good drizzle of extra-virgin olive oil for serving, and it's enough for 4.

fresh pea soup SERVES 4

If you've never had a soup made of fresh peas, you're in for a treat. It doesn't get much more refreshing than this.

The photo is on page 153.

Coarse salt

3 pounds English peas, shelled (see Note)

1/2 head tender lettuce (Boston, Bibb, leaf), chopped

3 cups water

2 tablespoons shredded fresh mint

Bring a large pot of water to a boil. Have ready a large bowl of ice water.

Salt the boiling water very well, so it tastes like sea water, then add the peas and lettuce. Bring back to a boil and cook for 1 minute. Taste a pea: it should be heated through. Drain the peas and lettuce in a colander and then plunge the colander into the bowl of ice water to refresh the vegetables. Drain again.

Puree the peas and lettuce in 3 batches in a blender (you'll get a smoother soup in the blender than you will in a food processor), adding 1 cup of the water to each batch. Check for salt and stir in the mint.

You can serve this immediately, or chill it for later.

Note: This soup will be better made with English peas from the garden, but I have to tell you that frozen peas are pretty damn good here. As they always are.

You need 3 cups of frozen peas. Put them in a strainer and rinse under hot water until they are no longer cold. You will still need to blanch the lettuce for a minute. Once you've done that, start pureeing and finishing the recipe.

zucchini cheddar soup SERVES 6

A better cheddar means a better soup, so opt for a good one (maybe from Vermont). The same goes for the squash. A lot of interesting varieties have been making their appearance at farmers' markets, including Leida, a pale green variety with a very tender skin, and avocado (or Korean) squash—it has the same shape as a Florida avocado. Both have less moisture and more flavor than your garden-variety zucchini.

If you don't know cheddar cheese soups, you should. They have nice body to them. This one is no exception.

FOR THE SOUP

4 tablespoons (1/2 stick) unsalted butter

2 onions, chopped

3 1/2 pounds mixed summer squashes (yellow squash, baby pattypan, zucchini, Leida, avocado squash), sliced

Coarse salt

1/2 cup dry white wine or dry vermouth

5 cups chicken or vegetable stock (page 20 or 21, or canned)

1/4 cup chopped fresh basil

1/4 cup chopped fresh flat-leaf parsley

Freshly ground black pepper

3/4 pound best cheddar, shredded

FOR THE CHEESE CROUTONS

2 large slices hearty bread (like farm bread)

1/4 pound best cheddar, shredded

FOR THE SOUP

Heat the butter in a large saucepan over medium-high heat. When it stops sizzling, add the onions, squash, and a good pinch of salt. Cook, stirring once in a while, until the vegetables have collapsed and released their juices, about 10 minutes.

Pour in the white wine and bring to a boil. Then pour in the stock and add the basil and parsley. Season with salt and pepper. Bring the soup back to a boil, then lower the heat and simmer for about 30 minutes. The squash should be *very* tender, almost falling apart. Let the soup cool for a while, so it doesn't erupt when you puree it.

FOR THE CHEESE CROUTONS

Heat the broiler while the soup simmers. Toast the bread in a toaster and place on a baking sheet. Cover with the shredded cheddar and slip under the broiler. Watch carefully, and leave it in just long enough for the cheese to melt and start to brown. Let the toasts cool, then cut into squares—how big is up to you.

Puree the soup in batches in a blender. Make sure you've vented the top, or you'll make a mess. I rest the lid on the blender (plastic cap previously removed) and hold it in place with a kitchen towel. Wipe out the saucepan and return the soup to it.

Bring the soup back to a simmer. Stir in the cheddar by handfuls, letting each batch melt before adding the next. Check for salt and pepper.

Serve in deep bowls with the croutons.

cranberry bean and escarole soup SERVES 4

Fresh shell beans—those varieties like cannellini and Jacob's Ladder and cranberry that we usually see dried—are becoming more widely available. And they're a great way to start a hearty bean soup. No soaking, no long cooking.

Not being able to find fresh beans is not an excuse to skip over this soup. Dried beans are fine, though the soup will take longer to make. Use 1½ cups dried beans, picked over and rinsed, and add enough water to the pot after the stock to cover the beans by 2 inches. Depending on the age of the beans, it will take at least 1½ hours for them to become tender. Just make sure they are always covered with water.

Does it have to be a cranberry bean? Well, no. You can substitute any white bean.

1 onion, chopped fine

1 carrot, chopped fine

1 celery stalk, chopped fine

2 tablespoons olive oil

Coarse salt

1½ pounds cranberry beans, shelled

5 cups chicken or beef stock (page 20, or canned)

¾ pound escarole, well washed

Freshly ground black pepper

Extra-virgin olive oil, for serving

Put the onion, carrot, and celery into a large saucepan with the oil. Add a pinch of salt and cook over medium-high heat, stirring once in a while, until the vegetables have softened and are starting to turn gold at the edges, about 10 minutes.

Add the cranberry beans and stock and bring to a boil. Cover partway, reduce the heat, and simmer until the beans are tender, 35 to 40 minutes.

Chop the escarole and stir it into the soup. Bring it back to a boil, then simmer for about 15 minutes, until the escarole is tender. Season the soup with salt and pepper.

You can serve this now, or let it sit for a while and eat it at room temperature. Pass the good olive oil for drizzling.

variation

Not really a variation, but a way of jazzing up this simple soup.

Just before you're ready to serve the soup, heat 1 tablespoon olive oil in a skillet over medium-high heat. When it shimmers, add 1 garlic clove, minced, and cook for 30 seconds or so, until it is fragrant. Add 1 pound of shelled shrimp—small or medium ones—and season with salt, pepper, and a pinch of crushed red pepper. Cook, stirring often, until the shrimp are pink and cooked, 4 to 5 minutes. Turn off the heat and add the juice of half a lemon.

Divide the shrimp among four soup plates before ladling in the soup.

cream of mushroom soup SERVES 6

Slow-roasting concentrates the flavor in the mushrooms, making even button mushrooms rich and woodsy. From there, it's a quick trip to soup.

Use any combination of wild and tame mushrooms for this soup. And real sherry. There's a reason "cooking sherry" isn't sold with other fortified wines: it's got more salt than the Dead Sea and is designed to teach children who sneak a taste behind mother's back a nasty lesson.

1½ pounds mushrooms, trimmed and sliced thin
1 garlic clove, minced
4 shallots, chopped
½ teaspoon dried thyme
Coarse salt and freshly ground black pepper
2 tablespoons unsalted butter
2 tablespoons olive oil
Juice of 2 lemons
6 cups chicken or vegetable stock (page 20 or 21, or canned)
1 cup heavy cream
Dry sherry
Buttery Croutons (page 16), for serving

Heat the oven to 275 degrees.

Combine the mushrooms, garlic, and shallots in a baking dish large enough to hold the mushrooms in just about 2 layers. Add the thyme, season with salt and pepper, and toss. Dot with the butter and drizzle on the oil and lemon juice.

Bake for 1 hour. The mushrooms should be very tender and the juices thickened.

Put half the mushrooms into a blender and add 2 cups stock. Grind up to a smooth puree. Scrape out into a large saucepan and repeat with the remaining mushrooms and another 2 cups stock. Scrape this into the saucepan and add the remaining 2 cups stock. Bring to a boil, then reduce the heat and simmer for 20 minutes.

Add the cream to the soup and bring back to a simmer. Put a spoonful of sherry into each bowl before ladling in the soup, and garnish with the croutons.

LEFTOVERS

Yes, I make tuna noodle casserole with leftover mushroom soup. Here's how.

Slice an onion very thin. Cook it in 1 tablespoon unsalted butter with a pinch of salt in a medium saucepan over medium heat until the edges start to turn golden, about 7 minutes. Add 2 cups leftover mushroom soup. Drain a 6-ounce can of Italian tuna packed in olive oil and add it to the soup. Simmer gently while you cook ½ pound noodles until just tender (a little bit past al dente). Drain the noodles, reserving ½ cup of the cooking water.

Add the noodles and water to the pan with the soup. Stir well, then scrape into a buttered gratin dish. Sprinkle with about ½ cup (2 ounces) grated Gruyère and bake in a preheated 375-degree oven for 20 minutes, or until browned. Of course you can crush some potato chips on top if you want.

roasted tomato soup with grappa and orange

SERVES 4 TO 6

Roasting plum tomatoes intensifies their flavor and concentrates the juices, which means you can get away with using them out of season. And while I like this soup best served cold in September, I think it's pretty wonderful to be able to eat tomato soup on a cold winter night.

1 generous cup sliced carrots

3 pounds plum tomatoes, cored and halved lengthwise

1 garlic clove, unpeeled

Coarse salt and freshly ground black pepper

½ teaspoon dried thyme or oregano

3 tablespoons olive oil

½ cup minced shallots

1 (28-ounce) can plum tomatoes

1½ cups water

⅓ cup grappa or vodka

Grated zest and juice of 1 orange

Heat the oven to 350 degrees.

Oil a baking sheet and scatter the carrots over it. Set the tomatoes on top, cut side up. Stick the garlic clove in somewhere. Season with salt and pepper, crumble the thyme over the top, and drizzle with 2 tablespoons oil.

Bake for 1½ hours. The tomatoes will have collapsed, shrunk some, and started to dry out. Let the tomatoes cool down, so you can handle them.

Slip the skins off the tomatoes and discard. Pop the garlic out of its skin. Put the tomatoes, carrots, garlic, and any juices from the baking sheet into a food processor and process until smooth.

Heat the remaining 1 tablespoon oil in a large saucepan or small stockpot over medium-high heat. When the oil shimmers, add the shallots and cook for a minute or so, just to soften them. Pour in the pureed tomatoes and carrots.

Process the canned tomatoes until smooth and add them to the pot. Use the water to rinse out the food processor and the tomato can, and add to the pot. Bring to a simmer and cook for 20 minutes.

Pour in the grappa and simmer for another 5 minutes. Taste for salt and pepper.

You can serve the soup now, or you can chill it and serve it cold. Or you can reheat it later. Whichever way you choose, add the orange zest and juice right before serving.

cauliflower and tomato soup SERVES 6

Here's a meal in a bowl, with an Italian-American background.

Ask for the pancetta in one piece. Baby spinach comes in 6-ounce bags, so you could substitute that for the arugula.

1/4 pound pancetta, in one piece, cut into small dice

1 red onion, chopped fine

2 tablespoons olive oil

Coarse salt

2 garlic cloves, minced

1 (14.5-ounce) can plum tomatoes

Freshly ground black pepper

Crushed red pepper

1 large (2 1/2 pounds) cauliflower

7 cups chicken stock (page 20, or canned)

1/2 pound thin spaghetti or thin linguine, broken into 1 1/2-inch pieces

4-6 ounces arugula, torn into pieces (see headnote)

Freshly grated Pecorino and extra-virgin olive oil, for serving

Put the pancetta, onion, and oil in a stockpot or large saucepan. Add a pinch of salt and cook over medium-high heat, stirring once in a while, until the onion is softened and starting to turn golden at the edges, about 10 minutes. Add the garlic and cook for about a minute, just until you can smell it. Crush or chop the tomatoes and add them, with their juices. Season with salt and pepper and a good pinch of crushed red pepper, and bring to a simmer. Lower the heat and cook for about 10 minutes, until the sauce has thickened and is very fragrant.

While the tomatoes are cooking, cut the cauliflower up into very small florets. Think about eating them while you cut, and picture a little floret or two nestled in your spoon. When the sauce is thickened, add the cauliflower and stir well to coat all the florets. Cover and cook for about 10 minutes; the cauliflower should be crisp-tender.

Add the stock, season well with salt, and bring to a boil over high heat. Reduce to a simmer and cook for about 20 minutes; the cauliflower should be very tender. You can prepare the soup up to this point and store it for later if you like, or proceed.

Bring the soup back to a boil over high heat. Add the spaghetti and arugula and bring back to a boil. Reduce the heat to medium-high and cook for about 10 minutes, until the pasta is tender (you don't really want al dente here). Taste for salt.

You can serve this right away, or cover it and let it sit for a while. Pass the cheese and olive oil at the table.

butternut squash and roasted apple soup SERVES 6

This soup is one of the staples of fall—a kind of turning-leaves dish that is welcome when there's a chill in the air.

1 large (4–5 pounds) butternut squash

3 tart apples (like Granny Smith), peeled, cored, and quartered

1/2 pound shallots, peeled

Coarse salt and freshly ground black pepper

2 teaspoons fresh thyme leaves

1 3/4 cups cider

2 tablespoons unsalted butter

4 cups chicken or vegetable stock (page 20 or 21, or canned)

1/2 teaspoon ground coriander

Freshly grated nutmeg

1 cup heavy cream

Buttery Croutons (page 16), for serving (optional)

Heat the oven to 350 degrees, and line a baking sheet with foil.

Cut the squash in half down its length and scoop out the seeds with a spoon. Place the halves cut side down on the baking sheet and roast for at least 1 1/2 hours. When it's done, the neck of the squash will feel soft to the touch, the skin will be wrinkled and browned in spots, and the juices will have caramelized. Leave the squash on the pan until it's cool enough to handle.

Meanwhile, combine the apples and shallots in a roasting pan. Season with salt and pepper and the thyme, pour in 3/4 cup cider, and dot with the butter. Cover the pan with foil and roast for 1 hour.

Take off the foil and roast for another 30 to 45 minutes; the shallots should be very tender and most of the juices should be absorbed. Let cool for a few minutes, then puree in batches in a food processor until smooth (there may be small bits of shallot left). Pour into a stockpot.

Cut the peel off the squash and puree the flesh in batches in the food processor until very smooth. Scrape into the stockpot. Whisk in the stock and the remaining cup of cider, the coriander, and nutmeg to taste and bring to a boil. Reduce to a simmer and taste for salt and pepper (a good hit of pepper is nice as a counterpoint to the sweetness of the squash).

Pour in the cream, bring back to a simmer, and cook for about 1 minute. It's ready to serve. Garnish with some croutons if you're in the mood.

lovely lentil soup SERVES 6 TO 8

This may not be the lentil soup you're expecting. It's earthy, of course, but the lentils don't cook long enough for them to break apart in the soup. The result is a good clean flavor.

When you're buying the pancetta, ask to have it cut in one or two pieces rather than slices, so you can have nuggets of the bacon in the soup. As for the tomatoes, see if you can find cans of cherry tomatoes for this soup; they should be drained and added whole. If you can't, it won't be the end of the world, but remember that the tomatoes from San Marzano in Italy are the best.

1 pound brown lentils, picked over and rinsed

1/4 pound pancetta (see headnote), diced

2 tablespoons olive oil

1 cup chopped shallots

2 celery stalks, chopped fine

2 carrots, chopped fine

1 (14.5-ounce) can tomatoes (see headnote), lightly drained and chopped

6 cups chicken stock (page 20, or canned)

1 teaspoon fresh thyme leaves

Crushed red pepper

Coarse salt and freshly ground black pepper

1/2 pound spinach, stemmed and big leaves ripped

Extra-virgin olive oil and freshly grated Pecorino, for serving

Put the lentils in a stockpot and cover with cold water by about 2 inches. Bring to a boil over medium-high heat, then lower the heat and simmer for 15 minutes. Drain them and set them out of the way.

Wipe out the pot and add the pancetta and oil. Cook over medium heat for about 5 minutes, until the pancetta has started to go gold at the edges. Add the shallots, celery, and carrots and cook until the vegetables have softened and the shallots are translucent, another 5 minutes. Then add the tomatoes, stock, thyme, a pinch of crushed red pepper, and salt and pepper to taste. Bring this up to a simmer, lower the heat, and let it cook for 30 minutes.

Add the lentils and spinach, bring back to a simmer, and cook for 20 minutes. Taste for salt and pepper. The soup is ready to go now, or you can let it sit and reheat it later on.

Have a cruet of olive oil and a bowl of grated cheese on the table for the cognoscenti.

white bean soup SERVES 6

What is it about white food, like mashed potatoes and rice pudding, that's so comforting? This soup has that same mysterious allure, with the bonus of the perfume of rosemary.

1 onion, chopped

2 tablespoons olive oil

1/2 cup dry vermouth or dry white wine

1 recipe Basic White Beans (page 256)

4 1/2 cups chicken stock (page 20, or canned)

2 teaspoons minced fresh rosemary

Coarse salt

Extra-virgin olive oil, for serving

Cook the onion in the oil in a large saucepan over medium heat until it is starting to turn gold at the edges, about 12 minutes. Pour in the vermouth and cook for a few minutes, to reduce it by half.

Meanwhile, put the beans and their liquid in a food processor, in batches, and pulse to make a coarse puree. Add the bean puree to the pan, stir in the stock and rosemary, and season with salt. Be generous with the salt, please—if you are using unsalted stock, you'll want at least 1 1/2 teaspoons. Bring to a simmer, and cook gently for 30 minutes.

Check for salt and serve, with a cruet of extra-virgin olive oil for drizzling.

LEFTOVERS

I like turning this into a kind of gratin. Cook about ½ pound of some pasta, like shells. Drain, reserving some pasta water to thin the soup. Combine the pasta and leftover soup, with pasta water as needed, scrape it into an oiled gratin dish, and sprinkle with grated Parmesan. Bake in a preheated 350-degree oven until bubbling and browned, about 30 minutes.

But you could just as well heat the soup and use it as a pasta sauce, and skip the baking.

yellow split pea soup SERVES 4 TO 6

My grandmother Anne Gorman called split pea soup laundry-day dinner. It was something you could put to simmer on the stove while your attention was elsewhere. And when she made it for us, she also made a batch of pancakes to serve with it.

1 onion, chopped
1 tablespoon olive or vegetable oil
1 pound yellow split peas, picked over and rinsed
7 cups water
1 meaty ham bone or 2 smoked ham hocks
1 bay leaf
6 sprigs flat-leaf parsley
1 sprig sage
2 cups diced (1/4-inch) carrots
1 cup diced (1/4-inch) golden turnip or rutabaga
Freshly ground black pepper
Coarse salt
Chopped fresh flat-leaf parsley, for serving (optional)

Cook the onion in the oil in a stockpot over medium-high heat until softened and starting to brown at the edges. Add the split peas, water, and ham bone. Tie the bay, parsley, and sage together with kitchen string, and add the herb bouquet to the pot. Bring to a boil, then reduce to a simmer. Let the soup bubble gently for 1 1/2 hours, skimming when you need to.

Add the carrots and turnip and simmer for another 1 to 1½ hours. The vegetables will be very tender and the peas will have pretty much dissolved.

Discard the herb bouquet. Take out the ham bone (or hocks) and pull off the meat. Chop it, and return the meat to the soup. Season the soup well with pepper, and check it for salt (you might not need it).

Serve hot, garnished with chopped parsley, if you like.

three-onion panade SERVES 6

Winter comfort at its best: an onion soup that's thick and rich enough for you to stand a spoon in it. I first made Richard Olney's version of this dish years ago, when I got his great book *Simple French Food,* and I've been playing with it ever since. His advice: "The thing to remember is that there should be lots of onion, lots of bread, and lots of cheese."

Find bread that's dense and chewy. And you'll need a wide casserole so you can make as much rich brown gratin as possible. It is so much more a gratin than a soupy soup, you know.

The photo is on page 160.

- 5 tablespoons unsalted butter
- 1½ pounds onions, sliced thin
- 3 leeks (white and light green only), sliced thin
- ¾ pound shallots, sliced thin
- Coarse salt
- 2 teaspoons sugar
- ¾ pound dense country bread, cut into 2-inch cubes
- 6 cups chicken or beef stock (page 20, or canned)
- ½ pound Gruyère, shredded
- 1–2 tablespoons brandy

Melt 4 tablespoons butter in a large heavy pot over medium-low heat. Add the onions, leeks, shallots, and a couple of pinches of salt. Stir, then cover the pot and cook for 1 hour, stirring a few times. The onions will reduce by half, and they will be very limp and wet.

Take off the lid, sprinkle in the sugar, and crank the heat up to high. Cook, stirring frequently, for about 15 minutes. The juices will brown and stick to the sides of the pot—use a wooden spoon to scrape this good stuff into the onions. And be sure to scrape the bottom of the pot too. The onions will be creamy and light brown when ready. Turn off the heat and cover the pot.

Heat the oven to 350 degrees.

Spread the cubed bread on a baking sheet and toast lightly in the oven. This should take about 15 minutes.

Bring the stock to a boil.

Add the bread to the onions and stir. Scrape into a wide casserole. Use the stock to rinse out the onion pot, and pour the stock into the casserole. Leave this to rest for about 5 minutes. The bread will have absorbed some of the stock, but the stock should still barely cover the bread. If it doesn't, pour in some hot water.

You can make the panade up to this point and leave it covered on the stove for an hour or two, or you can bake it now.

Spread the cheese evenly over the top of the casserole and sprinkle with the brandy. Dot with the remaining tablespoon of butter. Slide the casserole into the oven and bake for 1 hour, or until the cheese has formed a rich, dark crust.

Spoon the panade out into bowls and serve hot.

chicken soup SERVES 4

Everyone's got a recipe for chicken soup, but it's also the kind of recipe you can use lots of, I think, because there are all sorts of ideas you can mine.

I start my chicken soup with stock, which I've made when I've had the time and frozen. So when I'm in the mood for this soup, I can have it on the table quickly and I don't even have to bother with skimming fat, since I took care of that when I made the stock.

1 large onion, chopped fine
3 celery stalks, minced
2 large carrots, minced
2 tablespoons olive oil
Coarse salt
6 cups Chicken Stock (page 20)
2 whole skinless, boneless chicken breasts (about 2 pounds), cubed
1 teaspoon fresh thyme leaves
1 tablespoon minced fresh flat-leaf parsley

Put the onion, celery, carrots, and oil into a stockpot over medium heat. Add a big pinch of salt and cook, stirring once in a while, until the onion is translucent, 10 to 12 minutes. Pour in the stock and bring to a boil. Once the stock is boiling, add the chicken and thyme and bring to a simmer. Lower the heat and simmer the soup for 20 minutes.

Stir in the parsley and serve.

garnishes

- ✧ If you want, cook 1 cup of rice and stir it into the soup before serving.
- ✧ The same goes for noodles or soup pasta like pastina or orzo. Cook ½ pound of dried pasta separately and add it to the soup right before serving.
- ✧ Grated Pecorino is a nice garnish for the soup, with or without rice or noodles.
- ✧ If I've got some cooked white beans in the refrigerator, I'll add these to the soup with the chicken.
- ✧ I like greens in chicken soup too; maybe ½ pound of baby spinach or tender Swiss chard (no stems) or escarole, torn into small pieces and added with the chicken.
- ✧ For Tortilla Soup, cut corn tortillas into ½-inch-wide strips and fry them in a deep skillet in about ½ inch of vegetable oil. Make sure the oil is hot, 360 degrees, before adding the strips. Stick a bamboo chopstick into the center of the skillet, right to the bottom, to test the oil: if bubbles appear instantly around the chopstick, the oil is ready. Drain the tortilla strips on paper towels, and put a big pinch of tortillas into each soup bowl before ladling in the soup. Serve with bowls of diced tomato, diced avocado, peeled and chopped roasted poblanos, and wedges of lime.

weeknight dinners

weeknight dinners

This is my idea of an easy weeknight supper:

Skillet-Roasted Char, Chinois Noodles, Apples and Arugula, and doctored-up pound cake from the store for dessert. The menu might be a bit adult for the littlest of kids, but it's pretty fast. You have to pay attention in the kitchen, but not for a long time. Chances are you aren't completely stocked up for this; at least I hope you don't have some char sitting in the refrigerator waiting for you to do something with it—fish is something you should cook the day you buy it. So you stop on the way home. No char? Substitute salmon. The ingredients for the noodles are available in most big grocery stores and in all Asian markets.

Take off your coat and put out a bowl of cashews, so you'll have something to nibble on while you cook.

The first thing I would do is to get the peppercorns into the fish. The fish, incidentally, is a superb dish: the flesh is sweet and silky, and the skin is as crisp as you could want. Make fun of anyone who dares to leave any skin on the plate.

Next, put up the water for the noodles. Then make a quick lemon glaze by beating some fresh lemon juice into confectioners' sugar. Put your favorite store-bought pound cake on a platter, surround it with sliced berries, and glaze the cake. Drizzle any glaze left in the bowl over the berries, and that's it—dessert's done.

Start melting the butter for the fish. Once you have the fish in the skillet, make the salad and the sauce for the noodles. When the water boils, cook the noodles. All that's left is plating the fish and dressing the noodles. And you'll see in the recipe that you can make the noodles even earlier, if that's the kind of schedule you have. They might be even better.

You don't have to make a dessert for dinner every night—particularly when there's fresh fruit to be had. And not all the recipes in this chapter are quite as quick as the char. But they're all suitable for the middle of the week. The marinated steaks—like the London broil and the skirt steaks—will be at their very best if you start the marinade in the morning, but if you don't plan that far ahead, they'll still be delicious after an hour on the counter. That gives you time to make some sides and set the table. And the meat cooks in a flash.

Dishes like the Sumac Chicken do take longer to cook, but that's a one-dish meal, and a beautiful one at that. The sumac stains the chicken and the bread that cooks underneath it an intriguing red and lends an elusive lemon flavor.

Quickest of all are the pastas, which can be made in the time it takes to bring the water to a boil and cook the pasta.

Not a bad thing to know that you can put something good on the table that fast.

chicken milanese SERVES 4

Crunchy breaded chicken hidden under a mountain of tart salad is just the kind of thing I want to eat on a warm summer night. Perhaps you agree.

These don't take long to make, but if you have some extra time, make extra chicken breasts so you'll have them in the refrigerator for sandwiches.

If you don't have summer tomatoes, skip the tomatoes altogether. You want flavor.

The photo is on page 278.

FOR THE CHICKEN

2 whole boneless, skinless chicken breasts (about 2 pounds)

Coarse salt and freshly ground black pepper

3/4 cup all-purpose flour

2 large eggs

1/3 cup freshly grated Pecorino

1/4 cup milk

About 1 1/2 cups dried bread crumbs

Olive oil, for frying

FOR THE SALAD

4 big handfuls arugula

2 ripe summer tomatoes, cored and cut into wedges

1 small red onion, sliced thin

1/4 cup extra-virgin olive oil

Coarse salt and freshly ground black pepper

2 tablespoons balsamic vinegar, or to taste

FOR THE CHICKEN

Cut the breasts into halves, and trim away any cartilage or visible fat. Lay the chicken pieces out on plastic wrap, cover with another sheet of plastic, and pound to about 1/3 inch thick. If you don't have a classic meat pounder, use a rolling pin.

Season the chicken with salt and pepper. Set out three shallow bowls. Put the flour in one; beat the eggs in the second, then beat in the Pecorino and milk; and put the bread crumbs in the third. Dredge the chicken pieces in the flour and pat them, so you have just a thin dusting of flour. Then dip in the egg wash and dangle the chicken over the bowl to let the excess drip off. Finally, coat the chicken in the crumbs, pressing well to get a good coating. As you finish breading, put the chicken on a rack. You can prep the chicken this far a few hours in advance. Set the rack on a baking sheet, cover loosely with wax paper, and refrigerate.

Set a large skillet over medium-high heat and fill with about $^1/_3$ inch oil. Heat until the oil is shimmering. Fry the chicken 2 pieces at a time—no crowding—until golden brown on each side, and drain on another rack set over a baking sheet.

FOR THE SALAD

Rip the arugula into pieces and drop them into a mixing bowl. Add the tomatoes and onion and spoon on the extra-virgin olive oil; season with salt and pepper. Toss to get the salad coated with oil. Spoon on the vinegar and toss again. Taste a bit of the arugula and add more vinegar if you want.

To serve, put a chicken cutlet in the center of each dinner plate and top with a big heap of salad.

variations

The classic preparation is with a veal chop. You could substitute veal cutlets or pork chops—with or without bones—for the chicken.

chicken with vinegar and onions SERVES 4

This is what my grandmother called chicken cacciatore. And it does seem pretty likely that hunters wouldn't be carrying a lot more than some onions and wine with them when they went out into the woods.

My grandmother rarely had wine in her house, so she made this with vinegar. I've toyed with it over the years, and I've found that champagne vinegar and some dry vermouth give the dish the tang I like. If you want, use more wine than vinegar, but keep the same amount of liquid. Remember, this should be sharp. Champagne is a gentle vinegar. If you use white wine vinegar, you may want to lean toward more wine than vinegar.

Use your own hot cherry peppers (see page 390), or commercial ones from the pickle aisle.

Tangy and juicy, this calls out for rice on the plate with it.

5 chicken thighs (about 2 1/2 pounds)

Coarse salt and freshly ground black pepper

3 tablespoons olive oil

3 large onions, sliced thin

1 large garlic clove, minced

1 hot cherry pepper in vinegar, or more, seeded and torn into pieces

1/2 cup champagne vinegar

1/2 cup dry vermouth or dry white wine

Season the chicken with salt and pepper. Heat the oil in a large skillet over medium-high heat until it shimmers. Brown the chicken in batches—don't crowd it in the skillet—on both sides, and transfer the pieces to a bowl as they're done.

Spoon out excess oil or fat, leaving about 2 tablespoons in the skillet. Add the onions and a big pinch of salt, lower the heat to medium, and cook until the onions are soft and lightly colored, 10 to 12 minutes. They will release their juices, so scrape the bottom of the pan while they cook to dissolve any of the browned bits from the chicken. Add the garlic and hot pepper and cook for about a minute, then pour in the vinegar and wine and bring to a simmer.

Bury the chicken pieces in the onions and vinegar, and pour in any juices from the chicken bowl. Cover and simmer for 25 minutes, checking and monitoring the heat to make sure you're at a simmer and not a boil. You want small, steady bubbles. Turn the chicken pieces and cook for another 10 minutes.

Spoon the chicken and all the onions and juices out onto a deep platter and serve.

LEFTOVERS

If I've got leftovers, I'll shred the chicken and mix it with the onions and juices and store it that way. Then I make rice timbales.

Butter some ramekins and coat with dried bread crumbs (make sure you've got a good coating on the bottom). Heat the leftovers and mix them with hot rice; stir in some grated Pecorino and chopped fresh parsley. Pack into the ramekins and bake at 350 degrees for 20 minutes. Turn the timbales out onto plates and serve.

DINNER

Chicken with Vinegar and Onions

White Rice

Asparagus

Drop a bay leaf into the rice when you make it. Take your pick of asparagus: Lemon Roast (page 252) or Asparagus and Prosciutto (page 253). Or substitute Broccoli Cooked Forever (page 258).

sumac chicken with bread salad SERVES 4

Traditional in Middle Eastern cooking, the spice sumac brings a clean, tart flavor—think of a flowery lemon—to chicken as well as a deep rose color. As the chicken roasts, it will dye the bread underneath it too. My friends Zaid and Haifa Kurdieh, organic farmers from Norwich, New York, introduced me to sumac and told me about this recipe.

Armenian or Persian cucumbers, if you can find them, are delicious in this salad and, like Kirbys, don't need to be peeled or seeded. If neither is available, your basic cucumber will be fine—just peel and seed it before slicing. Ripe summer tomatoes are ideal. If you're making this out of season, substitute halved cherry tomatoes, which usually have some semblance of flavor in winter.

Buy a 1-pound loaf of very crusty bread, carve off the heavy bottom crust, trim edges that are particularly ragged—remember that some crust is nice—and you'll have just what you need.

If you can, start the dish in the morning by seasoning the chicken.

The photo is on page 280.

1 (3- to 3½-pound) chicken

Coarse salt and freshly ground black pepper

2 tablespoons ground sumac (see Note)

5 tablespoons olive oil

2 large red onions (about 1 pound), sliced thin

2 large garlic cloves, minced

2 tablespoons chopped fresh flat-leaf parsley

¾ pound dense bread (something like farm bread or pane de casa), cut into 1-inch cubes (see headnote)

3 Kirby cucumbers, quartered lengthwise, cut into ¼-inch slices, and tossed with a big pinch of salt

1 large ripe summer tomato, cored and cut into chunks

Juice of ½ lemon, or to taste

Cut the backbone out of the chicken with kitchen shears and flatten the chicken. Season it generously with salt and pepper on both sides. Make a paste with the sumac and 2 tablespoons oil and rub the paste into both sides of the chicken. Refrigerate on a plate—no need to cover—for about 8 hours. Or, if you haven't planned ahead, just leave the seasoned chicken on the counter while you prepare the onions and bread.

Heat the oven to 375 degrees.

Put the onions and the remaining 3 tablespoons oil into a large skillet over medium-high heat. Salt the onions and cook, stirring once in a while, until they are limp and turning gold at the edges, around 9 minutes. Add the garlic and parsley and cook until fragrant, about 30 seconds. Scrape the onions into a large mixing bowl and add the cubed bread. Toss.

Oil a casserole large enough to hold the bread in a single layer (I use a 12-inch round terra-cotta dish). Scrape in the bread and onions and spread them out. Set the chicken on top of the bread and roast for 1 hour.

Set the chicken on a cutting board and let it rest for 10 minutes.

Scrape the bread out into a big mixing bowl and let it cool for about 5 minutes. Add the cucumbers and tomato, squeeze in the lemon juice, and toss. Check for salt and pepper, and add more lemon juice if you want.

Pile the salad onto a platter. Cut the chicken into quarters and arrange it around the salad. It's ready to serve.

The leftover salad is great as a snack. Check to see if it needs another shot of lemon.

Note: You can find ground sumac in Middle Eastern markets or by mail from Kalustyan's (www.kalustyans.com or 800.352.3451).

DINNER

This is pretty much a meal in itself, but if you want, start with a simple soup.

broiled chicken with ginger and lime SERVES 6 TO 8

This is a take on Buffalo chicken wings, made with cut-up chicken so you can serve it for dinner. The chicken gets marinated with ginger and lime so it's flavorful but not incendiary.

You won't dip the chicken pieces in blue cheese dressing either, the way you would with Buffalo wings. Cut wedges of iceberg lettuce and pour the dressing over them (see page 321). Go on—your friends will be impressed.

FOR THE MARINADE

- 2/3 cup soy sauce
- 2/3 cup fresh lime juice (from about 4 limes)
- 1/4 cup vegetable oil
- 1/2 cup sugar
- 1/4 cup minced ginger
- 2 garlic cloves, smashed

2 (3 1/2-pound) chickens, cut into serving pieces

FOR THE DIPPING SAUCE

- 4 tablespoons (1/2 stick) unsalted butter
- 1/3 cup fresh lime juice (from about 2 limes)
- Crushed red pepper

FOR THE MARINADE

Whisk the soy, lime juice, oil, sugar, ginger, and garlic together in a small bowl. Pack the chicken pieces into a large sealable plastic bag and pour in the marinade. Close the bag and let the chicken marinate on the counter for 1 hour.

Position a rack near the middle of the oven so the chicken will be about 8 inches from the heating element, and heat the broiler. Line a baking sheet with aluminum foil. Arrange the chicken pieces on the baking sheet—skin up and thicker pieces in the middle of the pan—and slide the pan under the broiler. Broil for 10 minutes.

Turn the pieces over and broil for another 10 minutes.

MEANWHILE, FOR THE DIPPING SAUCE

Melt the butter in a small skillet or saucepan over low heat. Add the lime juice and a big pinch of crushed red pepper.

Roll the chicken pieces in the lime butter. Transfer to a platter and serve.

DINNER

Broiled Chicken with Ginger and Lime

Chinois Noodles (page 310)

Roasted Italian Peppers (page 333)

Iceberg Wedges with Blue Cheese Dressing (page 321)

flounder baked with tomatoes SERVES 2

This recipe is easily doubled, and if you're making it in tomato season, by all means substitute slabs of heirloom tomatoes for the cherry tomatoes.

The photo is on page 159.

1 pint cherry tomatoes, halved

1 small onion, sliced thin

3 tablespoons olive oil

1 bay leaf, torn in half

Coarse salt and freshly ground pepper

1 slice close-textured white bread (like Pepperidge Farm)

1/2 cup freshly grated Parmesan

3/4–1 pound flounder fillets

DINNER

Flounder Baked with Tomatoes

Creamy Spinach (page 292)

Crusty bread

You can add to the side dishes, if you want. Roast Peppers with Capers and Anchovies (page 332) or Peperonata (page 283), Skillet Corn (page 267), or Saffron Cauliflower (page 265). Rice, mashed potatoes, maybe Mushroom Pilaf (page 300).

Heat the oven to 350 degrees, and oil a casserole with low sides—one just large enough to hold the fish comfortably in one layer.

Put the tomatoes, onion, 2 tablespoons oil, and the bay leaf in the casserole, season with salt and pepper, and toss. Bake for 25 to 30 minutes, until the tomatoes have started to collapse. Take the casserole out of the oven and turn on the broiler.

Meanwhile, crumble the bread into crumbs or whir it in a food processor. Mix with the cheese.

Once the broiler is good and hot, lay the flounder on top of the tomatoes, strew with the cheese crumbs, and drizzle with the remaining 1 tablespoon olive oil. Broil for 3 to 4 minutes, until the crumbs are browned and the cheese is bubbling a bit. Let sit for about 5 minutes for the fish to finish cooking before serving.

Serve hot.

bluefish dijonnaise SERVES 4

You can't really go wrong with this technique and with this flavoring. Can't find bluefish? No problem. Substitute mackerel, black sea bass, even flounder.

The key to success here is the griddle. Broiler pans are designed for cooking meat: their accordion-pleated surface isn't fish-friendly. A searingly hot griddle sets the skin quickly, so it will be crisp when the fish is cooked, and the flat surface means you can slide your spatula under the fish with ease. It also means the fish takes only a few minutes to cook.

1½ pounds bluefish fillets, cut into 4 portions

Coarse salt and freshly ground black pepper

¼ cup mayonnaise

2 tablespoons Dijon mustard

1 tablespoon chopped fresh flat-leaf parsley

Place a rack in the upper third of the oven, set a flat cast-iron griddle on the rack (you want it about 5 inches from the heat source), and turn on the broiler. Let it heat for 15 minutes.

Season the fish on both sides with salt and pepper. Stir the mayonnaise and mustard together and spread over both sides of the fish.

Place the fish skin side down on the smoking-hot griddle and broil for about 3 minutes. The topping should be bubbling and browned in spots.

Use a big spatula to transfer the fish to four dinner plates. Sprinkle with the parsley, and serve.

DINNER

Bluefish Dijonnaise

Oniony Orzo (page 299)

Peperonata (page 283)

skillet-roasted char SERVES 4

I learned this no-fuss method from the French chef Georges Blanc. The result: silky-smooth fish with buttery, crunchy skin.

The kind of peppercorns is your choice. Black will give nice flavor, but if you have pink and white in your spice cabinet, use some combination that strikes your fancy. Big grains of sea salt are really what you want to finish the fish, but coarse kosher is fine.

If you can't find Arctic char, buy salmon. Salmon is usually thicker, so it will take longer.

4 (6-ounce) skin-on Arctic char fillets

Peppercorns (see headnote)

4 tablespoons (1/2 stick) unsalted butter

Coarse sea salt

Check the fish for pinbones and pull them out with tweezers if you find them. Stick a few peppercorns into each fillet and let the fillets sit on the counter for 15 minutes or so.

Choose a heavy skillet that's large enough to hold the fish comfortably in one layer. Melt the butter in it over medium heat. When the butter stops sputtering, slip in the fish, skin side down. Now leave it alone for about 12 minutes. The fish is done when it has turned opaque almost all the way up to the top; the top should remain pink and rare.

Use a large spatula to remove the fish to a platter or to dinner plates, and sprinkle the fish generously with salt. This can sit for a few minutes before serving.

DINNER

Skillet-Roasted Char

Chinois Noodles (page 310)

Apples and Arugula (page 324)

Toasted Israeli Couscous with Red Pepper and Saffron (page 306) is a nice companion to the fish. So are The Simplest Cooked Greens (page 282).

cod simmered in milk SERVES 4

Think about this for a cold winter night. It's plain, simple, and nursery good.

$^{3}/_{4}$ cup milk

2 large shallots, sliced very thin

2 bay leaves

Coarse salt

$1^{1}/_{2}$ pounds skinless cod fillet, about 1 inch thick, pinbones removed and cut into 4 equal portions

Freshly ground white pepper

Sweet paprika

2 tablespoons unsalted butter

DINNER

Cod Simmered in Milk

Company Mashed Potatoes (page 286)

Broiled Tomatoes (page 293)

Honey-Glazed Turnips and Pears (page 298)

I go with the variation in the recipe for the tomatoes and have a honey feast with the sweet cod.

Pour the milk into a deep skillet just big enough to hold the fish comfortably and add the shallots and bay leaves. Season with salt. Bring to a simmer, reduce the heat to as low as possible, and let infuse, partially covered, for 30 minutes. This should not bubble, so use a flame tamer if you need to.

Meanwhile, season the cod well with salt and pepper and sprinkle lightly on top with paprika. If necessary, fold the tail end under so the fish is an even thickness. Let the fish sit on the counter while the milk infuses.

Bring the milk back to an active simmer and stir to break up the skin on the milk. Slide in the cod, paprika side up, top with thin slices of the butter, reduce the heat, cover, and cook for 10 minutes.

Remove the fish with a slotted spoon or spatula. The milk sauce will have curdled, so either whisk it or puree it in the blender. Spoon some mashed potatoes onto each dinner plate, lean a piece of fish on the potatoes, and spoon on some of the milk sauce. Pass the other side dishes.

cod, puttanesca-style SERVES 4

Here we've got the ingredients, but not the proportions, of a traditional puttanesca pasta sauce. I'm sure you've heard the story about that sauce: quick enough for prostitutes to make between customers. This takes a bit longer, but then, I don't have those time constraints. And it's worth the extra time to simmer the fish in the sauce, rather than just serving the sauce on top of it.

1½ pounds skinless cod fillet, pinbones removed and cut into 4 equal portions

Coarse salt and freshly ground black pepper

All-purpose flour, for dusting

¼ cup olive oil

1 large onion, sliced thin

1 garlic clove, minced

3–4 anchovy fillets, chopped

1 tablespoon tomato paste

½ cup dry white wine or dry vermouth

¼ cup water

1 pint cherry tomatoes

12 oil-cured olives, pitted and chopped coarse

Crushed red pepper

⅓ cup chopped fresh flat-leaf parsley

Season the fish with salt and pepper and dust it with flour. Pat off any excess flour.

Heat the oil over medium-high heat in a skillet large enough to hold the fish in one layer. When the oil is shimmering, add the fish and cook until light golden brown, about 3 minutes a side. Remove the fish to a plate and cover loosely with a piece of foil.

Add the onion and a pinch of salt to the oil in the skillet and cook until the onion is limp and starting to turn gold at the edges, about 6 minutes. Add the garlic and anchovies and cook for 1 minute. Stir in the tomato paste and cook, stirring, until the paste has turned brick red, about 2 minutes. Add the white wine and water and let it bubble up. Stir well. Add the cherry tomatoes, olives, and a pinch of crushed red pepper. Bring to a boil, then reduce the heat, cover, and simmer the sauce for 20 minutes.

Uncover the skillet and use a potato masher or the back of a wooden spoon to smash any of the tomatoes that haven't collapsed. Nestle the fish into the sauce, spooning some sauce on top, and cover the pan. Simmer for 10 to 15 minutes, until the fish is cooked through.

Transfer the fish and sauce to a platter, shower with the chopped parsley, and serve.

DINNER

Cod, Puttanesca-Style

Riso with Peas (page 303)

Green Salad

If you've got the time and the inclination, try serving the cod over Polenta (page 311). I won't tell if you use the quick stuff. But if you do, then I think you should have time to make dessert.

A simple oil-and-vinegar dressing is all you need for the greens.

If you're not in a hurry and are feeling generous, make some Fried Eggplant (page 270) to go with the fish.

bacon-wrapped shrimp SERVES 6

Sweet and finger-licking good.
The photo is on page 154.

2 pounds extra-large (16–20 count) shrimp, shelled

2 tablespoons olive oil

1 tablespoon chopped fresh basil (Thai, if you can find it)

Coarse salt and freshly ground black pepper

8–10 slices bacon, cut into quarters

3 tablespoons maple syrup

2 tablespoons ketchup

2 teaspoons fish sauce or soy sauce

DINNER

Bacon-Wrapped Shrimp

Corn Custard (page 269)

Tomato Tomato Salad (page 326)

These shrimp may seem summery, but they're good year-round. In winter, I might serve them with Roast Pumpkin with Sage (page 291).

Soak at least 10 bamboo skewers in water for about 30 minutes.

Toss the shrimp with the oil, basil, and salt and pepper to taste.

Wrap each shrimp around the middle with a piece of bacon, kind of like a girdle, and spear it with a skewer—you may need to stretch the bacon to make sure both ends meet to be captured by the skewer. I fill each skewer with 4 wrapped shrimp, leaving a bit of breathing room between them, but you can pack more or fewer shrimp onto each skewer. And you can prep these way in advance and refrigerate them until you're ready to cook them.

Prepare an outdoor grill or heat the broiler.

Make a quick little sauce by whisking the syrup, ketchup, and fish sauce together in a small bowl.

Brush the shrimp on both sides with the sauce and grill or broil until the bacon is crisp and the shrimp is just cooked through, about 3 minutes a side. If you want, brush the shrimp again with the sauce right after you turn them.

You can serve the shrimp on the skewers or not.

inside-out cheeseburgers SERVES 6

Sure, you can always slice some good cheddar or Emmenthal or pepper Jack and melt it on a burger, but burying some butter and blue cheese inside suffuses the meat with flavor. Have plenty of napkins handy.

1/4 pound blue cheese, softened

4 tablespoons (1/4 stick) unsalted butter, softened

2 pounds ground round

Coarse salt and freshly ground black pepper

1 tablespoon Worcestershire sauce

Mash the cheese and butter together with a fork.

Crumble the beef into a bowl and season with salt and pepper. Sprinkle the Worcestershire over the meat and toss, as if you were tossing a salad.

Divide the beef into 12 patties. Divide the cheese and butter among 6 of the patties. Top the adorned with the unadorned, pinching the edges together. Do a thorough job enclosing the cheese in the meat, but don't squish; the more you compact the meat, the less tender and juicy your burgers will be.

Prepare an outdoor grill or heat a ridged cast-iron grill pan, and cook the burgers. About 3 minutes a side will give you a rare burger.

DINNER

Put out all your pickles, a big bag of potato chips, and Spicy Watermelon Salad (page 337) if it's a grown-up night.

LEFTOVERS

I like cold burgers, and these make a great sandwich. Toasted white bread, refrigerator pickles, sliced tomato, escarole or another sturdy lettuce, and some ketchup will do it.

broiled rib-eye steaks with gorgonzola butter

SERVES 4

Steak is one of the easiest proteins to come up with on a weeknight. It's quick, and it's flavorful. But steak is steak. So hearken back to the old days, when a pat of a compound butter—the classic was *maître d'hôtel,* with parsley and lemon juice—melted down into a hot piece of grilled meat. Gorgonzola butter adds much more in the way of flavor and texture, but you have many other options. See the box that follows.

The photo is on page 275.

FOR THE GORGONZOLA BUTTER

8 tablespoons (1 stick) unsalted butter, softened

½ pound Gorgonzola dolce, at room temperature

Coarse salt and coarsely ground black pepper

FOR THE STEAKS

2 teaspoons herbes de Provence

2 (1-pound) boneless rib-eye steaks

Coarsely ground black pepper

Coarse salt

Chopped fresh flat-leaf parsley, for garnish

FOR THE GORGONZOLA BUTTER

Beat the butter in a small bowl with a wooden spoon until it's smooth. Add the Gorgonzola and stir to combine, but leave some lumps of cheese. Season with salt and pepper.

Scrape the butter out onto a sheet of wax paper or aluminum foil and use a spatula to form it into a rough log 5 or 6 inches long. Wrap the paper around the butter, using the paper to shape the butter into a uniform log as you roll. Twist the ends closed and refrigerate until firm and well chilled, at least 2 hours.

FOR THE STEAKS

Crumble the herbes de Provence and rub into both sides of the meat. Season the steaks generously with pepper. Leave them on the counter for 30 minutes to 1 hour.

Heat the broiler, with the broiler pan about 5 inches from the heat source.

Broil the steaks, turning them once and salting them when you turn them, to your desired doneness. Broiling steaks that are 1 inch thick for 5 minutes per side should result in meat that is medium-rare.

Top the steaks with a few pats of the Gorgonzola butter and let them rest on a cutting board for at least 5 minutes.

Slice the steaks and arrange the slices on a platter. Garnish with more slivers of Gorgonzola butter and a shower of parsley.

DINNER

Broiled Rib-Eye Steaks

Mushroom Pilaf (page 300)

Butter-Braised Cauliflower and Turnips (page 264)

Or do the meat and potatoes thing and serve the steaks with Company Mashed Potatoes (page 286) and a tomato salad.

compound butters

If you have one or two of these flavored butters in the refrigerator, you can easily transform the simplest and most plainly prepared food into something really tasty. Put a pat onto any broiled or grilled steak or chops, or broiled fish, or steamed vegetables and potatoes. You could also halve tomatoes through the equator, nudge out the seeds, dust with fresh bread crumbs, and top with a pat of one of the butters; broil until the crumbs are browned. Two teaspoons or so are not unwelcome inside a burger before you cook it.

Here are some ideas for other butters. Follow the instructions in the recipe on page 134 to prepare them. They all make about ½ cup.

✧ **Anchovy Butter** Combine 1 stick of butter with 6 to 8 minced anchovies, 1 teaspoon fresh lemon juice, and salt and pepper. Go light on the salt.

✧ **Herb Butter** Combine 1 stick of butter with 3 tablespoons minced fresh herbs (parsley, chives, and thyme), 1 teaspoon fresh lemon juice, and salt and pepper. Using very coarse sea salt will give you crunch in your butter.

✧ **Dill-Lemon Butter** Combine 1 stick of butter with 2 tablespoons chopped fresh dill, 1 small minced shallot, 1/2 teaspoon grated lemon zest, 1 teaspoon fresh lemon juice, and salt and pepper. As with the herb butter, coarse sea salt is a nice touch.

✧ **Caper-Rosemary Butter** Combine 1 stick of butter with 2 tablespoons capers (rinse, drain, and chop them), 1 tablespoon minced fresh rosemary, and salt and pepper.

✧ **Roasted Garlic Butter** Combine the roasted garlic (below) with 1 stick of butter and salt and pepper.

✧ **Roasted Garlic** Separate half a head of garlic into cloves. Put the unpeeled cloves on a piece of foil, drizzle with 1 teaspoon of olive oil, and season with salt and pepper. Seal into a tight package and roast in a preheated 350-degree oven for 30 minutes or so, until the garlic is soft. Unwrap the package and let the garlic cool. Squeeze the garlic out from the skins, and mash it.

skillet flank steak SERVES 4

Flank steak responds well to pan-roasting and rewards you with crusty, juicy meat. If you haven't stockpiled the herbed salt, add a sprig of rosemary or a few sprigs of thyme to the skillet with the butter.

1 (1½-pound) flank steak

Freshly ground black pepper

1 tablespoon vegetable oil

Herbed Salt (page 19) or coarse salt

3 tablespoons unsalted butter

Take the steak out of the refrigerator about 30 minutes before you're going to cook it. Season it with pepper—go for it—and press the pepper into the steak.

Put a 10-inch cast-iron skillet over medium-high heat and heat it for a few minutes. Spoon in the oil. Let it heat until the oil is almost smoking, then lay the steak in the skillet. Leave it alone for 4 minutes to get a good brown crust on the meat.

Turn the steak over and season it well with herbed salt. Leave the heat on medium-high for 2 minutes. Add the butter to the skillet and turn the heat to medium-low. Cook the steak, basting often with the butter, for 10 minutes. Let the steak rest on a cutting board for at least 5 minutes before carving into thin slices on a sharp angle.

DINNER

Skillet Flank Steak

Riso (page 302)

Tomatoes and Lemon (page 325)

Riso in any of its permutations is a fine accompaniment to this steak, but then, so too are mashed potatoes or Oniony Orzo (page 299).

new year's eve steak SERVES 4

Every New Year's Eve, when I visit friends in Virginia, I make a first course of homemade pasta tossed with butter and lemon zest and topped with caviar. One year, we had blade steaks to follow (local grass-fed ones that had been aged). Following the Tuscan tradition, I grilled the steaks and squirted some lemon on them. Since I had some caviar left, I spread it over the steaks. That modest cut of meat turned into something truly celebratory.

I think Tuesday is a good night to celebrate. Use any steak you want, but do keep blade steaks in mind. They're inexpensive and they pack a lot of flavor. That central piece of gristle can taste a bit like liver, so cut it out. The method here is for the skillet, but grill the steaks if you want.

When it comes to caviar, go American.

4 (6-ounce) blade steaks (sometimes called flat-iron steaks)

Coarse salt and freshly ground black pepper

Vegetable oil

2 tablespoons unsalted butter

2 sprigs thyme or lemon thyme

1 ounce black caviar

Half a lemon

DINNER

New Year's Eve Steak

Lemon Potatoes (page 290)

Apples and Arugula (page 324)

You can certainly add more vegetables to the plate, and you can make just about any salad. Not in the mood for potatoes? Serve buttered noodles. Grate some lemon zest into them.

Heat a large heavy skillet over medium-high heat, and season the steaks with salt and pepper. When the skillet is hot, pour in a film of oil and let it heat until it shimmers. Add the steaks and let them brown for 3 minutes. Turn the steaks over, add the butter and thyme, and reduce the heat to medium. Cook, basting the meat with the butter, for another 3 minutes for medium-rare. Take the steaks out of the skillet and let them rest for 5 minutes.

Plate the steaks and smear each of them with some of the caviar. Squeeze the lemon over them and serve.

beer and molasses flank steak SERVES 8

Put molasses in a beef marinade, and you get some truly tasty browned and crunchy bits on the edges of the meat when you grill. Lager is my choice of beer in this recipe, but play around. Maybe a bottle of stout?

Most of the time, I use this marinade for flank steaks, since they're so easy to find. But, boy, is this good with skirt steaks.

There's a lot of meat here, so serve a crowd. Or stash the leftovers for sandwiches.

1 (12-ounce) bottle of beer (your choice)
1/3 cup molasses
1/4 cup soy sauce
Juice of 2 limes
3 garlic cloves, chopped
2 serrano chilies (or other hot peppers), halved lengthwise
2–3 slices ginger, smashed with the flat of your knife
2 (2-pound) flank steaks
Coarse sea salt and freshly ground black pepper

Combine the beer, molasses, soy, lime juice, garlic, chilies, and ginger in a large sealable plastic bag. Seal it and squish the bag with your hands to combine. Or put those ingredients in a pitcher and give them a whisk, then pour into the bag. Add the steaks and seal the bag, squeezing out the air. Squish it again to distribute the marinade. Put the bag on a big plate or in a bowl and refrigerate for 3 to 4 hours, turning it over every once in a while. Or, if you don't have that much time, marinate the steak on the counter for 1 hour.

Take the meat out of the refrigerator. Prepare an outdoor grill, or slip the broiler pan into the oven and heat the broiler. Grill or broil the steak to your desired state of doneness, about 5 minutes per side for rare, then let it rest on a cutting board for 10 minutes. Sprinkle with salt and pepper and slice on a sharp diagonal.

DINNER

Beer and Molasses Flank Steak

Fresh "Polenta" (page 268)

Tiny Tomatoes on the Grill (page 295)

or

Tomatoes, Kirby Cucumbers, and Feta (page 327)

tequila skirt steaks SERVES 4

Marinate some steaks in tequila, and turn Thursday night into fajita night at your house.

The marinade is a variation on a Margarita, with honey and orange juice standing in for the Triple Sec, and the honey ensures that you get some great caramelization on the meat. It's steak with a zing.

The photo is on page 157.

- 1 cup tequila
- 1/4 cup honey
- Juice of 2 limes
- Juice of 1 orange
- 4 garlic cloves, smashed
- 2 tablespoons olive or vegetable oil
- 1 1/2 teaspoons salt
- 1 teaspoon crushed red pepper
- 1 1/2 pounds skirt steaks (veal, if you can find them)

Combine all the ingredients in a sealable plastic bag. Seal the bag, squeezing out the air, and refrigerate for at least 4 hours, and up to 8. Or, if you haven't planned ahead, marinate the meat for 1 hour on the counter.

Prepare a grill or heat up a stovetop grill pan.

Grill the steaks for about 2 minutes a side for rare. Let the steaks rest for 5 minutes on a cutting board before cutting into strips and serving.

DINNER

Tequila Skirt Steaks

Flour tortillas

Roasted Corn Guacamole (page 356)

Apricot Salsa (page 358)

Sour cream

margaritas

You've marinated your steaks in tequila and lime, right? Continue the theme and serve Margaritas before dinner—and with it too, unless you want to move to beer.

Gary Regan, a king of cocktails and author of *The Joy of Mixology*, subscribes to the 3 : 2 :1 recipe: 3 parts tequila (and you want a silver tequila), 2 parts Cointreau or Triple Sec, and 1 part fresh lime juice. Here's his formula for a batch of Margaritas, when you're serving a crowd. You'll notice it has water in it. Tap water replaces the water you would get from the ice if you were shaking a single cocktail in a shaker. If you want to serve these on the rocks, cut out the water and forget about the chilling time. But please salt the glasses. Rub the outside of the rim with a wedge of lime and roll the glass in a saucerful of coarse salt.

9 ounces silver tequila
6 ounces Triple Sec or Cointreau
3 ounces fresh lime juice
5 ounces water

Stir it all up in a pitcher and chill for at least 6 hours. Serve in salt-rimmed cocktail glasses.

herb-marinated london broil SERVES 4 TO 6

The top round cut for London broil can be a very tasty cut of meat. Chewy, to be sure, which you compensate for by cooking it rare. And this marinade, which is like a very herby salad dressing, adds even more flavor to the meat. I adapted the marinade from one by my buddy John Martin Taylor, who is a very fine cook and an authority on the food of South Carolina's Lowcountry.

Cook this under the broiler or on the grill.

1/4 cup red wine vinegar

1/2 cup chopped tender fresh herbs (marjoram, summer savory, and basil—or your own mix), plus herb sprigs for garnish

2 garlic cloves, chopped

Coarse salt and freshly ground black pepper

Crushed red pepper or Tabasco sauce

1/2 cup olive oil, plus more for drizzling

1 (2-pound) London broil (top round)

Combine the vinegar, herbs, garlic, and salt and pepper to taste in a small bowl. Add a big pinch of crushed red pepper (or a few shots of Tabasco) and whisk in the oil.

Pour the marinade into a sealable plastic bag. Add the meat and seal the bag, squeezing out all the air. Refrigerate for at least 8 hours, or overnight, turning the bag over when you remember to. Or, if you haven't planned ahead, marinate the meat for 1 hour on the counter.

Take the meat out of the refrigerator if you need to, and heat the broiler or prepare an outdoor grill.

Broil or grill the meat for 5 minutes a side for rare. Let the meat rest on a cutting board for at least 10 minutes before slicing on the diagonal.

Drizzle the meat with some olive oil, garnish the platter with a bouquet of herbs, and serve.

DINNER

Herb-Marinated London Broil

Chinois Noodles (page 310)

Roasted Beets (page 257)

simple pork tenderloin SERVES 4 TO 6

Pork tenderloin used to be a fine piece of meat until pork producers started to pretend that pork was a white meat. The tenderloins ended up bland. But season some mustard with herbes de Provence and slather the meat with it, make a quick crust with bread crumbs, and you have flavor in next to no time—and the crust seals in the juices. Go ahead and tinker with the herbs: a heaped tablespoon of minced rosemary or thyme is nice. So too is flavoring the mustard with crushed coriander seeds and cracked pepper.

2 (1-pound) pork tenderloins

Coarse salt and freshly ground black pepper

2 teaspoons herbes de Provence

2 tablespoons Dijon mustard

$^1/_2$ cup dried bread crumbs

2 tablespoons olive oil

DINNER

Simple Pork Tenderloin

Roasted Beets (page 257)

Fennel à la Grecque (page 281)

Mushroom Pilaf (page 300)

If you've been stockpiling, you'll have the beets and fennel in the refrigerator. Take the fennel out when you start making dinner, so the chill will be off it. Slice the beets and dress them with some olive oil, salt and pepper, and herbes de Provence (or just thyme leaves). Better still, make some Aïoli (page 54).

Plain white rice is fine with this meal too. Maybe cook the rice with a bay leaf.

Heat the oven to 350 degrees.

Trim the silverskin from the tenderloins. Fold the thin ends under and tie or skewer them so the tenderloins have a consistent thickness. Season well with salt and pepper.

Crumble the herbes de Provence into the mustard and coat the tenderloins. Roll them in the bread crumbs.

Spoon the oil into a large heavy skillet that will go into the oven and heat over medium-high heat until the oil shimmers. Add the tenderloins and brown them on all sides, the work of 5 minutes or so. Slide the skillet into the oven and bake for 30 minutes.

Let the meat rest for 10 minutes before slicing. Diagonal cuts are nice; so are thin slices.

pork chops with fennel and tomato SERVES 4

Mashed potatoes are real good with this quick and juicy braise.

4 center-cut pork chops (about 8 ounces each)

Coarse salt and freshly ground black pepper

All-purpose flour, for dusting

2 tablespoons olive oil

2 tablespoons unsalted butter

2 fennel bulbs, cored and sliced thin

1 large onion, sliced thin

1 garlic clove, minced

1 teaspoon fennel seeds, crushed

½ cup dry white wine or dry vermouth

1 cup canned tomatoes, with their juice

Season the chops well with salt and pepper, and flour them, patting off any excess flour. (If you feel the need to dirty a plate, use one for the flour. Or use a piece of wax paper.)

Heat the oil and butter in a large skillet over medium-high heat. When the butter stops bubbling, add the chops and brown them on both sides. Don't jiggle them around in the pan—just leave them alone for 4 minutes or so on each side to get a good brown on them. Remove the chops to a plate.

Add the fennel and onion to the pan and season with salt and pepper. Cook, stirring once in a while, for 10 to 15 minutes, until the fennel and onion are limp, reduced in volume, and starting to brown. Stir in the garlic and fennel seeds and cook for 1 minute. Pour in the wine and bring to a boil, stirring to dissolve any of the good brown bits that might be left on the bottom of the skillet. Crush the tomatoes with your hands and stir into the skillet, with a bit of salt and pepper. Bring to a simmer.

Set the pork chops on top of the sauce, pushing them down some, and pour in any of the juices that have accumulated on the plate. Cover and simmer over low heat for 15 minutes. Turn the chops over, push them back into the sauce, and simmer, covered, for another 12 to 15 minutes.

It's nice to make plates with this, resting a chop over some mashed potatoes and spooning on the sauce, but there's no reason you can't serve this family-style.

DINNER

Pork Chops with Fennel and Tomato

Olive Oil Mashed Potatoes (page 284)

Dandelion Salad (page 318)

The fennel makes the pork chops a bit sweet, so I think a bitter salad is the way to go. Bitter Greens with Mustard Cream (page 316) could stand in well for the dandelion, and the salad can start or finish dinner. Add some peas to the plates if you're in the mood (see page 152).

sausages with onion and bay

Crisp sweet Italian sausages, perfumed with bay and charred a bit on the grill, are just plain good.

I'm not giving amounts; you can adjust depending on how many sausages you're grilling. The important thing is to use fresh bay leaves, which are usually available in markets like Whole Foods. Fresh leaves are flexible, which is good, and they release their flavor quickly. If all you can find is dry, don't despair. Soak them in hot water for about 30 minutes to reconstitute them the way you would dried mushrooms.

The photo is on page 159.

Sweet Italian sausages (with or without fennel)

Fresh bay leaves

Red onion, cut into wedges

Olive oil

Cover bamboo skewers with water and let them soak for at least 30 minutes.

Line up 4 sausages, making a block. Slip 1 or 2 bay leaves between each of the sausages. Break up the onion wedges and slip a piece of onion next to each bay leaf. Use two skewers to spear each block, one at either end of the block, spearing the bay leaves and onion as you push the skewers through.

Prepare an outdoor grill.

Brush the bay leaves and onion with olive oil, and grill the sausages over a medium-hot fire, turning once, until cooked through, about 20 minutes.

Pull out the skewers, pile the sausages, bay, and onion on a platter, and serve.

Note: Coils of thin Italian sausage are nice prepared this way too. Leave the sausage coiled, slip in the bay and onion, and secure them with two long skewers, pushed through in a cross.

DINNER

Since you've got to fire up the grill, you might as well grill some vegetables (page 296) and perhaps some Tiny Tomatoes (page 295). Or Grilled Squash with Onion and Mint (page 334).

Another option is a meal of the sausages, Olive Oil Mashed Potatoes (page 284), and a salad—maybe Mixed Greens with Buttermilk and Sun-Dried Tomato Dressing (page 317).

If you've got more time, think about serving Potato Tiello (page 288) and Peperonata (page 283). Greens—Grandma's Greens (page 282) or The Simplest Cooked Greens (page 282)—are good with sausage.

broiled lamb chops SERVES 4

Fast food at its finest.

The basic instructions and the rubs are for 4 chops, but it's all so easily doubled.

4 (1 1/2-inch-thick) rib lamb chops (about 1 1/2 pounds)

Coarse salt and freshly ground black pepper

One of the rubs for lamb chops (see page 150)

Season the chops with salt and pepper, and coat both sides of the chops with one of the rubs.

Leave them on the counter for 30 minutes. The chops will taste even better if you season them in the morning and refrigerate until dinnertime; take them out 30 minutes before broiling.

Position the broiler pan 5 to 6 inches from the heat source and heat the broiler. When the broiler and broiler pan are good and hot, put the chops in the pan and broil for 5 minutes. Turn and broil another 4 minutes for medium-rare. Let the chops rest for 5 minutes before serving.

DINNER

Tailor your vegetables to the flavor of the rub, but remember that asparagus is always welcome with lamb. At least, that is, if asparagus is in season. Any roasted vegetable can sit on the counter while you broil the chops.

Should you be in the mood to play, make a quick relish of chopped green olives, minced fresh parsley, and lemon segments dressed with a splash of olive oil to serve with the anchovy chops.

rubs for lamb chops

✧ Pile 1/4 cup chopped fresh herbs (lemon thyme, oregano, and chives is a nice mix) and 1 garlic clove, minced, on the cutting board. Chop together and slide the chef's knife over the mix, pressing down as you move the knife, to make a paste. Scrape the paste up and into a small bowl. Stir in 2 tablespoons olive oil.

✧ Combine 1 tablespoon Dijon mustard, 1 tablespoon dry vermouth, and 1 teaspoon olive oil. Crumble in 1 1/2 teaspoons herbes de Provence.

✧ Combine 1 tablespoon (or a bit more if you're in the mood for heat) chile de árbol powder with 2 teaspoons white wine vinegar and 2 teaspoons olive oil. (You don't need to pepper the chops when you use this rub.)

✧ Use 4 teaspoons anchovy paste.

lamburgers SERVES 4

Burgers get a kind of uptown treatment here. The meat is lamb, not beef, with lots of herbs and a quick rosemary cream sauce.

2 garlic cloves, minced to a paste or put through a press

1/3 cup chopped fresh flat-leaf parsley

1 tablespoon minced fresh rosemary

1/2 teaspoon herbes de Provence

1 1/2 pounds ground lamb

Coarse salt and freshly ground black pepper

1 tablespoon olive oil

2 tablespoons unsalted butter

1/3 cup minced shallots

1 cup heavy cream

1/2 teaspoon Dijon mustard

1 teaspoon fresh lemon juice

DINNER

Lamburgers

Riso (page 302)

The Simplest Cooked Greens (page 282)

Either the basic Riso or the Riso with Tomato and Zucchini would work. If you have the time, and the season is right, cranberry beans or cannellini are a fine addition to the plate.

Combine the garlic, parsley, 1 teaspoon rosemary, and the herbes de Provence in a mixing bowl. Crumble in the lamb, season with salt and pepper, and toss, as you would a salad. You don't want to compact the meat. Form into 4 patties.

Heat a large skillet over medium heat. Pour in the oil, and when it moves easily across the pan, add the burgers. Cook for 8 minutes on the first side and 7 minutes on the second. Check one for doneness: the meat should be barely pink inside. You really don't want a rare lamburger. Keep the burgers warm on a platter.

Pour out the oil in the skillet and add the butter, shallots, and a pinch of salt. Cook, stirring, for 1 to 2 minutes to soften the shallots. Add the remaining 2 teaspoons rosemary and cook until fragrant, about 30 seconds. Pour in the cream and bring to a boil. Season with salt and pepper. Let the cream reduce by about a third and thicken.

Turn off the heat, stir in the mustard and lemon juice, and check for salt and pepper. Pour the sauce over the burgers and serve.

frozen peas

A bag of peas, petite peas in particular, is a secret weapon no freezer should be without. But don't follow the instructions on the bag.

Pour the peas into a colander and run them under hot tap water to defrost them. Melt a knob of butter in a skillet or saucepan, add the peas, and roll them around until just warm. Stir in some chopped fresh mint if it goes with the rest of the meal.

fresh pea soup (page 91)

bacon-wrapped shrimp (page 132)

butter-braised cauliflower and turnips (page 264)

grilled squash with onion and mint (page 334)

riso with peas (page 303)

tequila skirt steaks (page 142)
with tortillas, roasted corn guacamole (page 356),
and apricot salsa (page 358)

gougère "pizza" (page 368)

sausages with onion and bay (page 148)

flounder baked with tomatoes (page 126)

three-onion panade (page 110)

quick pastas

It's been a long day. You got home late; you're hungry, maybe a bit irritable. What you don't want to do is start in on some involved cooking that means turning on the oven.

For me, I'll pour a glass of wine and put up a pot of water for pasta, and in the time it takes for the water to boil and the pasta to cook, I'll have a little sauce ready. Those are the recipes that follow. Well, there's one sauce that you'll start before you put up the water, but it's still very fast.

All you need to turn any of these into a meal is to make a quick salad, and there's time for that too. Of course, if you've been cooking ahead, you may have some greens in the refrigerator, or some Roasted Beets or Roasted Italian Peppers. Maybe some Broccoli (or Cauliflower) Cooked Forever or Fennel à la Grecque. If you do, dinner's that much easier, because you can just put out your leftover vegetables, warmed or not.

If you wanted to tease appetites, and you had the goods, you could nibble on crostini topped with cannellini or cranberry beans that you've warmed with a drizzle of olive oil and mashed coarsely, so the beans won't roll off the bread. Or topped with Broccoli Cooked Forever and sprinkled with some grated Parmesan. But this is all getting complicated. You could just put out a bowl of nuts. Don't forget the glass of wine.

ziti with ricotta SERVES 4

Here's a kind of mac and cheese without any effort. Adding goat cheese gives American ricotta the tang it has when it comes from sheep's milk. I learned this trick from Sicilian cooking teacher Anna Tasca Lanza.

Coarse salt

1 pound ziti or penne rigati

1 pound ricotta

2 ounces fresh goat cheese

2 tablespoons unsalted butter

Freshly ground black pepper

Freshly grated Pecorino, for serving

Bring a large pot of water to a boil. Salt the water and pour in the pasta. Stir. Set your serving bowl on top of the pot to warm it.

While the pasta cooks, whip the ricotta and goat cheese together with a fork.

Once the pasta is cooked al dente, ladle out about a cup of the pasta water. Drain the pasta and return it to the pot. Stir in the butter and the cheeses and season with pepper. Stir in enough of the pasta water—a little at a time—to make a smooth sauce.

Scrape the pasta into the serving bowl and serve immediately. Pass the grated cheese at the table.

variation

Wash about 1/2 pound of greens, something like dandelion or curly endive or Swiss chard, and cut into ribbons. Sauté the greens in a combination of olive oil and butter, about 1 tablespoon of each, until tender. Season with salt and pepper, and a pinch of crushed red pepper if you'd like, and add to the pasta when you add the cheeses.

Easier still is to tear 1/2 pound of arugula or dandelion greens into small pieces and boil them along with the pasta.

salting the water for pasta

Pasta needs a lot of water to cook, and that water needs to be well salted, or the pasta won't taste right. I use 2 tablespoons coarse salt for 4 quarts of water, which is about enough to cook 1 pound of pasta—unless you're cooking dried fettuccine, which is happier with 6 quarts of water and 3 tablespoons salt.

quickish pasta and beans SERVES 4

This pasta is almost a soup and perfect for a cool night.

If you can find canned cherry tomatoes, use them here. If you've got your own cooked beans in the fridge, pull them out.

1 onion, chopped fine

1 carrot, chopped fine

1 celery stalk, chopped fine

1 tablespoon olive oil

Coarse salt

1 (19-ounce) can cannellini beans, rinsed and drained, or about 2 cups homemade (page 254 or 256), with their juices

1 (14.5-ounce) can tomatoes

Freshly ground black pepper

Crushed red pepper

Pinch of dried oregano

3/4 pound spaghettini or linguine fini, broken into 2-inch lengths

1/3 cup chopped fresh flat-leaf parsley

Extra-virgin olive oil, for drizzling

Freshly grated Pecorino, for serving

Put the onion, carrot, celery, and oil into a large saucepan. Season with salt and cook over medium heat until the vegetables have softened and the onion is translucent. This should take 8 to 10 minutes.

Stir in the beans. Crush the tomatoes with your hands and add them, along with any juice from the can. Fill the tomato can with water and pour that in. Season with salt, black pepper, and crushed red pepper and crumble in the oregano. Bring the sauce to a boil over high heat, then reduce to a simmer.

Fill a large pot with water and bring it to a boil. Salt the water and add the pasta. Cook until the pasta is almost al dente; it will finish cooking in the sauce. Scoop out about a cup of the pasta water, then drain the pasta.

Pour the pasta into the sauce, kick up the heat, and bring to a boil. Stir in the parsley and enough of the pasta water to keep the dish on the soupy side.

Divide among four bowls, drizzle with extra-virgin olive oil, and serve right away. The cheese goes on the table for passing.

linguine with burst tomato sauce and fried eggs SERVES 4

This dish is pretty, and you've got some surprising textures as well. The yolks run and combine with the chunky sauce, the potato offers a slight resistance (potatoes and pasta are traditional with pesto, but I've expanded that tradition), and the edges of the egg whites have crispy bits.

If you can find it, buy Barilla thin linguine for this dish. It will cook to al dente in 4 minutes—no matter what the package says—which is just the time you need to prepare the eggs.

The photo is on page 67.

7 tablespoons olive oil

1 garlic clove, minced

2 anchovy fillets, chopped

1 pint cherry tomatoes

Pinch of crushed red pepper

Coarse salt and freshly ground black pepper

1 yellow-fleshed potato, peeled and cut into tiny dice

1 pound linguine fini (see headnote)

4 large eggs

10–12 fresh basil leaves, torn into bits

Freshly grated Parmesan, for serving (optional)

Put a large pot of water up to boil.

Meanwhile, spoon 3 tablespoons oil into a large skillet and add the garlic. Turn the heat to medium and cook until the garlic is sizzling and fragrant. Add the anchovies and cherry tomatoes, and season with the crushed red pepper and salt and pepper to taste. Cook, stirring once in a while, until the tomatoes burst and make a sauce. Ripe tomatoes in season will cook in 5 to 10 minutes. Out-of-season tomatoes are stubborn—you'll need to help them along. After about 7 minutes, smash them with a potato masher or with the back of a wooden spoon. Turn the heat to very low while you cook the pasta and fry the eggs.

When the water boils, salt it well and add the potato and pasta. Cook until the pasta is al dente.

Meanwhile, heat the remaining 4 tablespoons oil in a large skillet over medium-high heat. When the oil is shimmering, almost smoking, crack in the eggs and cook them, spooning the oil over the eggs, just until the whites are set. The whites should be crisp and browned at the edges, and the yolks should be barely set. Take the eggs off the heat.

Ladle out about 1 cup of the pasta water, then drain the pasta and add it to the skillet with the sauce. Turn the heat to high and toss the pasta with the sauce, adding pasta water as needed. Don't make soup; just add enough water to make sure the sauce is evenly distributed.

Toss in the basil, and divide the pasta among four dinner plates or wide pasta bowls. Top each serving with an egg and eat right away. Pass the Parmesan, if you want, but I don't find that the dish really needs it.

linguine with tuna SERVES 4

Beloved by Italian-American Catholics who remember meatless Fridays, this is a classic in the canon of easy fish sauces for pasta. Add a bit of fresh mint with the tuna if you feel adventurous.

Just to be on the record: Italians would never consider eating tuna packed in vegetable oil or, worse yet, in water. Those tunas have an off flavor and taste more of tin than tuna. There are more and more brands of tuna in olive oil available nationally. Find one you like. Or, better, use the Oil-Poached Tuna (page 190).

I think this sauce marries best with linguine, but penne and ziti are very acceptable options.

1 (28-ounce) can plum tomatoes, preferably from San Marzano
2 tablespoons olive oil
1 garlic clove, minced
1 small hot pepper, minced, or a pinch of crushed red pepper
3 tablespoons chopped fresh flat-leaf parsley
Coarse salt and freshly ground black pepper
1 pound linguine
1 (5½-ounce) can Italian tuna packed in olive oil
Freshly grated Pecorino, for serving (optional)

Put a large pot of water on to boil. Pour the tomatoes and their juice into a bowl and crush the tomatoes with your hands.

Spoon the oil into a big skillet, large enough to hold all the pasta once it's cooked. Add the garlic and hot pepper and turn the heat to medium. Cook until the garlic is very lightly colored, then add the parsley and let it sizzle for about 1 minute. Pour in the tomatoes, season with salt and pepper, and bring to a boil. Turn the heat down so the sauce cooks at a steady, active simmer.

Once the water boils, salt it well and add the linguine. Stir the pasta right away, and give it a stir once in a while as it boils.

Drain the tuna and stir it into the sauce.

When the linguine is cooked just shy of al dente, ladle out about a cup of the pasta water. Drain the pasta and add it to the sauce. Turn the heat to high and finish cooking the pasta in the sauce, tossing, and adding pasta water if you need it to loosen the sauce a bit, about a minute. Don't go overboard with the pasta water; you're not making soup.

Serve immediately. Pass the grated Pecorino if you're not afraid of violating one of the cardinal rules of Italian cooking—the one about not serving cheese with fish pastas. I'm not shy about breaking it with this dish.

pasta with shrimp and chorizo SERVES 4

Use a Spanish chorizo for this chunky sauce, or better yet, a Portuguese chouriço. Andouille and kielbasa are also fine options; their smokiness marries well with the sweet shrimp.

Choose a big juicy Brandywine—or a beefsteak.

1 pound medium shrimp, shelled

Coarse salt and freshly ground black pepper

4-5 tablespoons olive oil

1/4 pound smoky sausage (see headnote), chopped coarse

1 garlic clove, minced

2 large ripe tomatoes (about 1 1/4 pounds), seeded and chopped

Crushed red pepper

1 pound linguine

1/3 cup chopped fresh flat-leaf parsley and chives

Bring a large pot of water to a boil. Season the shrimp with salt and pepper.

Meanwhile, heat 3 tablespoons oil in a large skillet over medium-high heat until it shimmers. Add the sausage and cook for a couple of minutes, until it smells fragrant and just starts to brown. Stir in the garlic, cooking for 30 seconds or so, until it's fragrant. Add the tomatoes, salt and pepper to taste, and a big pinch of crushed red pepper. Cook for about 2 minutes, until the tomatoes release their juices. Turn down the heat and let the sauce simmer actively while you cook the pasta.

Salt the boiling water well and add the linguine. Cook until just shy of al dente. About 2 minutes before the pasta is done, bury the shrimp in the sauce. Crank the heat up to high.

Scoop out about a cup of the pasta water, then drain the pasta. Give the sauce a stir and pour in the pasta. Still over high heat, toss the pasta in the sauce, adding pasta water as you need it, for 30 seconds to a minute. Drizzle in another 1 to 2 tablespoons oil and toss in the herbs.

Serve right away.

fettuccine with corn and tomatoes SERVES 4

This quick pasta so benefits from a farmers' market. Find the freshest corn, the ripest tomatoes. Homemade pasta certainly shines with the sauce, but if all you have is dried, go for it.

4 tablespoons (1/2 stick) unsalted butter
3 ears corn, kernels cut from the cobs
Coarse salt
2 large ripe tomatoes, seeded and chopped
1 cup heavy cream
1 pound fettuccine
1/4 cup chopped fresh basil
Freshly grated Parmesan, for serving

Bring a very large pot of water to a boil.

Meanwhile, melt the butter in a large skillet over medium-high heat. Add the corn, season with salt, and cook, stirring often, until the corn makes a film on the bottom of the skillet and that film starts to brown. Add the tomatoes and salt to taste. Cook for 1 minute to heat the tomatoes, then pour in the cream. Bring to a boil and boil to reduce the cream by half. You've got your sauce. Turn the heat to as low as possible while the pasta cooks.

When the water boils, salt it well and add the pasta. Cook until it's just shy of al dente. Reserve about 1 cup of the pasta water, and drain the pasta. Pour the pasta into the skillet with the sauce and cook, stirring constantly, for about 1 minute. Add some of the pasta water if you need to loosen the sauce.

Toss in the basil and serve immediately. Pass the Parmesan.

weekend cooking

weekend cooking

Weekends are the time for cooking something big, something slow, something that you need time for.

That big batch of stew, the big braised ham, the big Sunday Sauce. Some of these weekend projects might keep you in the kitchen for a few hours, but with most of them, once you've finished your prep, the dish will just take care of itself while it cooks. And you should have plenty of leftovers to get you started for the rest of the week.

Take Alice's Picnic Chicken, a big, plump bird poached in dry vermouth with a lot of mushrooms. You devote Sunday afternoon to poaching your chicken and letting it cool in the wine broth. Toward dinnertime, you skin the chicken and pull off the breasts and save them for Tuesday, when you'll make Chicken Hash, or Chicken and Artichoke Pie, or Curried Chicken Salad. Dinner will be the meat from the wings, legs, and thighs and all those little bits on the carcass, heated in the broth and served in soup dishes with boiled potatoes and some of the mushrooms. The leftover mushrooms can be turned into a spread for sandwiches or used to fill deviled eggs. You can take the same approach with roast chicken too. Roast two of them, or three, so you've got extra for another meal.

Piggy is another dish that can feed you for days, with plenty of meat left for sandwiches and maybe a casual dinner of hash. Heat up a cast-iron skillet and soften an onion in a few tablespoons of vegetable oil. Dice some cold boiled potatoes and season them and some chopped leftover pork with salt and plenty of pepper. Pile them into the skillet and press down with the back of a spatula. Let the hash cook for a while over medium heat, pressing down with the spatula a few times, until a crust forms; then pour in a few tablespoons of cream and turn the hash with the spatula. Press down again and cook until a crust forms again. Turn it one last time with the spatula, cook until the crust re-forms, and you're done. Poach some eggs to go on top.

The biggest weekend project in this chapter is Sunday Sauce, the ultimate in Italian-American cooking. You cook a lot of meat with the sauce, plenty for several meals. For this recipe, you might want to call in some help. With meatballs to make and braciole (stuffed meat rolls) to roll and tie, it can easily be turned into a community project. And if you've got a room of helpers available, you can go completely overboard and make the cavatelli too. If you don't freeze a lot of the meat, you can reheat it later in the week to serve with roast peppers and cooked greens—both recipes you'll find in the Salads chapter.

In fact, you'll find recipes for weekend cooking in several places in the book. The roast peppers and Fennel Slaw can both be made in larger batches to serve later in the week. The beets and the basic shell and white beans in Sides are meant to be made when you've got time and then turned into something even tastier a day or two later.

One other thing that comes to my mind for the weekend is an afternoon barbecue. While grilling a hot dog is quick, on Saturday you might find the time to make a pot of chili so you can serve up those dogs Southern-style.

my roast chicken SERVES 3 TO 4

It may be nothing fancy, but a good roast chicken is a very satisfying thing to sit down to at the dinner table. My niece Hanna Finamore Rossler says she likes the skin on the legs of this one because "it's so lemony." Now, if only she'd eat potatoes.

I think of this chicken as weekend food, since it needs to marinate in the fridge for a while before you roast it. But there's no reason you can't season the chicken before you go to work on a Tuesday morning and leave it in the refrigerator all day.

1 ($3\frac{1}{2}$- to 4-pound) chicken, preferably organic

Coarse salt and freshly ground black pepper

6 sprigs lemon thyme or regular thyme

3 tablespoons olive oil

1 onion, peeled and halved

2 lemons, scrubbed

$\frac{3}{4}$ cup dry vermouth

1–2 tablespoons unsalted butter

Wash and dry the chicken. Season the cavity liberally with salt and pepper. Stick your fingers under the skin over the breast to release it, and slip in 2 sprigs of thyme. Flip the chicken over, push your fingers under the skin along the backbone, and slip in 2 sprigs of thyme up by the thighs.

Rub the chicken all over with the olive oil, and fold the wings under the chicken. Season the back liberally with salt and pepper, flip the chicken over, and put it on a plate. Put the onion and the remaining 2 sprigs of thyme into the cavity. Halve the lemons, and juice them over the chicken. Stuff 2 of the lemon shells into the cavity and put the other 2 onto the plate. Tie the legs together or, if your butcher has left you with a skin flap, poke the legs through that. Season liberally with salt and pepper. Add the neck, heart, and giblets to the plate (they'll give great flavor later to the pan juices), and refrigerate uncovered for at least 2 hours and up to 8.

Take the chicken out of the refrigerator 30 minutes before you're ready to cook it, and heat the oven to 400 degrees. Transfer the chicken, with the extra lemon shells, and the neck, hearts, and giblets, to a large cast-iron skillet. Spill any juices over the chicken.

Roast the chicken for 30 minutes. Pour the vermouth over the chicken and roast for another 45 minutes, basting every 15 minutes.

Put the skillet on the stove, and lift the chicken out with a big fork, tilting it over the skillet so any juices run out of the cavity. Let the bird rest on a cutting board for 15 minutes.

Tilt the skillet and spoon out any fat, and remove the neck, heart, and giblets—they're a cook's treat. Take out the lemon halves and discard.

Carve the chicken and arrange the pieces on a platter.

Reduce the juices in the pan by half, and taste for salt and pepper. Swirl in the butter. Spoon the pan juices over the chicken, and serve.

variation

Substitute an orange for the lemons, and red wine for the vermouth.

LEFTOVERS

Make more than one chicken, so you'll have leftovers. Use two skillets, or a large roasting pan, so the chickens have plenty of breathing room to cook and brown evenly. Then you'll have enough for Chicken and Artichoke Pie (page 182). Or make Curried Chicken Salad (page 57). Or butter toasted English muffins (see page 38 for homemade) and top with sliced tomatoes, lettuce, and sliced chicken.

SIDES

Pretty much everything goes with roast chicken, so keep with the season. Fresh "Polenta" (page 268) and Tomato Tomato Salad (page 326) in the height of summer. Creamy Spinach (page 292) and Lemon Potatoes (page 290) in spring. Roast Pumpkin with Sage (page 291) and Riso (page 302) in fall.

springtime chicken fricassee SERVES 4

Fricassee has that kind of grandma-ish comfort that makes me smile. It can be on the stodgy side, though. This one isn't. It has a clean, bright taste.

3 spring onions

6 tablespoons olive oil

1 (3 1/2-pound) chicken, cut into serving pieces

Coarse salt and freshly ground black pepper

All-purpose flour, for dusting

8 small heads green garlic, peeled, or 1 large garlic clove, sliced thin

1 cup grape or cherry tomatoes, halved

4 tablespoons (1/2 stick) unsalted butter

Grated zest and juice of 1 lemon

1 1/4 cups Prosecco (or other dry sparkling wine)

3/4 pound mushrooms (your choice of wild or tame), trimmed and halved or quartered, depending on their size

Trim off the tops of the spring onions, leaving an inch or two of green. Halve the onions through the stem.

Heat 2 tablespoons oil in a large skillet over medium-high heat. When the oil is shimmering, add the onions, cut side down. Cook for about 2 minutes, until browned, then turn the onions over and cook for another minute. Transfer the onions to a plate.

Add the remaining 4 tablespoons oil to the skillet and heat it until it shimmers. Season the chicken with salt and pepper, dust it lightly in flour, and brown it until golden on all sides. Pour out the oil from the pan.

Pack the onions in between the chicken pieces and add the garlic and tomatoes. Cut 2 tablespoons butter into pieces and add that to the skillet as well. Season with salt, pepper, and the lemon zest (reserve the juice for later) and pour in 1 cup Prosecco. When the wine comes to a boil, lower the heat so it just simmers, cover the skillet, and cook gently for 45 minutes. About halfway through the cooking time, turn the chicken pieces over in the sauce.

While the chicken simmers, cook the mushrooms. Heat a large skillet over medium-high heat. Add the remaining 2 tablespoons butter, and when the butter has stopped sizzling, add the mushrooms. When the mushrooms have browned, season them with salt and pepper, then pour in the lemon juice and the remaining 1/4 cup Prosecco. Cook, stirring often, until the liquid thickens and reduces to about 1 tablespoon. Take the mushrooms off the heat and let them sit until the chicken's done.

Arrange the chicken and onions prettily in a wide shallow serving dish. Spoon in the sauce, spoon the mushrooms on top, and serve.

SIDES

Asparagus, either to start or on the plate with the fricassee, and buttered noodles. Make Shortcake (page 418) for dessert if strawberries or rhubarb are ready.

alice's picnic chicken SERVES 4, WITH LEFTOVERS

This big, beautiful chicken braised in vermouth can be a classic Sunday dinner: a few slices of chicken in a soup plate, some mushrooms from the pot, and a boiled potato, moistened with a spoon or two of the braising liquid. Or you can turn all the parts of the dish into different meals for the week: Chicken Hash (page 35), chicken salad (page 57), chicken pie (page 182).

Inspiration here comes from Alice B. Toklas, who had great ideas for making tasty food. Alice made sandwiches with her chicken. I do too, and with the mushrooms as well.

I get my chickens at the farmers' market, but I've also made this successfully with a grocery store roaster.

1 (7 1/2-pound) chicken

Coarse salt and freshly ground white pepper

1 lemon, scrubbed and halved

2 tablespoons unsalted butter

2 small onions, peeled

4 carrots, peeled

5 or 6 sprigs flat-leaf parsley

1 bay leaf

1 cup dry vermouth or dry white wine

1 1/2 pounds cremini mushrooms, trimmed and quartered

Heat the oven to 325 degrees.

Wash and dry the chicken. Season it well with salt and pepper, inside and out. Stick the lemon into the cavity, and tie the legs together. Leave it on the counter while you start on the vegetables.

Put the butter, onions, and carrots in a large heavy ovenproof pot, big enough for the chicken, over medium-low heat. Cover and sweat the vegetables for 15 minutes. Add the parsley, bay leaf, vermouth, and mushrooms. Bring to a boil, then turn off the heat.

Rest the chicken on the vegetables, cover it with a piece of parchment or wax paper, and put the lid on the pot. Slide it into the oven and braise for 1 hour and 45 minutes to 2 hours, basting the chicken every 30 minutes.

If you're serving this for dinner, let it rest for about 10 minutes before carving. Serve in soup plates with the mushrooms, carrots, and braising liquid.

If you've made this for leftovers, lift the chicken out of the pot and let it cool down before removing the skin and pulling the meat off the bones. Strain out the mushrooms (see below) and vegetables. Reserve the broth to add to the pot when you're making Chicken Stock (page 20); it freezes beautifully. Toss out the onions. The carrots are the cook's treat.

SIDES

Serve this with some boiled potatoes if you want.

the mushrooms

Mushroom Spread. Put the mushrooms in a food processor while they're still warm and process to a smooth puree. You'll need to scrape the sides a few times. Let it cool for 15 minutes or so in the processor. Add 1 stick of softened unsalted butter and process to mix the mushrooms and butter completely. Taste for salt and pepper. Pack into a crock and cover. This will keep for about 5 days in the refrigerator, and it makes about 2 cups.

Toast some bread for Crostini (page 16) and top with some of the spread, and maybe a dollop of crème fraîche and a bit of fresh dill. Or toast white bread and make a sandwich with the spread and some sliced chicken—or ham. Use it as a filling for Deviled Eggs (page 360). Put a tablespoon on a grilled steak or inside a burger.

chicken and artichoke pie SERVES 3 TO 4

So you've made Alice's Picnic Chicken (page 180), or an extra roast chicken (page 176). Pull off both breasts (or the legs), skin them, and cut the meat into big chunks. Enrobe them with a creamy sauce and bake with little potatoes and artichokes.

FOR THE PASTRY

1 cup all-purpose flour

Grated zest of 1 small lemon

Salt

8 tablespoons (1 stick) cold unsalted butter

Cold water

FOR THE FILLING

3 tablespoons unsalted butter

1 onion, chopped

Coarse salt

3 tablespoons all-purpose flour

2 cups chicken stock (page 20, or canned)

Freshly ground black pepper

1/4 teaspoon dried tarragon

1 (13.75-ounce) can artichoke bottoms, drained and quartered

Half a leftover roast chicken, skin removed and meat cut into chunks

1/2 pound small red-skinned potatoes, boiled until tender and halved

3 or 4 large eggs, hard-cooked (see page 59)

Milk

Coarse sea salt

FOR THE PASTRY

Toss the flour, zest, and a pinch of salt together in a bowl, or stir with a fork. Unwrap the butter and drop it into the flour to coat it, then pick it up and cut it into bits. Work the flour into the butter with your fingers, two knives, or a pastry cutter until it looks like coarse oatmeal, with a few bigger bits of butter still left. Stir in a tablespoon or two of very cold water with a fork until the pastry comes together. Form it into a disk, wrap it in plastic wrap or wax paper, and pop it into the refrigerator for about 30 minutes. (Remember as you form the disk that it will be easier to roll out a circle if you start with a circle.)

Heat the oven to 375 degrees, and butter a 1½-quart gratin dish or a casserole.

FOR THE FILLING

Melt the butter in a large saucepan over medium heat. Add the onion and a good pinch of salt and cook, stirring once or twice, until the onion is soft and translucent. Spoon in the flour, stir, and cook for about 2 minutes, until bubbling. Pour in the chicken stock, stirring well to dissolve the roux, and bring to a boil. Reduce the heat, season with salt, pepper, and the tarragon, and simmer for 15 minutes.

Stir in the artichokes, chicken, and potatoes. Taste for salt and pepper. Scrape into the gratin dish. Slice the eggs, big slices, and nestle them into the filling.

Unwrap the pastry and roll it out on a floured surface to a couple of inches larger than your dish. Lay it over the filling and push it in just along the rim, so the edge of the pastry sticks up. Crimp the pastry, brush it with milk, and sprinkle with some coarse sea salt. Cut in a steam vent or two.

Bake for about 1 hour, until the pastry is golden and the filling is bubbling. Serve this hot.

SIDES

It might be nice to start out with a celery salad (page 342)—with or without the Ricotta Fritters.

stuffed little birds SERVES 4

Little spring chickens are supremely tender and juicy, and, let's face it, they're just plain cute. They're not particularly easy to find, though. Game hens are, and they're relatively inexpensive, so you don't have an excuse for not making this. Game hens aren't always big on flavor, though, so they benefit from early seasoning and a kind of cure in the refrigerator, which tenderizes the meat and opens it up to accept the flavors of the stuffing. Salt well, inside and out, early in the day and refrigerate.

This dish is elegant enough for entertaining and homey enough for family dinner.

2 spring chickens (also called poussins) or Cornish game hens (1½–2 pounds each)

Coarse salt and freshly ground black pepper

FOR THE SAUSAGE STUFFING

1 small red onion, chopped fine

1 tablespoon olive oil

Coarse salt

½ pound sweet Italian sausage, casings removed

⅓ cup dry vermouth

1 heaped cup cubed farm bread (about 2 slices)

¼ pound ricotta salata (or Emmenthal), cut into small cubes

Freshly ground black pepper

1 large egg, beaten

1–2 tablespoons olive oil

1 cup dry vermouth

FOR SERVING

Livers from the chickens

1 tablespoon unsalted butter

Coarse salt and freshly ground black pepper

2 tablespoons vinegar (your choice)

4 big handfuls arugula

3 tablespoons extra-virgin olive oil

Check the chicken cavities: if you have the neck, giblets, and heart, save them for the roasting pan; they'll give great flavor to the sauce. Reserve the livers for later. Wash and dry the birds and season them liberally with salt and pepper. Set them on a plate and refrigerate, uncovered, for 8 hours. Or, if you haven't planned ahead, season the birds and let them sit on the counter for 1 hour.

FOR THE SAUSAGE STUFFING

Put the onion and oil in a skillet with a pinch of salt. Cook over medium heat until the onion has softened, about 5 minutes. Crumble in the sausage and cook, continuing to break up the sausage into smaller and smaller bits with your spoon, until it has browned. Pour in the vermouth and bring to a boil. Scrape this out into a mixing bowl and add the bread. Give it a stir, and let the sausage cool for a few minutes.

Add the ricotta salata to the stuffing. Season with salt and pepper (be generous with the pepper) and stir in the egg.

Fill the cavities of the birds with stuffing (don't pack it in; leave some room for it to expand). If your butcher has left you a little flap of skin at the cavity, slip the legs through it. Otherwise, tie the legs together with some kitchen string. If there's a flap of skin at the neck, turn the birds over and stuff the necks with the rest of the stuffing. Pull the skin over this stuffing and fold the wing tips back under themselves to hold the skin in place. If you don't have that extra flap of skin at the neck, just put the rest of the stuffing in a small baking dish and cover it with foil. You'll bake it next to the birds.

Rub the birds all over with the olive oil, and put them in a roasting pan with the necks and giblets and hearts, if you have them. Leave the pan on the counter while you heat the oven to 400 degrees.

Slide the pan into the oven and roast for 30 minutes. Pour in the cup of vermouth and baste the birds. Roast for another 30 minutes, basting once or twice.

Transfer the birds to a cutting board and let them rest for 15 to 20 minutes. Leave all the juices in the roasting pan for now.

FOR SERVING

Chop up the livers. Heat the butter in a small skillet over medium-high heat, and when it stops sizzling, add the livers. Season with salt and pepper and cook, stirring, until the livers have lost all traces of pink. Add the vinegar and bring to a boil. Take the skillet off the heat.

Toss the arugula with the oil and season with salt and pepper.

Put the roasting pan over medium-high heat and reduce the pan juices by half.

When you're ready to plate this up, add the livers and the juices in that skillet to the arugula and toss. Divide the salad among four big dinner plates. Cut the birds in half—along the breastbone and down through the backbone—with a chef's knife (yes, you can) and set on top of the salad. Spoon some of the reduced pan sauce over the birds and serve.

variation

Here's the mushroom–red wine version. Play around with the mushrooms. Maybe use a combination of cremini and oyster. Or chop up portobellos. And, sure, you can use button mushrooms too.

Heat 3 tablespoons olive oil in a large skillet over medium-high heat until it shimmers. Add 1/2 cup chopped shallots and cook for a minute or two to soften them. Add 1 pound mushrooms, sliced, season with salt and pepper and a pinch of crushed red pepper, and cook until the mushrooms are tender and browned. There shouldn't be any juices left in the pan. Add 1 teaspoon fresh thyme leaves and stir in 1 tablespoon tomato paste. Cook for about a minute, and add 1/3 cup dry red wine. Bring to a boil, then scrape the mushrooms out into a mixing bowl. Add 1 heaped cup cubed farm bread and give it a stir. Let the stuffing cool for about 5 minutes, then season with salt and pepper and stir in 1 beaten egg and the grated zest of 1 orange.

Stuff the birds as in the main recipe, pouring the juice of the orange that you got the zest from over the birds. Substitute red wine for the vermouth for basting.

buttermilk fried chicken SERVES 4

I don't know anything that compares to fried chicken: crunchy on the outside, moist and juicy inside, and designed to be eaten with your fingers—the ideal guilty pleasure.

I've written this for thighs and breasts, but use the parts you love best. Although you can buy a special deep cast-iron skillet that's designed for frying chicken, I don't like them. Nothing beats a plain old cast-iron skillet.

4 chicken thighs (about 1½ pounds)

2 bone-in chicken breast halves (about 1½ pounds), split in half

Coarse salt and freshly ground black pepper

2 cups buttermilk

2 tablespoons Dijon mustard

1 teaspoon Tabasco sauce

About 4 cups all-purpose flour

Peanut or corn oil, for frying

Lay the chicken pieces in a glass baking dish and season liberally on both sides with salt and pepper. Whisk the buttermilk, mustard, and Tabasco together in a large measuring cup or small bowl and pour over the chicken. Slide the dish into the refrigerator and leave it there for at least 3 hours.

When you're ready to fry, pull the chicken out of the refrigerator, put the flour in a big bowl, and pour not quite an inch of oil into a large cast-iron skillet. Heat the oil to 375 degrees. You can test this with a thermometer, or stick a wooden chopstick into the oil, touching the bottom of the skillet: if the oil bubbles up around the chopstick immediately, the oil's ready for frying. Have ready a baking sheet with a cooling rack on it.

Pick the thighs out of the buttermilk and drop them into the flour. Coat very well in the flour, so there are no damp spots visible, and add to the oil. Fry, turning the pieces three or four times, until they are a deep, rich brown, 15 to 17 minutes. Repeat with the breast pieces; they will take 13 to 15 minutes. To be on the safe side, fry very large parts an additional 2 minutes. Let the pieces drain on the rack.

SIDES

Smashed Potato Salad (page 338), Fennel Slaw (page 322), and a big green salad works for me.

oil-poached tuna MAKES 1 QUART

Weekends are the time when you can stock up, filling the larder with good things to eat later on in the week. This tuna is so much better than anything you'll get in a can, and you can fit making it in between other chores. Make it a day ahead for best flavor. Albacore is the more reasonably priced tuna.

The photo is on page 277.

2 cups olive oil

4 bay leaves

2 large garlic cloves, smashed

1½ pounds tuna (use albacore for this if you can get it)

Pour the oil into a small saucepan. Add the bay leaves and garlic and turn the heat to medium. Cook just until the garlic starts to sizzle and has bubbles forming around it. Turn off the heat and let sit for 15 minutes.

Blot the tuna dry with paper towels and cut it into chunks that are about 1 inch square. Add them to the oil, and make sure all the tuna is submerged. Turn the heat to medium-low and bring to a bare simmer. Reduce the heat to very low, so you see just the occasional bubble, and poach the tuna for 10 minutes. Turn off the heat and let the tuna cool to room temperature.

You can eat this now, but believe me when I tell you that it will be better if you refrigerate it for a day first. I pack it, in the oil, into a quart jar. It keeps in the refrigerator for about a week.

tuna on the table

So, you've poached your tuna. Make Tuna Salad, Italian-Style (page 56) for lunches. Or Linguine with Tuna (page 168). Or tear up some curly endive, dress it lightly with oil and vinegar, season with salt and pepper, and make a bed of the lettuce on a platter. Top with room-temperature beans—Basic White Beans (page 256) or cranberry beans or cannellini beans (see page 254)—flaked tuna, and very thinly sliced red onion. Drizzle some oil from the tuna jar over the beans and throw on some chopped parsley. It's a fine dinner for a summer night.

beer-battered shrimp SERVES 4

Deep-fried shrimp is just too good to be left to let's-eat-out nights, particularly when you can make a simple batter that yields a shatteringly crisp crust.

FOR THE BATTER

1½ cups Bisquick

Coarse salt and freshly ground black pepper

1 (12-ounce) bottle of beer (pale ale is nice for this)

1 large egg white, beaten to soft peaks

FOR THE SHRIMP

2 pounds large (21–25 count) shrimp (in the shell)

1 tablespoon chopped fresh dill

¼ teaspoon ground coriander

Pinch of cayenne

Coarse salt and freshly ground black pepper

Peanut oil, for frying

FOR THE SAUCE

2 cups water

2 tablespoons olive oil

4 scallions (white and some of the green), chopped

6 or 7 sprigs dill, tied with kitchen string

1 (14.5-ounce) can diced tomatoes (in juice, not puree)

Coarse salt and freshly ground black pepper

1 tablespoon chopped fresh dill

1 teaspoon white wine vinegar

FOR SERVING

4 big handfuls mixed greens

1 tablespoon olive oil

2 teaspoons white wine vinegar

Coarse salt

FOR THE BATTER

Put the Bisquick in a bowl and season with salt and pepper. Whisk in the beer to make a perfectly smooth batter. Let it sit on the counter for an hour.

FOR THE SHRIMP

Pull off the shells, but leave the tail bits intact. As you work, drop the shells into a small saucepan; you'll use them for the sauce. Make an incision along the back of each shrimp and remove the vein.

Put the shrimp into a bowl and add the dill, coriander, cayenne, and salt and pepper to taste. Toss well to distribute the seasoning, cover with plastic, and refrigerate for at least an hour.

FOR THE SAUCE

Pour the water into the saucepan with the shrimp shells. Bring to a boil, then lower the heat and simmer actively for 20 minutes.

Heat a saucepan over medium-high heat. Add the oil and scallions and cook for just a minute or so; you want to soften the scallions but not brown them. Strain the shrimp stock into the skillet and bring to a boil. Add the dill sprigs, and boil for about 4 minutes to reduce the stock to 3 to 4 tablespoons. Pour in the tomatoes and their juice and season with salt and pepper. Bring to a boil, then lower the heat and cook at an active simmer until the sauce has come together and thickened a bit, about 15 minutes. Let cool.

When you're ready for dinner, heat at least 3 inches of peanut oil (don't fill the pot more than one-third full) in a large saucepan or wok to 350 degrees. Set a rack on a baking sheet and have it ready near your frying station.

Pull the dill sprigs out of the sauce, and stir in the chopped dill and vinegar.

Give the batter a whisk, then fold in the egg white. Hold a shrimp by the tail and dip it into the batter, coating it evenly. Shake off any excess batter, then drop the shrimp into the hot oil. Fry 4 to 6 shrimp at a time, so you don't crowd them in the oil, until golden brown, about 2 minutes. Remove with a slotted spoon and drain on the rack.

SIDES

There's something about fried shrimp that says potato salad (see page 338) to me, but Two-Rice Salad (page 340) is also a fine accompaniment.

FOR SERVING

Toss the greens with the oil, vinegar, and salt to taste. Divide the salad among four dinner plates, and surround with the shrimp. Put a few dollops of the sauce on each plate, in between the shrimp, and serve immediately. Pass the rest of the sauce.

hot dogs and hamburgers

You can make a hot dog or hamburger anytime, but there's something about making both that says Sunday afternoon cookout. Invite a crowd. All you need to do to turn this into something special is make sure you've got as many fixings as possible.

Bring out all your pickles and relishes, sliced onions and tomatoes, lettuce, mustard, mayonnaise, and ketchup. Or take it even further and set out plates and bowls of:

- ✧ Strips of crisp bacon
- ✧ Guacamole (page 356) or sliced avocado
- ✧ Sliced cucumbers
- ✧ Sautéed mushrooms
- ✧ Sautéed onions
- ✧ Sliced cheddar and Swiss (the good stuff)
- ✧ Coleslaw (page 322)
- ✧ Chili (page 196)
- ✧ Salsa (page 355)
- ✧ Sauerkraut

For mustard, make sure you've got the full range: bright yellow, ballpark, and Dijon. For ketchup, I think Heinz is the only option, but that's me.

My absolute favorite rolls are Martin's potato rolls—toasted, of course. Martin's is in Pennsylvania, though, and they ship to only a few states. You might be able to find a good potato roll locally, but who's to say that hard rolls, sesame buns, rye bread, and toasted English muffins (mine are on page 38) don't have their place?

To fill out the buffet table, I'd put out Mac and Cheese (page 308) or Smashed Potato Salad (page 338) and Beets, Tomatoes, and Peaches (page 328) or Spicy Watermelon Salad (page 337). Because the grill will be going, I'd probably grill some zucchini, peppers, and scallions too.

For dessert, Ice Cream Sandwiches (page 454).

chili for hot dogs MAKES ABOUT 5 CUPS

Hot dogs piled with chili and coleslaw—ketchup and yellow mustard optional—are the rule in the South. Here's a nice easy chili to pile on.

2 tablespoons vegetable oil

1½ pounds ground chuck

Coarse salt and freshly ground black pepper

1 large onion, chopped

2 tablespoons chili powder

1 teaspoon dried oregano, crumbled

1 teaspoon ground cumin

1 tablespoon cider vinegar

1 teaspoon sugar

1 (28-ounce) can tomatoes, juice drained and reserved, tomatoes chopped

1 cup stock (chicken or beef) or water

Heat 1 tablespoon oil in a saucepan over medium-high heat. When the oil is shimmering, crumble in the ground beef. Season with salt and pepper. Cook the beef, stirring often to break it up, until it is no longer pink and is very crumbly. Scrape the beef into a colander and let the fat drain out.

Return the saucepan to the heat and add the remaining tablespoon of oil and the onion. Season with salt and cook, stirring often, until the onion softens and starts to turn golden at the edges, about 7 minutes. Stir in the chili powder, oregano, and cumin and cook for about 1 minute. Add the beef, vinegar, sugar, tomatoes and juice, and stock, season with salt and pepper, and bring to a simmer. Lower the heat and let the chili simmer slowly for 2 hours, stirring once in a while, until very thick.

Aficionados will puree the chili in a food processor before presenting it for hot dog use.

chili for dinner

Of course you could just make this for dinner. Cook it for $1\frac{1}{2}$ hours (it doesn't need to be as thick), and have bowls of "fixings" on the table: shredded cheddar, diced onion, chopped tomato, chopped black olives, shredded lettuce, sour cream, and tortilla chips. This recipe makes enough for 4.

lemonade

There is simply no way to get through the summer without lemonade. I don't often have it with a meal, but in the middle of a steamy Sunday afternoon, I need some.

John Martin Taylor, authority on all things Southern, makes it best, and simplest. When the mood strikes, I make it pink.

Scrub 6 of the heaviest, and therefore juiciest, lemons you can find with a brush under hot water. Halve them, and put them in a big heatproof bowl or a pot. Add a cup of sugar and 6 cups of boiling water. Stir to make sure you dissolve the sugar, then leave it sit for an hour or two.

Pull out the lemon halves and squeeze them into the water. Then pour the lemonade through a strainer into a pitcher. To make it pink, stir in a cup or so of cranberry juice.

Either way, pour it into tall glasses packed with ice, and garnish with mint.

real good meat loaf SERVES 6 TO 8, WITH LEFTOVERS

Oh, I know: you've got a meat loaf recipe already. Well, I think there can never be too many meat loaf recipes, and I wish you'd try mine. It's an Italian-American one, with sausage meat in it. This is a big meat loaf, so you'll have leftovers (see page 200), and that is good.

1 large red onion, chopped
4 tablespoons olive oil
Coarse salt and freshly ground black pepper
3 garlic cloves, minced
1 pound mushrooms (tame or wild), trimmed and halved
2 tablespoons tomato paste
1/2 cup dry white wine or dry vermouth
1 (28-ounce) can tomatoes
3/4 cup packed freshly grated Pecorino
1 1/2 cups fresh bread crumbs
2 large eggs
1/4 cup chopped fresh flat-leaf parsley
2 tablespoons chopped fresh basil
2 teaspoons chopped fresh thyme (or 1/2 teaspoon dried)
1 pound sweet Italian sausage, casings removed
2 pounds ground round
2 or 3 bay leaves

Heat the oven to 350 degrees, and oil a large casserole, say a 3-quart rectangular one.

Combine the onion with 2 tablespoons oil in a large skillet over medium heat. Season with salt and pepper and cook, stirring once in a while, until the onion is turning gold at the edges, about 8 minutes. Add the garlic and cook for a minute or two, until fragrant. Scrape into a large mixing bowl. Set the pan aside.

Meanwhile, process the mushrooms in batches in a food processor until minced very fine. Add the remaining 2 tablespoons oil to the skillet and turn the heat to medium-high. When the oil is shimmering, add the mushrooms and season with salt and pepper. Cook, stirring and scraping, until the mushrooms brown. They will throw off a lot of liquid as they begin to cook; don't fret—it will cook away. When the mushrooms are browned and sticking to the skillet, stir in the tomato paste. Cook for a minute or two, until the tomato paste turns brick red. Pour in the wine and turn off the heat. Stir and scrape the pan to release any bits of mushroom, and scrape into the bowl with the onion.

Put the tomatoes in the food processor and whir them around until they are chopped pretty fine. Add about 1½ cups of the tomatoes to the mixing bowl, along with the Pecorino, bread crumbs, eggs, parsley, basil, and thyme. Season well with salt and pepper. Crumble in the sausage and get your hands in. Mix very well, breaking up the sausage as small as you can.

Crumble the ground round over the meat loaf base and toss it in gently with your hands—as if you were tossing a salad. Don't go overboard, though; if you overwork the beef, you end up with a tough meat loaf. Of course, if you don't mix it well enough, the slices will break. So just be gentle and thorough. Keep breaking the clumps of beef up with your fingers and tossing until completely mixed, but don't squish the meat with your hands.

Put the bay leaves in the casserole and form the meat loaf on top of them. Season the rest of the tomatoes with salt and pepper and pour over the top.

Slide the meat loaf into the oven and bake for about 1½ hours. Take out your handy instant-read thermometer; you want an internal temperature of 155 degrees.

SIDES

What makes more sense than meat loaf and mashed potatoes? But get something green on the plate, and match it to the season.

Let the meat loaf rest for about 20 minutes before transferring it to a big platter. Tilt the pan and spoon off any fat from the juices. Pour the juices over the meat loaf, and serve. When you come across the bay leaves, leave them on the platter.

LEFTOVERS

There's nothing better than a meat loaf sandwich. The question is what kind of sandwich are you going to make? Here are two ideas, but I'd bet you have some of your own.

Break up some escarole into small pieces, season with salt and pepper, and dress with olive oil and vinegar. Use a bit more vinegar than you would if you were going to serve this as a salad. Make a sandwich with cold sliced meat loaf and close-textured white bread.

Slice some meat loaf and heat it in a small skillet with the leftover pan juices. Slit open a hard roll and add the hot meat loaf and some of the juices. Eat it this way, or cover with a slice or two of mozzarella and run it under the broiler to melt the cheese.

Of course, if you have enough left over, you may want to have another dinner. Pour some of the pan juices into a large skillet. Slice the meat loaf and make a single layer of slices in the pan (or overlap them slightly). Spoon on more pan juices, cover, and heat over medium heat until piping hot.

smothered steaks SERVES 6

Lip-smacking good, this is one of those examples of long cooking turning an inexpensive cut of meat into something special.

If you want to fuss, you can cut out the vein of gristle that runs up the center of the steaks. But you needn't bother: with this amount of cooking it will soften into a very tasty bit.

Pounding the steaks after dredging (or dusting) rather than before is a trick I learned from reading James Beard. You get the good brown crust that comes from flouring meat without the bits of burned flour in the skillet. Clever, no?

6 blade steaks (sometimes called flat-iron steaks; about 2 pounds)

Coarse salt and freshly ground black pepper

All-purpose flour, for dusting

4 tablespoons olive oil

1½ pounds mushrooms (wild or tame or a mix), trimmed and quartered (if you're using portobellos, cut them into big chunks)

1 garlic clove, minced

2 large onions (Spanish or sweet), sliced very thin

½ cup dry vermouth

¼ cup plus 1 tablespoon chopped fresh dill

1½ cups beef or chicken stock

Juice of ½ lemon

Season the steaks on both sides with salt and pepper and dredge them (or dust) in the flour. Now pound the steaks (with a meat pounder, rolling pin, even a small skillet) to half their original thickness.

Heat a large skillet over medium-high heat. Spoon in 2 tablespoons oil and heat it until it shimmers. Working in batches so you don't crowd the meat and steam it, brown the steaks very well on both sides. Keep the steaks warm on a plate near the stove.

Add 1 tablespoon oil to the skillet and heat until it shimmers. Add the mushrooms and garlic, season with salt and pepper, and cook, stirring often, until the mushrooms brown. They will release their juices during this process, and the juices will thicken before browning starts. Once the mushrooms are browned, scrape them into a bowl.

Add the remaining 1 tablespoon oil to the skillet and heat it until it shimmers. Add the onions and a good pinch of salt. Cook, stirring often, until the onions are limp and lightly browned. Add the mushrooms back to the skillet, along with any juices in the bowl, and pour in the vermouth. Cook, scraping the bottom of the skillet, until the vermouth bubbles up and reduces by half.

Stir in the ¼ cup chopped dill, then pack the steaks into the mushrooms and onions. Pour in the stock and bring to a simmer, then cover, reduce the heat to low, and simmer gently for 1 hour. Check this once in a while to make sure you've got a gentle simmer and not a furious one, and adjust the heat if necessary.

Once the steaks have cooked completely, you can turn off the heat and let them sit on the stove for an hour, or let them cool and refrigerate them for tomorrow (when they'll be wonderful).

When you're ready for dinner, bring the sauce and meat to a steady simmer and cook until the steaks are hot. Transfer the steaks to a platter and cover them with foil to keep warm.

Turn the heat to high and cook the sauce, with the mushrooms and onions, for about 5 minutes to reduce it. Stir in the lemon juice and taste it for salt and pepper.

Spoon the sauce over the steaks, scatter with the remaining tablespoon of dill, and serve.

SIDES

I might broil some tomatoes (page 293) to serve with this and roast some asparagus (page 252). Or just make buttered peas (frozen ones, rinsed under hot water to thaw and then rolled around in a knob of butter over medium heat until they're hot). Buttered noodles too.

LEFTOVERS

You'll probably have plenty of sauce left over. The simplest leftover dish is a pilaf, with the warmed sauce (cut up any leftover steak into small pieces) stirred into the rice.

You can also make a macarronade. Cook some sturdy pasta like ziti or rigatoni, toss with the sauce, and put it in a buttered gratin dish. Cover it with shredded cheese, sharp cheddar, maybe, or Gruyère, and bake it at 375 degrees for 15 to 20 minutes, until the cheese is melted and the sauce is bubbling.

beef and carrot stew SERVES 6

You're buying a roast for this so you can have big chunks of meat in the stew, not the mingy ones you so often get when you buy stew meat. If your carrots are thicker than your index finger, slice them in half lengthwise.

As with any stew, this is even better when you've made it the day before (my friend Barry Estabrook says it should be the law to make it in advance), but that's not to say it won't be really good if you eat it the day you cook it. It does need to marinate for at least 8 hours, or overnight.

The photo is on page 279.

1 (4-pound) beef chuck roast

1 onion, peeled and stuck with 4 cloves, plus 2 onions, sliced thin

2 (5-inch) pieces orange zest

2 herb bouquets—each made with 10 parsley sprigs, 4 thyme sprigs, and a bay leaf, tied with kitchen string

2 tablespoons cognac or other brandy

1 bottle fruity red wine, like a Côtes du Rhône

Coarse salt and freshly ground black pepper

3–4 tablespoons olive oil

2 garlic cloves, minced

2 tablespoons tomato paste

1½ pounds small carrots, peeled

2 teaspoons grated orange zest

Cut the beef into big chunks, about 2 inches square. Trim off and discard any big pieces of fat. Put the beef in a large bowl, along with the onion you've stuck with cloves, the strips of orange zest, 1 of the herb bouquets, the brandy, and wine. Cover and stick it in the refrigerator to marinate for at least 8 hours (24 hours will be even better).

Strain, reserving the marinade and the onion. Discard the zest and herb bouquet.

Dry the beef well (damp meat sticks when you brown it) and season with salt and pepper. Heat 2 tablespoons oil in a wide saucepan or a large skillet over medium heat. Brown the meat—in batches, so you don't crowd and steam the beef. Remove the pieces as they brown and keep them in a bowl; add a bit more oil to the pan should you need it.

While the meat browns, take the cloves out of the marinade onion and discard them. Slice that onion thin. Add the remaining 1 tablespoon oil and all the sliced onions to the pan. Season with a pinch of salt and cook the onions, stirring once in a while, until they are very soft and beginning to turn gold at the edges, about 10 minutes. Add the garlic and tomato paste and cook, stirring, until the paste turns brick red, which will take a minute or two.

Put the beef and any juices that have accumulated into the pan, along with the reserved marinade and the other herb bouquet. Give the stew a stir and add the carrots, burying them in the marinade. Bring to a boil, then reduce the heat so the stew simmers gently, cover, and cook for 1½ hours, or until the beef and carrots are fork-tender.

If you've made the stew for serving tomorrow, let it cool before you refrigerate it, covered. Pull off any congealed fat, which will be a lovely orange, before reheating.

If you're serving the stew today, tilt the pan and spoon off the fat.

Stir in the zest right before you serve the stew.

SIDES

Buttered noodles, white rice, and boiled potatoes are all traditional and pretty nice with stew, so you have something to sop up the sauce. Follow it with a salad.

pot roast with porcini and beer SERVES 6

I've always loved Belgian beef stew, cooked in beer and thickened with a piece of bread. Judy Rodgers, in her wonderful *Zuni Café Cookbook*, does her spin on that dish by starting it with short ribs. I thought it would be even better as a pot roast, so I've adapted Judy's recipe.

1 (4-pound) beef chuck roast

Coarse salt and freshly ground black pepper

1 tablespoon olive or vegetable oil

1½ pounds onions, sliced thin

2 teaspoons fresh thyme leaves

1 bay leaf

1 (12-ounce) bottle of beer (a pale ale is good here)

½ cup water

1 bouillon cube (mushroom, if you've got it)

1 ounce (1 heaped cup) dried porcini mushrooms

2 tablespoons Dijon mustard

If you can plan ahead, season the beef with salt and pepper the night before you make this, covering it loosely and refrigerating it. Otherwise, try to season it at least an hour ahead and just leave it on the counter.

Heat the oven to 300 degrees.

Heat the oil in a deep heavy ovenproof skillet or a Dutch oven over medium-high heat. Brown the beef well, until it's crusty on all sides. Transfer the beef to a plate.

Add the onions, thyme, and bay to the pan, along with a big pinch of salt. Cook, stirring often, until the onions have softened and reduced in volume by about half. The onions will release some of their juices, so scrape the bottom of the pan and use these juices to release any of the browned bits from the beef.

Pour in the beer and water, and crumble in the bouillon cube. You might want to grind in some more pepper at this point; I usually do. Rinse the mushrooms under hot water, chop them, and add them to the pot. (Don't worry that you haven't reconstituted them; you'll be doing that directly in the sauce for the pot roast and getting all their flavor.) Bring the sauce to a boil.

Nestle the beef in the sauce, cover the pan, and slide it into the oven. Roast for 1 hour. Turn the meat over, cover the pan again, and roast for another hour, until a fork goes into the beef like butter.

Put the beef on a cutting board, tent it with foil, and let it rest for 10 minutes or so. Fold a couple of kitchen towels, and rest one side of the pan on them so it is tilted—any fat will gather at the bottom of the slope. Leave the sauce to sit for a few minutes, then spoon off the fat.

Most of the onions should have almost melted into the sauce. If you'd like the sauce a bit thicker, put the pan over medium-high heat for a few minutes, and stir a few times. When you've got the consistency you want, turn off the heat.

Stir the mustard into the sauce. Taste for salt and pepper.

Slice the beef and arrange the slices on a platter. Nap with some of the sauce. Serve with the rest of the sauce on the side.

SIDES

Boiled potatoes are probably your easiest choice, but you could serve mashed potatoes or even Polenta (page 311) as a starch. Honey-Glazed Turnips and Pears (page 298), Roast Carrots (page 262) or Roasted Beets (page 257), drizzled with olive oil, or Roast Pumpkin with Sage (page 291)—all good.

rib roast boulanger SERVES 6

This is the kind of thing you can play with, varying the root vegetables that sit under the roast. In the mood for parsnips? For beets? Add them. You have the same freedom with herbs too.

I admit it: the mushroom stock I use comes from a bouillon cube.

1 (4-pound) boneless beef rib roast, tied

Coarse salt and freshly ground black pepper

1 pound small carrots (as thick as your index finger), peeled and halved lengthwise

½ pound small onions, peeled

1 pound fingerling potatoes, scrubbed

½ pound Brussels sprouts, trimmed and halved

1 small head cauliflower, broken into florets

2 bay leaves

6 sprigs thyme

3 tablespoons olive oil

1 cup beef or mushroom stock (see headnote), heated to a simmer

If you've planned ahead, season the roast liberally with salt and pepper and let it sit, loosely covered (wax paper is fine), in the refrigerator for 24 hours. If not, get the salt and pepper on the meat as far ahead of roasting as you can. Either way, take the meat out of the refrigerator 1 hour before roasting.

Heat the oven to 450 degrees.

Drop the vegetables into a large roasting pan as you prep them. Add the bay and thyme, season with salt and pepper, and pour in the oil. Toss well to get all the vegetables coated with oil. Pour in the stock and set the beef on top of the vegetables. Slide the pan into the middle of the oven and roast for 1¼ hours for rare beef (120 degrees on your instant-read thermometer). Check at 1 hour. If the pan is dry, add a few tablespoons water.

Put the roast on a cutting board, tent it with foil, and let it rest for at least 15 minutes. Turn off the oven. Give the vegetables a stir and pop them back into the oven to keep them hot.

Slice the roast fairly thin and place the slices down the center of a big platter. Surround with the vegetables and serve.

SIDES

This is a one-pot meal, though it is a fancy one. So I'd start with something fancy too, such as Celery Salad with Ricotta Fritters (page 342).

beef tenderloin stuffed with summer salsa

SERVES 8, WITH LEFTOVERS

Impressive, pretty delicious, and easy. Easy, I tell you. You slice a piece of beef, fill it with salsa, and tie it up. Once you've grilled it, you're rewarded with tender rare beef permeated with the flavor of the salsa.

You could ask a butcher to trim the beef for you, but it's so simple to do, and untrimmed whole fillets are relatively inexpensive at places like price clubs.

1 (5- to 6-pound) whole beef tenderloin

3 tablespoons olive oil

1 recipe Summer Salsa (page 355)

Coarse salt and freshly ground black pepper

To trim the beef, start by cutting away the strip of meat along the side (save this "chain" to flash-fry for the start of a great steak sandwich). Trim off the visible fat and the silverskin (the shiny membrane), and trim away the narrowest piece of the tail (save it with the chain). Make a lengthwise cut almost all the way through the fillet and open the beef like a book.

Rub the inside of the beef with 1 tablespoon oil and pile on about 1½ cups of the salsa. Fold the beef around the salsa and tie it shut with kitchen string about every 1½ inches; keep poking any salsa that escapes back into the beef. You can do this hours ahead; just pop the beef into the refrigerator, and be sure to take it out 30 minutes before grilling.

Prepare an outdoor grill. You want a medium-hot fire (you should be able to hold your hand 5 inches away from the grill for 7 seconds).

Pat the beef dry with paper towels, then rub it with the remaining 2 tablespoons oil and season well with salt and pepper. Grill the beef, turning it so it browns evenly, to an internal temperature of 120 degrees for rare.

Let the fillet rest on a cutting board, tented under foil, for at least 10 minutes before slicing. (If you want, you can grill this well in advance and serve it chilled or at room temperature.)

Cut the tenderloin into thin slices, and serve with the rest of the salsa.

LEFTOVERS

This is a big piece of meat, and leftovers piled onto a baguette, with some salsa if there's any left, or sliced tomatoes if there's not, are good to pack for lunch.

You could also make beef salad. Sauté mushrooms in a little olive oil. Top with a heap of mixed greens dressed with your favorite vinaigrette and lay thin slices of the beef on the salad.

SIDES

It could be a potato salad (page 338) and Skillet Corn (page 267) day, or it could be a Two-Rice Salad (page 340) and Eggplant and Mint (page 329) day. Up to you.

sweet sausage with melted escarole SERVES 4

Long, slow cooking makes the escarole sweet and soft—unctuous, you could say. This is the kind of dish I might make early in the afternoon and leave covered on the back of the stove until dinner.

2 pounds (2 big heads) escarole

4 largish garlic cloves, peeled and bruised with the side of a big knife

2 dried hot peppers or a big pinch of crushed red pepper

1/4 cup olive oil, plus more for the table

1/2 cup dry white wine or dry vermouth

Coarse salt

8 sweet Italian sausages, with fennel or without, pricked all over with the point of a knife

Trim the root end of the escarole and cut or tear the leaves into thirds. Wash well in a couple of changes of water.

Put the garlic in a large wide saucepan that has a lid and crumble in the peppers. Add the oil and turn the heat to medium. Cook until the garlic is sizzling and you can smell it. Pour in the wine, which will start bubbling away immediately. Add half the escarole, salt it, and put the lid on the pan. Cook for 4 to 5 minutes, to start the greens wilting. Stir them, add the rest of the escarole and more salt, and cover again. After 4 to 5 minutes, give the escarole another turn or two—you'll find tongs are the easiest tool for this—and push the sausages into the escarole. Not under the greens, but so just the tops of the sausage are sticking up.

Turn the heat to very low, put the lid on, and leave this alone for 30 minutes or so. Turn the sausages over, put the lid back on, and cook for at least another 30 minutes. You can go as long as 45 minutes or more; just make sure the greens are silky and meltingly tender.

Have a cruet of olive oil on the table. This dish wants drizzling when it's served.

LEFTOVERS

If you've served this to four, you shouldn't have leftovers unless it's a sausage or two that you'll put in a sandwich. But the dish multiplies easily (though you may need to use two pans). And what I do is just sauce pasta with this, whether there are any sausages left over or not. Put up the pot of water for the pasta and slice up any sausages. Put the sausage and greens and all the juices in a largish pot (big enough to hold the pasta once it's cooked), cover it, and turn the heat to low. It'll be hot enough by the time the pasta is done.

What pasta depends on what you have on the shelf. It really doesn't matter. Just make sure the pasta is cooked less than al dente and that you save about a cup of pasta water. Drain the pasta, dump it into the greens, and add enough of the pasta water to make it slightly soupy. Turn the heat to high and cook for a minute or so to finish the pasta, marry it to the sauce, and reduce the excess liquid. Put it into a serving dish, drizzle with olive oil, and make sure there's grated Pecorino on the table.

SIDES

What to serve this with? The greens are soupy, so you want something that will drink the juices up. Rice, certainly. Maybe simple Riso (page 302). Olive Oil Mashed Potatoes (page 284) would be tasty as well. Simplest of all is just pulling apart a thick slice of peasant bread and putting it in a soup dish before spooning in the greens and sausage. If you have some beans in the refrigerator, by all means add them to the plate.

If you want a first course, keep it uncomplicated. Serving this dish with something fancy only confuses matters. Sliced tomatoes to start?

orange-maple-glazed pork chops SERVES 6

Brining pork chops makes them tender and juicy. Plan ahead, to give the chops enough time in the brine.

FOR THE BRINE

- 1/2 cup sugar
- 1/4 cup coarse salt
- 3 strips orange zest (fresh or dried)
- 2 teaspoons dried rosemary
- 1 teaspoon black peppercorns
- 2 teaspoons fennel seeds, crushed
- 3 bay leaves
- 1 tablespoon molasses
- 3 quarts water

6 (1-inch-thick) center-cut pork chops (about 4 1/2 pounds)

FOR THE GLAZE

- 1/2 cup maple syrup
- 1/4 cup prepared horseradish
- Juice of 1 orange
- 1 tablespoon bourbon

FOR THE BRINE

Put the sugar, salt, seasonings, and molasses in a large saucepan with 4 cups water. Bring to a boil, stirring. Remove from the heat, add 8 cups cold water, and cool to tepid.

Drop in the pork chops, cover, and refrigerate for 12 hours.

Remove the chops from the brine and pat them dry. If you brine them overnight, you can wrap them in plastic and leave them in the refrigerator until an hour before dinnertime.

Fire up an outdoor grill.

FOR THE GLAZE

Combine all the ingredients in a small saucepan and simmer for 20 minutes.

Once the grill is hot, pat the chops dry. Grill them on the first side for 6 minutes, then turn them over and brush the seared side generously with the glaze. Cook for another 6 minutes, and turn the chops again. Brush with the glaze and cook for 1 minute. Take them off the grill, arrange them on a platter, and serve.

SIDES

Try these chops with Corn Custard (page 269) and Zucchini all'Insalata (page 335).

variations

Actually, you don't need to fire up the grill if you don't want to. You can broil the chops and then brush with the glaze. Give them a minute on each side under the broiler for the glaze to bubble.

If you're not in the mood for a glaze, you could also pan-roast the brined chops, and serve them with Cabbage and Noodles (page 260), and maybe some Roast Carrots (page 262). Bring out whatever pickles you've got in the refrigerator.

Heat the oven to 400 degrees, and heat a heavy skillet over medium-high heat. Spoon 2 tablespoons olive oil into the skillet and when it shimmers, add half the pork chops. Brown well on both sides, and transfer to a baking dish. Brown the other 3 chops. Put these in the baking dish, slide it into the oven, and bake for 15 minutes.

slow-cooked pork stew SERVES 4 TO 6

Sure, it would be a lot easier to buy a boneless pork loin and cut that up for a stew, but you're just not going to get the flavor, or texture, you will from a shoulder. And there's something so satisfying about working your knife along the bone, releasing lobes of pork, then cutting them into big chunks; it's a feeling of accomplishment, isn't it?

1 (4 1/2-pound) bone-in pork shoulder

Coarse salt and freshly ground black pepper

3 tablespoons olive oil

2 carrots, chopped fine

1 onion, chopped fine

1 celery stalk, chopped fine

1 1/2 teaspoons fennel seeds, crushed

1/2 teaspoon dried sage

1 bay leaf

2 sun-dried tomatoes, chopped

1/2 cup dry white wine or dry vermouth

1 cup canned tomatoes, with their juice, chopped or crushed

1 cup chicken or beef stock

Heat the oven to 325 degrees.

Cut the rind off the pork and discard it. Cut the pork into large chunks, about 2 inches. Season the pork with salt and pepper.

Heat a heavy Dutch oven or other heavy ovenproof pot over medium-high heat. Add 1 tablespoon oil. When the oil shimmers, add the pork, in batches, and brown it. If you crowd the meat in the pan, it will steam and not get crusty brown, and you want that brown crust. Transfer the pork to a bowl as it browns.

Lower the heat to medium. Spoon in the remaining 2 tablespoons oil to the pan and when it shimmers, add the carrots, onion, and celery. Season with a pinch of salt and cook, stirring once in a while, until the vegetables are starting to brown at the edges, about 10 minutes. Stir in the fennel seeds, sage, bay leaf, and sun-dried tomatoes. Cook for 1 minute. Pour in the wine and let it bubble up. Stir and scrape the bottom of the pan to dissolve the browned bits that will have accumulated. Stir in the canned tomatoes and stock and bring to a simmer. Taste for salt and pepper, then stir in the pork and any juices in the bowl.

Cover the pan with parchment or foil, then cover tightly with the lid and slide the pan into the oven. Roast slowly for 2½ hours.

Fold up a kitchen towel and set one side of the pot on it, so the pot's on an angle. Leave it alone for about 5 minutes, then spoon off the fat that will have pooled.

Serve in wide shallow bowls.

SIDES

Very buttery Polenta (page 311) or just plain boiled potatoes. Some Saffron Cauliflower (page 265) on the side could be tasty too. Make a big salad for after the pork.

pork roast with fruit stuffing SERVES 6 TO 8

This is a fine company dish, succulent and sweet, and it fills the kitchen with aromas that announce "Sunday dinner." And the slices of pork, with their stained-glass stuffing, are kind of pretty too.

Chef Randall Price cooks in France, and he developed this refinement of pork stuffed with prunes.

The photo is on page 409.

FOR THE BRINE

6 cups water

1/4 cup coarse salt

1/4 cup light brown sugar

3 bay leaves

3 or 4 star anise

3 garlic cloves, peeled and smashed

1 dried hot pepper

2 teaspoons black peppercorns

1 teaspoon fennel seeds, crushed

1 (3-pound) boneless pork loin

FOR THE STUFFING

1/2 cup dried cherries

6 dried peach halves

Freshly ground black pepper

2 tablespoons vegetable oil

FOR THE GRAVY

2 cups chicken stock (page 20, or canned)

2 tablespoons unsalted butter

Coarse salt

FOR THE BRINE

Combine all the ingredients in a large wide saucepan and bring to a boil. Reduce the heat and simmer for 5 minutes. Let cool until tepid.

Make a long lengthwise cut almost all the way through the pork. Add the pork to the brine, cover, and refrigerate for 6 to 12 hours, giving it a turn once or twice.

FOR THE STUFFING

Cover the dried fruit with boiling water and let sit for about 5 minutes, until softened. Drain. Set aside ¼ cup of the cherries for the gravy. Chop the peaches coarse and combine with the remaining cherries. Season with pepper.

Heat the oven to 350 degrees.

Take the pork out of the brine and pat it dry. Open it flat, like a book, and cover with the stuffing, leaving a border of about an inch all around. Fold the pork closed and tie it shut with kitchen string, about every 1½ inches. The stuffing will try to escape, but just poke it back in when you've finished tying the roast.

Heat a large ovenproof skillet or a roasting pan over medium-high heat. Spoon in the oil, and when it shimmers, add the roast. Brown it on all sides, 10 to 15 minutes. Watch carefully and turn often so the roast doesn't scorch.

Cover lightly with a piece of aluminum foil and slide the pork into the oven. Roast for 50 minutes, or until an instant-read thermometer reads 165 degrees. Transfer the pork to a cutting board, tent it with foil, and let it rest while you prepare the gravy.

FOR THE GRAVY

Pour or spoon the fat out of the pan and place the pan over medium heat. When the pan is sputtering, pour in the chicken stock and bring to a boil. Scrape up any of the browned bits in the pan as they soften, then add the reserved 1/4 cup cherries. Reduce the stock to 1/2 cup, which will take 15 to 20 minutes.

Turn off the heat and add the butter to the pan. Tilt the pan back and forth to melt the butter and swirl it into the gravy. Check for salt.

SIDES

Cabbage and Noodles (page 260) and Roasted Beets (page 257).

Slice the pork into thinnish slices, say 1/3 inch, nap with the gravy, and serve.

piggy SERVES A CROWD, WITH LEFTOVERS

When I found this recipe by meat meisters Chris Schlesinger and John Willoughby, and then made it, it was eye-opening: the most tender, succulent pork with the crispiest skin imaginable. This is what weekend cooking is all about. You can dress it up or down, depending on what you do for side dishes. Schlesinger and Willoughby serve this with an oregano salsa, but I love it with my vinegar sauce.

What's important is that you get a shoulder with the skin on and the bone in. You start this the night before.

FOR THE BRINE

3 gallons warm water

3 cups coarse salt

3 cups sugar

1 (10- to 12-pound) bone-in, skin-on pork shoulder

FOR THE VINEGAR SAUCE

1 cup rice vinegar

$^1/_2$ cup champagne vinegar

1 garlic clove, smashed

2 teaspoons crushed red pepper

1 tablespoon soy sauce

1 teaspoon sugar

1 tablespoon vegetable oil

Coarse salt

FOR THE BRINE

Get out your largest kettle, suitable for cooking missionaries, and pour in the water. Dissolve the salt and sugar in it. Immerse the pig in the brine, make space for the kettle in the refrigerator, and let it sit there for 8 hours (you'll be doing this overnight).

In the morning, take the piggy out of the brine and dry it. If you're going to start roasting it in an hour or two, let it sit on the counter. Otherwise, put it back in the refrigerator.

Heat the oven to 350 degrees.

Put the shoulder on a rack in a roasting pan and then into the oven. Leave it there for 5 hours.

Turn the heat down to 275 degrees and roast for 2 more hours for a smaller shoulder, 3 hours for a larger one. It's done. The meat will be juicy and fork-tender and the skin will be crisp beyond your dreams. Let the piggy rest for 20 minutes.

MEANWHILE, FOR THE VINEGAR SAUCE

Combine the ingredients in a small pot over low heat and bring to a simmer. Let the sauce simmer for 3 to 4 minutes. Serve it warm or at room temperature.

To carve the roast, first pull off the skin and chop it into small pieces with a cleaver or heavy knife. The meat just pulls apart with a fork.

Serve with the vinegar sauce. You can pass a bowl of the sauce for people to drizzle on the meat, or set the table with little bowls of sauce at each setting.

SIDES

Coleslaw is essential, so try the Fennel Slaw (page 322). Mac and Cheese (page 308) is obvious, and good, but you might want to mix things up and serve your piggy with Toasted Israeli Couscous with Red Pepper and Saffron (page 306) or with Chinois Noodles (page 310).

LEFTOVERS

This pork makes incredible sandwiches, and there have been times when my friends and I have lunched on it happily for days. I might make a complicated sandwich like a Rueben: rye bread (seeded or not), slathered with Russian dressing out of a jar, piled with meat, and topped with sliced Swiss, put in the microwave to heat the meat and melt the cheese. But most often I pull the pork into shreds, heat it in the microwave for maybe 45 seconds, and pile the meat on soft hamburger rolls, with a good drizzle of the vinegar sauce and some leftover slaw. It doesn't get much better than that.

Sandwiches aren't the only option, though. Leftover piggy makes great hash too.

ham braised in marsala SERVES 10 TO 12

"Succulent" may be the best word to describe this ham. I've certainly made more than my share of baked hams, with lots of cloves and different sugary coatings, and I've yet to find one that compares to this.

The ideal pan for making it will be just large enough for the ham to fit, with the cover on—a 7-quart Dutch oven or braising pan. If you're making it in something larger, like a heavy stockpot (which I often resort to if the ham is on the bigger end of the scale), rip off a piece of parchment or foil and cover the ham with it before you cover the pan.

I've adapted this from a recipe by Molly Stevens, my cooking partner, teaching partner, and dear friend. It's from her amazing book, *All About Braising*.

2 tablespoons olive oil

3 carrots, chopped coarse

2 onions, chopped coarse

2 celery stalks, chopped coarse

1 (6- to 8-pound) fully cooked bone-in ham (see Note)

2 garlic cloves, smashed

4 (3-inch) sprigs rosemary

1 large bay leaf

1 handful celery leaves

1 1/2 cups dry Marsala

1/2 cup beef or chicken stock

1/3 cup raisins (optional)

Heat the oven to 300 degrees.

Put the oil, carrots, onions, and celery in a Dutch oven large enough to hold the ham. Turn the heat to medium-high and cook the vegetables, stirring once in a while, until they start to brown at the edges, about 10 minutes.

Meanwhile, cut the rind off the ham if it has one, and trim back the fat, leaving just a thin layer.

When the vegetables are starting to brown, add the garlic, rosemary, bay, and celery leaves and cook for 1 minute, or until you can smell the garlic. Pour in the Marsala and bring to a boil. Cook for 5 minutes or so, to reduce the wine by about half. Pour in the stock, lower the heat, and simmer for another 5 minutes to combine the flavors.

Nestle the ham, on its side, into the braising liquid. Cover the pot and slide it into the oven. Braise for 1 hour.

Turn the ham over, cover the pan again, and braise for another 30 to 45 minutes, until the ham is tender and heated all the way to the bone. Let the ham rest on a cutting board while you finish the sauce.

If you want to make a sauce, strain out the solids from the braising liquid and discard them (they will be pretty salty). Let the liquid settle for about 5 minutes, then skim off the fat. Pour it into a saucepan, add the raisins if you're using them, and simmer for about 10 minutes.

Slice the ham and serve it, warm or at room temperature, with a bit of the warm sauce spooned on top.

Note: Make sure you save the bone for pea soup (page 108). You can wrap it tightly in foil and freeze it.

SIDES

There are so many things to pair with a ham: Grandma's Greens (page 282), for something a little bitter to offset the sweetness of the ham, or Honey-Glazed Turnips and Pears (page 298). Or Roast Pumpkin with Sage (page 291). Or you could go the Mac and Cheese (page 308) route, with a big green salad and buttermilk dressing (page 317).

LEFTOVERS

Of course you make ham sandwiches. On rye, with mustard, Emmenthal, and lettuce. On country bread, with mayonnaise, cheddar, and bread-and-butter pickles. On Cream Biscuits (page 42), split and spread with a bit of mustard. And in grilled cheese sandwiches (see page 48).

You can also just make a nice plate of ham and Tipsy Onions (page 392) and cheddar. Or a chef's salad, with romaine and cubed cheese and all the rest of the fixings.

When you get to the smaller parts of the ham, the ones that don't make pretty slices, you can mince the meat in a food processor and make salads. My mother makes hers with India relish and mayo; I make mine with cream and mustard (page 371).

For something fancier, try the Ham and Oyster Pie that follows.

about hams

You don't need a fancy ham for this recipe; the ones from the grocery are fine. You're looking for half a ham (a whole ham is a lot bigger than 6 pounds). The shank end is easier to carve (and it has great bones for soup), but the butt end is fine. If the ham has been presliced—something I've noticed in too many stores lately—tie it with kitchen string so it doesn't fall apart while you braise it.

ham and oyster pie SERVES 4

Pies for dinner are a good thing. The biscuit topping means no rolling pastry on a floured surface. You can make this with leftover braised ham, or pick up a ham steak and start from scratch.

- $1^1/_4$ cups heavy cream, plus more for brushing the biscuits
- $^1/_2$ cup braising liquid from Ham Braised in Marsala (previous recipe) or beef stock
- 4 cups cubed ($^3/_4$-inch) ham
- Freshly ground white pepper
- Freshly grated nutmeg
- 1 teaspoon chopped fresh sage
- Coarse salt
- 1 (10-ounce) package frozen petite peas (2 cups)
- 1 pint shucked oysters, drained
- Dough for Cream Biscuits (page 42)

Combine the cream, braising liquid (stock if you used the raisins), ham, white pepper to taste, a few gratings of nutmeg, and the sage in a saucepan. (If you're using stock, add some salt.) Bring to a simmer over medium-high heat, then turn off the heat and let the cream infuse for about 20 minutes.

Meanwhile, heat the oven to 375 degrees, and butter a $1^1/_2$-quart gratin dish.

Rinse the peas under hot water, and stir them into the ham and cream. Scrape into the gratin dish, and nestle in the oysters. Top with the cream biscuits. Brush the biscuit tops with cream and put the gratin dish on a baking sheet. Bake for 35 to 40 minutes, until the biscuits have risen and browned and the filling is bubbling in the center and browning at the edges of the dish.

Serve hot, in soup plates.

SIDES

It's a meal in itself. I'd follow it with a big green salad, maybe with Strawberry Vinaigrette (page 320).

meaty lamb shanks SERVES 4

This is the best of winter food: rich and satisfying, and with the added attraction of being able to be made in just one pot. You'll pay attention to it while you brown the shanks and get the sauce going—which will take about 30 minutes—but then you'll slide the dish into the oven and pretty much forget about it for a couple of hours. The pot you prepare this in needs a tight cover and has to be able to live happily both on the stove and in the oven; it should also be just big enough to hold the shanks snugly in one layer.

Coarse salt and freshly ground black pepper
4 lamb shanks (about 1 pound each)
About $^{1}/_{2}$ cup all-purpose flour
2 tablespoons olive oil
3 onions, sliced very thin
2 garlic cloves, minced
6 anchovy fillets, chopped
2 tablespoons tomato paste
2 cups fruity red wine, like a Côtes du Rhône
1 sprig rosemary
1 bay leaf

Heat the oven to 350 degrees.

Put a heavy flameproof casserole or Dutch oven on the stove over medium-high heat. Salt and pepper the shanks, then flour them lightly. Pour the oil into the casserole and heat it until it starts to shimmer. Brown the shanks in batches (don't do them all at once, or they'll steam and never get a crust), and hold them on a plate as they're browned.

Add the onions to the casserole and turn the heat down to medium. Season with a pinch of salt and a few grinds of pepper and cook, stirring as you need to, until the onions are limp and translucent. This should take 5 to 7 minutes. Add the garlic and anchovies and cook, stirring, until the garlic is fragrant and the anchovies have melted, about 1 minute. Stir in the tomato paste and cook until the paste turns brick red, a minute or two.

Pour in about half the wine and stir, scraping the bottom of the pot to release any browned bits that didn't dissolve when the onions released their liquid. Add the rest of the wine, the rosemary and bay, and the shanks, along with any juices from the plate. Bring up to a simmer, cover the casserole tightly, and slide it into the oven.

After about 1 hour, turn the shanks over in the sauce. It will take 2 to 2½ hours for the meat to be just about falling off the bone—which is what you want. Test the shanks with a small sharp knife. The blade should slip in and out without any resistance.

These are great served in wide shallow bowls, with a big spoonful of sauce napping them.

LEFTOVERS

Don't you dare toss any leftover sauce. Heat it up the next day (you can first lift off any congealed fat), and stir it into rice, maybe with some frozen peas that you've run under hot water to defrost.

SIDES

Serve something alongside that will sop up the sauce. It might be mashed potatoes or Polenta (page 311), but it could just as easily be rice or buttered noodles. String beans on the side: Just trim the tops and put them in a skillet with a knob of butter. Pour in enough water to barely cover the beans. Cover, bring to an active simmer, and cook until the water has just about cooked away. Take the cover off and keep cooking until the water's gone and the butter starts to sputter. Season with coarse salt.

white beans and lamb SERVES 6

What we have here is my cassoulet: no goose, no duck confit, no pork. Just white beans and lamb chops, cooked into a very rich and satisfying casserole. And you can use canned beans.

Six 1½-inch-thick loin lamb chops

Coarse salt and freshly ground black pepper

6 tablespoons olive oil

3 turnips, preferably golden (about 1¼ pounds), peeled and cut into ½-inch dice

4 carrots, cut into ½-inch dice

½ cup water

½ cup dry white wine or dry vermouth

2 onions, chopped

2 garlic cloves, minced

1 tablespoon chopped fresh rosemary

1 (14.5-ounce) can tomatoes, chopped or crushed, with their juice

1 recipe Basic White Beans (page 256) or 2 (15.5-ounce) cans cannellini beans

3 cups chicken stock (page 20; if you're using canned beans)

1 cup fresh bread crumbs (from about 1 slice country bread)

Season the chops with salt and pepper.

Heat 2 tablespoons oil in a large skillet over medium-high heat. When the oil shimmers, lay in the chops and brown them on both sides, 3 to 4 minutes a side. Transfer the chops to a plate, cover with foil to keep warm, and discard the oil in the skillet.

Spoon 1 tablespoon oil into the skillet and add the turnips, carrots, and a pinch of salt. Cook the vegetables over medium-high heat, stirring once in a while, until they start to brown, 8 to 10 minutes. As the vegetables release some of their juices, they will pick up color from the browned bits in the skillet. Pour in the water and wine. Bring to a boil, then reduce the heat to a simmer, cover the pan, and cook until the vegetables are just tender, about 15 minutes. Scrape the vegetables out into a large bowl.

Wipe out the skillet, put it back over medium-high heat, and spoon in 2 tablespoons oil. When it shimmers, add the onions and a pinch of salt. Cook until the onions are softened and starting to turn gold at the edges, about 5 minutes. Add the garlic and rosemary and cook just until the garlic is fragrant, about 30 seconds. Pour in the tomatoes and bring to a boil. Reduce the heat so the tomatoes cook at an active simmer, and cook until the sauce is very thick and aromatic, 10 to 15 minutes.

Heat the oven to 350 degrees.

Scrape the tomato sauce into the bowl with the vegetables. Put the beans and their cooking liquid into the skillet and bring to a simmer. Or, if you are using canned beans, drain and rinse them and heat them in the chicken stock.

Drain the beans, reserving the liquid. Add the beans to the bowl with the vegetables and sauce and stir it all up.

Put half the beans into a deep casserole, something that will hold 3 to 3½ quarts. Layer the lamb chops on top, adding any juices that have accumulated, and spoon in the rest of the beans.

Measure the bean liquid and add enough water to make 3 cups. Pour it into the casserole. Scatter the bread crumbs over the top and drizzle with the remaining 1 tablespoon oil.

Slide the casserole into the oven and bake for 1 hour. Take it out and break up the crust with the side of a big spoon, pushing some of the crumbs into the juices. Bake for another 45 minutes to 1 hour, until richly browned and bubbling.

Serve in wide soup plates.

SIDES

You really don't need more than a salad to make this a meal.

summertime ragù SERVES 6

Here's a Bolognese-type sauce for those summer days when you're in the mood for a meat sauce but want something lighter and a bit brighter in flavor than the classic three-hour version.

FOR THE RAGÙ

- 2 tablespoons olive oil
- 2 tablespoons unsalted butter
- 1/3 cup chopped scallions
- 1 garlic clove, minced
- 1 pound ground veal
- Coarse salt and freshly ground black pepper
- 1 cup rosé
- 2 tablespoons tomato paste
- 1 (28-ounce) can plum tomatoes, preferably from San Marzano
- 1 cup water
- 2 teaspoons minced fresh rosemary

- Coarse salt
- 1 1/2 pounds ziti or penne (or other tubular pasta)
- Freshly grated Parmesan, for serving

FOR THE RAGÙ

Heat the oil and butter in a large saucepan over medium-high heat. When the butter has melted, add the scallions and cook for about 1 minute to soften them up. Add the garlic and cook for about 30 seconds, until fragrant. Crumble in the veal and season it with salt and pepper. Cook, stirring often, until the veal is no longer pink and is very crumbly.

Pour in the rosé and bring it to a boil. Cook, stirring once or twice, until the wine has reduced to about 1/3 cup. The meat will start looking like rice as it cooks, with little holes over the surface. Stir in the tomato paste and cook for about 2 minutes.

Meanwhile, put the tomatoes and their juice into a blender or food processor and whir them until you have a smooth puree. Pour the pureed tomatoes into the pan, rinse the blender container with the water, and stir that into the pan, along with the rosemary. Season with salt and pepper. Bring to a boil, then reduce the heat and simmer the sauce for 45 minutes to 1 hour. The ragù should be thick.

SIDES

Eggplant and Mint (page 329) might be a nice way to start the meal. Or The Simplest Cooked Greens (page 282).

Bring a large pot of water to a boil. Salt the water well and add the ziti. Cook until the pasta is just shy of al dente. Scoop out about 1 cup of the pasta water, then drain the pasta. Return it immediately to the pot and stir in about 3 cups of the ragù. Add enough of the pasta water to loosen the sauce and cook, stirring, for a minute or two to marry sauce and pasta.

Serve immediately, with a spoonful of the remaining sauce on top of each serving. Pass the cheese.

grandma called it gravy

Weekend cooking was something I learned about early on in life. When I was born, my parents lived in the apartment upstairs from my dad's mother. Grandma Finamore, who was Italian, was a seamstress, and while she could be counted on to get a good, quick dinner on the table during the week, it was on the weekends, when she had more time to devote to the kitchen, that her skills shone.

Her Sunday sauce was the ultimate in weekend cooking, the Italian-American dream. She called it gravy. The process would start after she had gone to early Mass on a Sunday morning. The aromas of the meats browning would carry to our place upstairs, and they were exquisite torture. I was a good Catholic boy, which meant no eating until after Mass, and we were on the late-morning church schedule. I'd knock on Grandma's door as soon as we got home, and she'd answer it with a meatball on a fork for me to taste.

Over the years, I've played with the recipes, but then, so did Grandma. "There are a lot of ways to skin a cat" was a favorite saying of hers in the kitchen, her answer when I'd ask why she was braising the braciole instead of putting it in gravy. Or why sometimes she'd brown garlic in oil and add the greens and other times she'd boil the greens and dress them with oil she'd heated garlic in. That was how I started learning to play in the kitchen.

sunday sauce SERVES AT LEAST 8, WITH LEFTOVERS

You too can be an Italian grandmother.

Sure there's a lot of prep here, but you'll also feed a crowd with meatballs and sausages, chicken, and the Italian meat rolls called braciole, all cooked slowly in tomato sauce, and then you'll have leftovers for days.

You'll need a really big pot for this, at least 10 quarts. Tall and wide (rather than tall and narrow) is what you want, and it's best if the pot is stainless steel or something else nonreactive.

game plan

You've got a lot to do to get this sauce going.

- ✧ Prep the braciole (you can do this the day before if you want, and refrigerate, covered, overnight. Blot the rolls dry with paper towels before browning them).
- ✧ Start the sauce, and get it up to a simmer.
- ✧ Prep the meatballs once the sauce is starting to simmer.
- ✧ Brown the meatballs and chicken. These can sit in a baking dish on the counter until it's time to add them to the sauce.
- ✧ Definitely reward yourself with a glass of wine.

FOR THE BRACIOLE

1 small onion, minced

1 tablespoon olive oil

Coarse salt

1/4 cup pine nuts

1 1/2 cups fresh bread crumbs

1 (6-ounce) jar marinated artichoke hearts, drained and chopped fine

1/3 cup freshly grated Pecorino

Freshly ground black pepper

Freshly grated nutmeg

6 very thin slices top round of beef (about 4 by 10 inches, total weight about 1 pound)

1/4 pound sliced prosciutto

FOR THE SAUCE

2 meaty beef soup bones (3/4–1 pound each)

Coarse salt and freshly ground black pepper

1/4 cup olive oil

1 1/4–1 1/2 pounds sweet Italian sausages

2 red or yellow onions, sliced thin

2 garlic cloves, chopped

1 (4.5-ounce) tube tomato paste (5 tablespoons)

1 cup dry red wine

2 (35-ounce) cans plum tomatoes, preferably from San Marzano

About 1 cup water

Crushed red pepper

2 bay leaves

FOR THE BRACIOLE

Put the onion and olive oil in a small skillet with a pinch of salt. Cook over medium-high heat until the onion has softened and is starting to turn golden at the edges, about 7 minutes. Add the pine nuts and cook, stirring often, until the nuts start to brown, just a minute or two. Scrape this all out into a mixing bowl.

Add the bread crumbs, artichoke hearts, and Pecorino to the bowl. Season with a bit of salt, a good hit of pepper, and a few gratings of nutmeg. Mix well with your hands to make a slightly moist stuffing.

Lay the beef slices out on your counter and season them with salt and pepper. Cover the beef with a single layer of prosciutto (you probably won't use it all). Cover the meat with plastic wrap and give each slice a few whacks with a meat pounder. Toss out the plastic and then sprinkle each piece of meat with an even layer of stuffing, leaving about a ½-inch margin along the long sides and one short side. Pat the stuffing down with your hand. Roll up the slices, working from the stuffed short side to the short side with the margin. Tie each roll in two places with kitchen string, or secure with toothpicks.

FOR THE SAUCE

Season the soup bones with salt and pepper. Heat 2 tablespoons oil in a big nonreactive pot over medium-high heat. Add the soup bones and brown until they're good and crusty on both sides. Transfer them to a big platter or a baking sheet. Add the braciole to the pot and brown them well on all sides. Transfer them to the platter too. Prick the sausages with the tip of a knife, or slash the casings, and add them to the pot. Brown on all sides and transfer to the platter.

Add the onions and a pinch of salt to whatever fat is left in the pan. Cook, stirring often, until the onions soften and start to brown at the edges. Add the garlic and cook until fragrant, maybe 1 minute. Scrape the onions and garlic out into a food processor.

Pour the remaining 2 tablespoons oil into the pot—still over medium-high heat—and when it shimmers, add the tomato paste. Cook, stirring often, until the paste turns brick red. Pour in the wine and bring to a boil.

Meanwhile, add about half a can of tomatoes and their juice to the onions in the processor. Whir to a smooth puree. Pour into the pot. Process the rest of the tomatoes in batches and add to the pot. Use a cup of water to rinse out the cans and the processor and add to the pot. Season with salt and pepper, a big pinch of crushed red pepper, and the bay leaves.

Now add the braciole, soup bones, and sausages to the sauce and bring to a boil. Reduce the heat so the sauce will simmer actively. Cook for 2 hours, stirring once in a while. If the sauce seems to be thickening quickly, stir in some water. This sauce shouldn't become dense. You're going for something the consistency of slightly thickened heavy cream.

I start making the meatballs once the sauce is at a simmer. Or you can take a break for about half an hour.

FOR THE MEATBALLS

3 slices white bread (something like Pepperidge Farm)

1/2 cup milk

2 large eggs

3/4 cup freshly grated Pecorino

1/4 cup chopped fresh flat-leaf parsley

Crushed red pepper

Coarse salt and freshly ground black pepper

1 3/4 pounds ground round

1/2 cup water

Olive oil

1 garlic clove

6 chicken thighs

Coarse salt and freshly ground black pepper

FOR SERVING

Coarse salt

2 pounds rigatoni

Freshly grated Pecorino

SIDES

A very big salad, sharp with vinegar, is mandatory with this. Italian bread won't hurt.

When I was growing up, we ate the salad after the pasta and meat, on the same plates, so it mixed with any leftover sauce. I haven't changed that practice.

FOR THE MEATBALLS

Rip up the bread and put it into a mixing bowl. Pour in the milk and work this into a fairly smooth paste. The genteel will use a fork; I use my fingers. Add the eggs, cheese, parsley, and a big pinch of crushed red pepper, then season with salt and black pepper (a heaped teaspoon of salt and a good amount of pepper). Mix this very well with your hands.

Crumble the meat into the bowl and toss it with the seasonings, then mix gently but thoroughly with your hands until the mixture is smooth and holds together. Take a bit of care here: undermix, and the meatballs will likely fall apart; overmix, and you'll end up with something as tender as golf balls.

Set out a small bowl of water and a plate. Dip your hands in the water and start rolling out meatballs about the size of a walnut, putting them on the plate as you roll them. Wet hands make it easier to roll, and they leave the meatballs damp, which helps browning. You'll end up with 25 to 30 meatballs. When you've rolled out the meatballs, pour the ½ cup water into the mixing bowl and swirl it around. Keep it for later.

Heat about ¼ inch of olive oil in a large skillet over medium-high heat until it shimmers. Peel the garlic and add it to the oil. It should sizzle immediately. If not, wait a moment for the oil to become hot enough. Brown the meatballs in batches, transferring them to a platter or baking sheet as they're done. Discard the garlic when it gets very brown.

Season the chicken thighs with salt and pepper and brown them on both sides in the same oil used for the meatballs. Remove them to the platter. Pour the oil out of the skillet and return the skillet to the heat. Pour in the water you've got in the mixing bowl and deglaze the skillet, scraping up all the browned bits in the pan. Pour into the sauce.

Once the sauce has simmered for 2 hours, add the meatballs and chicken. Poke all the meats down into the sauce. Cook for another hour, stirring gently once or twice and adding water if the sauce thickens too much. There will likely be fat that has risen to the surface; skim it off. Capture the soup bones. Pull the meat off the bones, chop it, and return the meat to the sauce. The marrow can be a cook's treat or can be added to the sauce.

You can leave the sauce on the stove for an hour or so, until you're ready for dinner. Come dinnertime, bring a large pot of water to a boil and bring the sauce back to a simmer.

Salt the water well and add the rigatoni. Cook until just shy of al dente.

Meanwhile, take the meats out of the sauce with a slotted spoon or spider and pile on a platter. Spoon some of the sauce on top. Fill a small bowl with some sauce for the table.

When the pasta is almost cooked, scoop out about 1 cup of the pasta water. Drain the pasta and return it to the pot, still a bit wet. Put the pot back on the heat and ladle in about 2 cups of the sauce. Cook, stirring, for about a minute to marry the pasta and sauce. Add some of the pasta water if you need to loosen the sauce, but don't overcook the pasta. It should still be round and proud, not flabby and collapsed.

Scrape the pasta into a big bowl and serve at once with the meats. Pass the Pecorino and the bowl of sauce.

LEFTOVERS

Store the meats and sauce together. Do rinse out the pot with some water and add it to the sauce. There will always be good stuff stuck to the bottom or sides of the pot.

You could make heroes with the leftover meat and sauce, or make the meal with pasta again. Tradition mandates that you do this on Wednesday.

on the reheating of pasta

Purists say you're not supposed to do it. And to that I say, in the words of Nero Wolfe, pfui. Pasta that's been sitting in the refrigerator, marrying completely with the sauce, is just too good not to be eaten.

Cookbook author Lee Bailey used to stir eggs into leftover pasta and turn it into some kind of casserole. Me, I just oil a casserole or gratin dish, put a meatball or two in the bottom, and cover them with leftover pasta. Strew on some grated cheese—Pecorino or Parmesan, maybe some shredded mozzarella—and top with more pasta: spaghetti, rigatoni, whatever. If you have some leftover sauce, spoon on a little. Sprinkle, say, 3 tablespoons of water over the pasta and top with more cheese. Cover the dish with foil and bake in a 350-degree oven for about 30 minutes. Take off the foil and bake for another 10 or 15 minutes, until the pasta is, as they say, piping hot and browned in spots. I love the crunchy bits best.

You may not want to go through the bother, of course. If you haven't discovered this, cold leftover pasta is even better than leftover pizza.

homemade ricotta cavatelli

SERVES 4 AS A MAIN COURSE; 6 AS A FIRST COURSE

This sturdy and toothsome pasta is easy to make. With practice, you'll get the hang of shaping the pieces on a fork, and you'll find it goes quickly.

If you bought grocery-store ricotta and you have the time, put the cheese in a strainer lined with dampened cheesecloth, set it over a bowl, and let it drain in the refrigerator for an hour or two. You'll need less flour to make the pasta, and less flour means lighter pasta.

Cavatelli are meant to go with rich meat sauces. Try them with Sunday Sauce (page 235) or with Summertime Ragù (page 232). They're also pretty good with a quick raw tomato sauce (recipe follows).

The photo is on page 274.

1 pound ricotta (see headnote)

3 large eggs

1/2 cup freshly grated Pecorino

Coarse salt

About 2 1/2 cups all-purpose flour, plus more for shaping

Whisk the ricotta, eggs, Pecorino, and 1 teaspoon salt together in a large bowl until smooth. Start stirring in the flour, about a cup at a time, with a wooden spoon. As you add more flour, you'll need to switch over to your hand as mixing tool. Add just enough flour to make a firm, only slightly sticky dough.

Flour your work surface and scrape out the dough. Knead the dough a few times, only long enough to smooth it out. Pat the dough out into a rectangle that's about 1/2 inch thick. Rub some flour over the rectangle, and cut it into 1-inch-wide strips. Now, use your palms to roll each strip into a rope about 1/2 inch in diameter, or a bit bigger—no need to obsess over this. Just keep the counter well floured. Cut the ropes into 3/4-inch lengths.

Hold a fork in one hand, tines resting on the counter. Pick up a piece of the dough, set it at the top of the fork, and use your thumb to roll the pasta down the tines, applying a little pressure. Do it with the right amount of pressure, and the pasta will curl around your thumb, making a little cup with ridges on the outside from the tines—the perfect shape for capturing sauce. Too much pressure, and the pasta will just break apart, so roll it back into a ball and try again. Keep the counter and the fork well floured as you shape the pasta, and transfer the cavatelli to a well-floured baking sheet. What you are doing here is making the same shape as gnocchi. And I know some people will always push too hard on the pasta when they roll it down the fork. But don't worry: if you are having difficulties, just stay with the ¾-inch lengths, and put them on the baking sheet.

You can hold these for a couple of hours on the baking sheet in the refrigerator (don't cover them). They also freeze well: freeze them on the baking sheet, uncovered for an hour or two, then transfer to sealable plastic bags.

Bring a big pot of water to a boil over high heat. Salt it well and add the cavatelli. Stir, making sure that none stick to the bottom of the pot. Boil for about a minute after the cavatelli rise to the surface (taste one for doneness; they should be a bit chewy), then drain. Return the pasta to the cooking pot, add your sauce, stir, and dish up.

salsa cruda

Cut up some perfectly ripe and juicy tomatoes. Put them in a big serving bowl with a minced garlic clove and a minced hot pepper (or a big pinch of crushed red pepper). Season with salt and pepper, pour in about 1 tablespoon extra-virgin olive oil, and stir. If you want, add some chopped fresh basil or parsley or mint. Let the sauce sit for 30 minutes. Drain the cooked pasta, pour it on top of the sauce, stir, and serve.

lasagne with greens SERVES 8

I first made this one Thanksgiving for my vegetarian sister, Barbara. Now, for just about any family gathering, the word comes that I should make it, please. It's creamy with an Italian white sauce, and packed with sautéed greens like escarole and chard, and the spicy tomato sauce lends a bit of zing.

I use store-bought fresh lasagne noodles in the recipe; they're much more tender than the dried, and you want that tenderness in this dish. When I feel very generous, I'll make the noodles myself (3 eggs worth is enough).

This is a production, but it's so worth the effort. You can make the casserole in advance, even the day before, and refrigerate it. Bake it when you plan to serve it, though.

FOR THE GREENS

2 pounds mixed greens (Swiss chard, escarole, chicory, spinach), washed and stemmed

Coarse salt

3 tablespoons olive oil

1 garlic clove, minced

Freshly ground black pepper

FOR THE TOMATO SAUCE

1 (28-ounce) can plum tomatoes, preferably from San Marzano

2 tablespoons olive oil

1 garlic clove, minced

Coarse salt and freshly ground black pepper

Crushed red pepper

FOR THE BESCIAMELLA

3 tablespoons unsalted butter

3 tablespoons all-purpose flour

3 1/2 cups milk, plus more if needed

Coarse salt and freshly ground black pepper

Freshly grated nutmeg

1/2 cup freshly grated Parmesan

Coarse salt

1 pound fresh lasagne noodles

1 cup freshly grated Parmesan

1 tablespoon unsalted butter

FOR THE GREENS

Bring a big pot of water to a boil. Add the greens and a big pinch of salt and boil the greens until tender, about 10 minutes. Drain the greens, refresh them in cold water, drain again, and squeeze them dry. (No need to try to get out every drop of liquid.) Chop the greens.

Heat the oil in a large skillet over medium-high heat. When it shimmers, add the garlic and cook just until you can smell it, about 30 seconds. Add the greens and stir. Season the greens with salt and pepper. Cook a minute or two, stirring, to season the greens. Turn off the heat.

FOR THE TOMATO SAUCE

Put the tomatoes and their juice in a blender or food processor and puree.

Heat the oil in a saucepan over medium heat. When it shimmers, add the garlic and cook until it's fragrant, about 30 seconds. Pour in the tomatoes, season with salt, pepper, and a good pinch of crushed red pepper, and bring to a boil. Reduce the heat and cook the sauce at an active simmer until it thickens and smells completely wonderful, about 20 minutes. Turn off the heat on this too.

Put a big pot of water up to boil for the lasagna.

MEANWHILE, FOR THE BESCIAMELLA

Melt the butter in a medium saucepan over medium-high heat. Spoon in the flour, stir well, and cook for a minute or two, stirring often. If you have a microwave, zap the milk to take the chill off it; if you don't, don't fret. Pour the milk into the pan, whisking briskly to dissolve the roux you just made with the butter and flour. Cook, stirring often, until the sauce just comes to a boil. Reduce to a low simmer and cook for 5 minutes. Reduce the heat to as low as possible, stir in the salt, pepper, and nutmeg to taste and the Parmesan, and keep the sauce warm.

The water for the pasta should be boiling by now. Set out a large bowl almost filled with cold water. Salt the boiling water very well and put in a few of the pasta sheets. Cook until the pasta is just tender, which should be about 1½ minutes after the water comes back to a boil. Scoop the pasta out with a skimmer or a smallish strainer and drop it in the cold water. Swirl it around, then lift it out and lay flat on kitchen towels. Repeat, cooking the pasta in batches. It's perfectly fine, preferable really, to stack the pasta between towels.

You're ready to assemble. Oil a casserole—about 9 by 13 inches—and ladle in 1 cup of the besciamella. Tilt the casserole so you have an even layer of the sauce across the bottom. Cover the bottom and sides of the casserole with pasta, with some of the sheets overhanging the edges by about an inch. Spread ½ cup of the besciamella over the pasta, then scatter a quarter of the greens on top. Spoon on about ¾ cup of the tomato sauce—just try not to make puddles—and strew with 2 tablespoons of the Parmesan. Add another layer of pasta, but don't overlap the pasta this time—trim it so it will just fit inside the pan. Repeat making layers, just as you did the first one: 1/2 cup besciamella, a quarter of the greens, 3/4 cup of the tomato sauce, and 2 tablespoons of the Parmesan, ending up with a top layer of pasta.

Fold over the overhanging edges of pasta. If the besciamella has thickened, add a few tablespoons of milk—up to 1/4 cup—and bring it back to a boil. Cover the top layer completely with the besciamella and strew with the remaining Parmesan. Dot the top with the butter. Cover with foil. You can bake this now, or refrigerate until tomorrow.

Heat the oven to 350 degrees.

When the oven is hot, slide in the casserole and bake it for 30 minutes (45 minutes if you've made the casserole in advance). Take the foil off and bake another 15 minutes or so, until browned and puffed up.

This needs to sit for 15 minutes before you cut it into pieces and serve.

SIDES

You've got lots of greens in the lasagne, so think about Eggplant and Mint (page 329), or Zucchini all'Insalata (page 335). Or Roasted Beets (page 257), dressed with olive oil and fresh thyme.

sides

sides

One little serving of meat or fish surrounded by a lot of vegetables and salads is my ideal.

And you'll find, in this chapter and elsewhere, that I really like to cook vegetables—I mean *really* cook them. Roast a beet until it yields to the slightest pressure of your fork, simmer cauliflower so when you take a bite it melts on your tongue—well, that goes against the grain in these days of 30-minute meals. I'm not a 30-minute guy. Longer cooking is not just about texture; when you take your time cooking a vegetable, you're rewarded with flavor.

As I'm writing this, spring is supposed to be here, but that's just on the calendar. The farmers are selling the last of their storage crops—turnips and cabbages—and I'm eager for the first sign of the new crops. In the meantime, I'm cooking cabbage. Sometimes I'll shred it like I would for coleslaw, then sauté it quickly in some butter. Or I'll cut it into wedges and rub them with olive oil and roast them in a 350-degree oven until the thick parts are creamy and the edges are crisp and almost burnt. The markets still have good broccoli and cauliflower, so I'll cook them forever (see page 258).

Soon dandelions will arrive, and spring garlic, and early spinach. Then comes the first of the new potatoes, with the soft, wispy skins that almost wash off—so delicious cooked just in butter and a spoon or two of water, and showered with fresh herbs when they're tender.

Most of all, I'm waiting for tomatoes—real summer tomatoes, with tender skins and heavy with juice, still warm from the sun.

Much as I love food in season, though, I can't do without frozen peas. As the English cook and writer Nigel Slater says, "They will get you out of no end of trouble," and I always have a bag in the freezer.

Not every side needs to be a vegetable, though. Polenta (page 311) is a very satisfying dish to make, the kind of thing you can be proud of. Cooking rice like pasta and then dressing it with some butter and lemon and egg is also a very handy thing to know. And you can experiment with adding all kinds of vegetables and make the Riso on page 302 your own.

And that's what it's all about.

lemon roast asparagus SERVES 6

This is best with thin spears. Peel thicker ones.

If you want to eat the lemon (and I always do), try to find an organic one, which won't have been sprayed with something unfortunate. Otherwise, scrub the lemon very well with soap and hot water.

2 pounds asparagus, tough ends trimmed

1/4 cup olive oil

Coarse salt and freshly ground black pepper

1 lemon, scrubbed

Heat the oven to 400 degrees.

Toss the asparagus with the oil and salt and pepper to taste—I do this prep on the baking sheet, rather than dirtying a bowl. Slice the lemon very thin. Push the asparagus to one side and make a layer of lemon slices on the bottom of the baking sheet. Spread the asparagus on top of the lemon, and roast for 15 minutes, until the asparagus is tender and browning a bit.

Serve hot or warm.

asparagus and prosciutto SERVES 6

You roast the asparagus in bundles, each one wrapped with a piece of prosciutto. It's a pretty dish.

1 pound asparagus

Coarse salt and freshly ground black pepper

1 tablespoon olive oil

6 slices (about 1/4 pound) prosciutto

Lemon wedges, for serving

Break the tough ends from the asparagus, and peel any thick stalks.

Bring about 1/2 inch of water to a boil in a large skillet. Add a good pinch of salt and the asparagus. Bring the water back to a boil and blanch the asparagus for 2 minutes. Drain, refresh the asparagus in cold water to stop the cooking, and drain again. Dry on paper towels.

Oil a baking sheet. Season the asparagus with salt and pepper and the olive oil. Divide the stalks into 6 piles, and wrap each pile with a piece of prosciutto. The ham will stick to itself and make a neat packet. Put the packets on the baking sheet. You can finish the dish now, or let it sit on the counter, lightly covered with plastic wrap or waxed paper, for a couple of hours.

When you're ready, heat the oven to 350 degrees.

Slide the baking sheet into the oven and roast for 10 minutes, or until the asparagus is tender.

Serve with lemon wedges.

variation

If you're in the mood to gild the lily, smear about 1 tablespoon of fresh goat cheese on each slice of prosciutto before you wrap the asparagus.

basic shell beans—two ways

MAKES ABOUT 6 CUPS

Fresh cannellini and cranberry beans in their pods have been showing up at farmers' markets for a few years now. I hope you can find them at yours; they make a wonderful side dish. Besides the great flavor, they cook so much more quickly than dried. And shelling beans is good for the soul.

VERSION 1

1 tablespoon olive oil

1 thick slice pancetta or prosciutto (about 2 ounces), diced

2 pounds cannellini or cranberry beans, shelled (about 3 cups)

1 large garlic clove, lightly crushed with the side of a knife

6 or 7 parsley sprigs, tied with kitchen string

3 cups water

Coarse salt

VERSION 2

1 tablespoon olive oil

1 thick slice bacon, cut into matchsticks

1 onion, chopped fine

2 carrots, chopped fine

1 celery stalk, chopped fine

Coarse salt

2 pounds cannellini or cranberry beans, shelled (about 3 cups)

2 cups chicken or beef stock (page 20)

VERSION 1

Put the olive oil and pancetta in a saucepan and cook over medium heat until the pancetta just starts turning golden at the edges. Add the beans, garlic, parsley, and water and bring to a simmer. Reduce the heat so the beans will cook very gently, and simmer until the beans are tender, about 30 minutes. Remove the garlic and parsley, taste for salt, and serve hot or at room temperature.

VERSION 2

Put the olive oil and bacon in a saucepan and cook over medium heat, stirring once or twice, until the bacon has softened and is just starting to brown. Add the onion, carrots, celery, and a pinch of salt. Cook, stirring once in a while, until the vegetables are soft and starting to brown, about 10 minutes. Add the beans and stock and bring to a simmer. Reduce the heat so the beans will cook very gently, and simmer until the beans are tender, about 30 minutes. Taste for salt, and serve hot or at room temperature.

variation

It's very easy to turn these beans into a gratin. Spoon the cooked beans into a gratin dish, keeping them juicy with the cooking liquid. Mix some bread crumbs with grated Parmesan and scatter over the beans. Drizzle with a little olive oil and bake in a preheated 375-degree oven until the beans are hot and bubbling and the crumbs have browned.

buying shell beans

These are a late-summer item in New York. Look for firm, plump pods, filled their entire length (why pay for pods without beans?). Look for pods with good color too.

basic white beans MAKES ABOUT 6 CUPS

These beans are a staple in my kitchen. Once I've got them made, it's a snap to turn out a soup or two, or a quick pasta for dinner. Or I might just heat them up to serve as a side dish. Parmesan rind adds such good flavor to white beans. Cut the rinds off the hunks of Parmesan you buy to grate as needed, and keep them in the freezer. And vary the herbs. Thyme is also wonderful in beans, and so is winter savory.

Make this on a day when you'll be around the house for a while. The beans aren't soaked—the texture is much better without soaking—and older beans can take a lot of cooking.

1 pound Great Northern or cannellini beans, picked over and rinsed

1 large onion, peeled and stuck with 3 whole cloves

2 carrots, cut into large chunks

1 celery stalk, cut into large chunks

1 large sprig rosemary

1 bay leaf

A big piece of Parmesan rind

Put all the ingredients into a stockpot and cover with cold water by about 3 inches. Bring to a boil over medium heat, reduce the heat to low, and simmer, partly covered, until the beans are very tender. This can take anywhere from 1½ to 4 hours. Skim any foam that rises in the pot as the beans simmer and keep an eye on the water level. Add boiling water if you need to, to keep the beans covered.

Toss out the rind, onion, carrots, celery, rosemary stem (don't worry about the needles), and bay leaf. You can leave the beans, in their liquid, covered, in the refrigerator for 3 or 4 days. The beans will keep in the freezer for a couple of months.

roasted beets SERVES 4 TO 6

Double this recipe, or triple it, but make at least one packet for each bunch of beets. If you overstuff the foil packets, you'll be roasting the beets forever before they become tender. I make these all summer, whenever I have the oven on for something else. The oven temperature really isn't critical; if the oven is on at 400 degrees, fine.

1 bunch beets (4 or 5 medium)

2 tablespoons olive oil

3 or 4 sprigs thyme

Coarse salt and freshly ground black pepper

Heat the oven to 350 degrees. Tear off a large piece of heavy-duty aluminum foil. (If lightweight is all you have, use a double layer.)

Cut off the beet tops, leaving about 2 inches of stem. Scrub the beets and place them in the center of the foil. Drizzle with the oil, stick in the thyme sprigs, and season with salt and pepper. Wrap the beets in the foil—make a double fold on all the open ends so the packet won't leak—and roast them for 1 hour, or until tender.

Peel the beets when you're ready to use them.

You'll find several recipes elsewhere in this book—like Beets, Tomatoes, and Peaches on page 328—that call for roasted beets. Once you have some in the refrigerator, you can make all sorts of dishes.

Slice the beets and heat them in butter. Season with salt and pepper and a splash of red wine vinegar.

Bring them to room temperature and serve them sliced, on a bed of Aïoli (page 54), or dress them with your best olive oil, your best salt, some pepper, and fresh thyme. My parents are particularly fond of pickled beets, which are sliced, tossed with sliced red onion, a pinch or two of ground cloves and some pepper, and covered with vinegar, and served icy cold.

broccoli (or cauliflower) cooked forever SERVES 4 TO 6

When you cook broccoli forever, it gets meltingly soft and mellow. I've adapted this from a recipe by the San Francisco chef Nancy Silverton. She uses it for sandwiches; I use it as a side dish. I've found that cooking cauliflower the same way is just as wonderful.

2 bunches (2–2¼ pounds) broccoli or 2 heads cauliflower

1 cup olive oil

3 garlic cloves, sliced thin

2 small hot peppers, halved lengthwise

4 anchovy fillets, chopped

Coarse salt and freshly ground black pepper

Bring a large pot of water to a boil.

While the water is heating, cut the florets off the broccoli. Peel the stems and cut them into rather thick slices, about ⅓ inch. (If you're making cauliflower, break the heads into large florets.)

When the water comes to a boil, add the broccoli (or cauliflower) and cover the pot to bring it back to a boil quickly. Blanch the broccoli for 5 minutes. Drain.

Put the oil and garlic in a large skillet over medium heat. When the garlic starts to sizzle, add the hot peppers and anchovies. Cook, giving a stir or two, until the anchovies melt. Add the broccoli, season with salt and pepper, and stir well. Cover the skillet, turn the heat to very low, and cook for 2 hours. Use a spatula to turn the broccoli over in the skillet a few times, but try not to break it up. It will be very tender when done.

Use a slotted spoon to transfer the broccoli to a serving dish. It's delicious hot or at room temperature.

LEFTOVERS

To tell the truth, this is so good you probably won't have any left over. But if you do, you can make amazing sandwiches with it. Try it on Italian bread, with some Fontina, and maybe some leftover roast pork. Or put the leftovers in an oiled gratin dish, strew with grated Parmesan or Gruyère, and bake until crusty and hot.

If you had some leftover Polenta (page 311), you could also make a great first course. Slice the polenta and fry it until the slices are browned and crispy. Top the slices with broccoli and some grated Parmesan, and bake at 400 degrees for 15 to 20 minutes, to melt the cheese.

This broccoli also makes a wonderful sauce for pasta. Try it with something sturdy, like rigatoni. And you'll want to save some of the pasta water to loosen the broccoli into a sauce.

cabbage and noodles SERVES 6

This is good with just about any kind of pork, but I have to tell you I could make a meal of just this and a glass of white wine.

4 tablespoons (1/2 stick) unsalted butter

1 (2-pound) green cabbage, cored and shredded

1 teaspoon caraway seeds, crushed

Coarse salt and freshly ground black pepper

1/2 pound egg noodles

1 cup sour cream

Melt the butter in a very large skillet over medium heat. Add the cabbage and caraway seeds and season with salt and pepper. Cook, stirring and tossing often, for about 30 minutes, until the cabbage is completely limp and starting to brown.

Meanwhile, cook the noodles in a pot of boiling well-salted water until al dente. Scoop out about 1/2 cup of the pasta water and drain the noodles.

Add the noodles to the cabbage and toss. Stir in the sour cream and cook just long enough to heat. If the sauce is very tight, you might want to stir in a few tablespoons of the pasta water to loosen it. Check for salt and pepper, and serve right away.

braised red cabbage SERVES 6

This dish of melting cabbage is a fixture on our Christmas dinner table in Virginia, where it is a foil for a roast goose. But I love it with roast pork too, and brined pork chops. You can make it early in the day or even a day in advance.

1 large red onion, sliced thin

2 tablespoons unsalted butter

1 tablespoon olive oil

2 tablespoons red or black currant jelly

1 medium ($1\frac{1}{2}$–2 pounds) red cabbage, cored and shredded

1 Granny Smith apple, peeled, cored, and sliced thin

1 cup fruity red wine, like a Côtes du Rhône

1 tablespoon red wine vinegar

Coarse salt and freshly ground black pepper

Cook the onion in the butter and oil in a large skillet over medium heat until it is limp and translucent, about 5 minutes. Stir in the jelly and cook for a moment to dissolve it. Add the cabbage, apple, wine, and vinegar, and season well with salt and pepper. Toss as well as you can (the skillet will be rather full), cover, and turn the heat down to low. Cook, stirring once in a while, for 1 hour, until the cabbage is very tender. Check for salt and pepper.

You can serve this right away or let it sit, covered, on the stove for a couple of hours. If the cabbage is soupier than you like, turn up the heat and reduce the wine sauce.

roast carrots SERVES 4 TO 6

Look for thin carrots with their tops; the chunky ones that are so good for soup aren't right here. Make these while you have something else in the oven.

12 carrots

1 tablespoon olive oil

Coarse salt and freshly ground black pepper

1 teaspoon sugar

2 or 3 sprigs thyme (or 1/2 teaspoon dried thyme)

1 tablespoon unsalted butter

1/4 cup dry white wine or dry vermouth

Heat the oven to 350 degrees.

Leave about an inch of the tops attached, and peel the carrots. Cut them lengthwise in half and drop them into a large gratin dish or low-sided casserole—something large enough for them to be in a single layer. Drizzle on the oil, season with salt, pepper, and the sugar, and toss. Tuck in the thyme and dot with the butter.

Roast the carrots for 30 minutes. Pour in the wine, shake the pan, and roast for another 30 minutes, or until the carrots are tender and browned. Serve them hot or at room temperature.

orange-seethed carrots SERVES 4

When you seethe, which is a great way to cook potatoes and root vegetables, you combine a liquid with butter or oil and cook until the liquid disappears. It leaves the vegetable—as you'll see with these carrots—imbued with flavor.

1 pound carrots, peeled and cut into thin coins

1 cup orange juice

3 tablespoons unsalted butter

Coarse salt and freshly ground white pepper

2 tablespoons chopped fresh flat-leaf parsley

Put the carrots into a wide saucepan or deep skillet, add the orange juice and butter, and season with salt and white pepper. Bring to a boil over high heat. Cover, reduce the heat to medium or medium-low, and cook at an active simmer for 20 to 25 minutes, until the carrots are crisp-tender.

The orange juice and butter should have reduced to a creamy sauce. If they haven't, uncover the pan and boil for a minute or two. Taste for salt, stir in the parsley, and serve.

variations

Replace the orange juice with dry vermouth or dry white wine, and the butter with 2 tablespoons olive oil. Once the carrots are crisp-tender, uncover the pan and cook at high heat until the wine has just about evaporated; listen for a sizzle in the pan.

With either recipe, you should think about varying the herb. Fresh dill and basil are both nice; so are chives. You might add a teaspoon of grated ginger to the orange juice too.

butter-braised cauliflower and turnips SERVES 6

I first tasted something like this at Prune, Gabrielle Hamilton's wonderful little restaurant in New York City's East Village. Bliss. I had to figure out how to make it the next day, and it's been a staple ever since. If you can find small, sweet Japanese turnips in your farmers' market, use them here.

The photo is on page 155.

1 (2-pound) cauliflower

1 bunch white turnips or 2 bunches (about 14) Japanese turnips

½ cup water

8 tablespoons (1 stick) unsalted butter, cut into pieces

Coarse salt and freshly ground white pepper

Core the cauliflower and break it into florets. Halve the larger florets, so they're all about two-bite–sized. Trim the tops off the turnips, leaving about 1½ inches of stem. If the greens are nice, reserve some for a garnish. Peel the turnips and cut lengthwise in half, then cut into wedges—try to have some of the tops with each wedge. (Leave the little Japanese turnips whole.)

Bring the water to a steady simmer in a wide saucepan. Whisk in the butter piece by piece, making sure each piece is incorporated before adding the next. Season with salt and white pepper, and add the cauliflower and turnips. Stir. Cover the pot and cook the vegetables gently for 45 minutes, or until very tender. Check them from time to time to make sure the sauce isn't bubbling too vigorously, and to stir the vegetables.

Spoon the vegetables into a bowl. If you've saved some of the turnip greens, cut them into thin strips and stir them in. Serve hot.

saffron cauliflower SERVES 6

I really like cauliflower when it's been cooked a lot, until almost mushy. But you've also got the option here of cooking it more quickly, which will leave it a bit more crisp.

This is really nice with steaks or chops.

3 tablespoons unsalted butter

1 onion, chopped

1 (2-pound) cauliflower, broken into medium to large florets

Coarse salt

A big pinch of saffron threads

1½ cups chicken or vegetable stock

1 tablespoon chopped fresh flat-leaf parsley

Melt the butter in a wide saucepan (or a deep skillet) over medium heat, and add the onion. Cook for 4 to 5 minutes, until the onion is starting to soften. Turn the heat to medium-high, add the cauliflower and a good pinch of salt, and cook, stirring once in a while, for about 10 minutes, until the cauliflower has taken on some color. The florets are an irregular shape, so don't expect even browning.

Crumble in the saffron and pour in the stock. Bring to a boil, reduce the heat to low, cover, and cook for 20 minutes. Take off the cover, turn the heat to high, and cook until most of the liquid has evaporated. (For crisper cauliflower, use only 1 cup stock and cook covered for 12 minutes. Then uncover and proceed as above.)

Spoon the cauliflower into a serving bowl and sprinkle with the parsley.

celery gratin SERVES 4 TO 6

Celery has a good, clean taste, but it's often overlooked as anything other than an aromatic in soups and braises or something to gnaw on raw. This quick gratin is in the Italian tradition of side dishes to be served at room temperature, but it's equally good hot.

1 bunch celery
Coarse salt
$^1/_2$ teaspoon celery seeds
Freshly ground black pepper
2 tablespoons olive oil
$^1/_2$ cup freshly grated Parmesan

Heat the oven to 400 degrees, and bring a large skillet of water to a boil. Oil a $1^1/_2$-quart gratin dish or low-sided casserole.

Trim the celery. Peel the stalks and cut them lengthwise in half.

Once the water is boiling, salt it and boil the celery until just tender, about 10 minutes. Pull the stalks out with tongs and drop them into the gratin dish. Don't obsess about drying them. And you'll be adding some cooking water to the dish, so save it.

Season with the celery seeds and pepper and toss. Pour about $^3/_4$ cup of the cooking water over the celery and drizzle on the oil. Strew with the Parmesan and bake for 30 minutes. The cheese should form a golden crust.

You can serve this hot, warm, or at room temperature.

skillet corn SERVES 4

Much as I love fresh corn, I just don't care for eating it right from the cob. My solution? Cutting the kernels off the cob and cooking them quickly in a hot skillet. The result: sweet, almost fluffy kernels that are a treat to eat.

Bring out your best salt.

3 tablespoons unsalted butter
4 cups fresh corn kernels (cut from 4 or 5 ears)
Sugar
Coarse sea salt

Melt the butter in a large skillet over medium-high heat. Add the corn and a big pinch of sugar and cook just until the corn is searingly hot and starting to brown. Season with coarse salt, scrape into a serving bowl, and serve immediately.

fresh "polenta" SERVES 4 TO 6

Sure, you can make this creamy side dish with fresh corn (you'll need a total of 6 cups kernels), but frozen corn is one of those things like frozen peas: a kitchen essential with pretty good flavor all through the year.

2 (1-pound) bags frozen white corn

2 tablespoons unsalted butter

1/2 cup heavy cream

1/2 cup water

Coarse salt and freshly ground white pepper

Rinse half the corn under hot water to defrost it quickly. Drain it well, then put it in a food processor. Process to make a thick puree.

Melt the butter in a large saucepan over medium heat and scrape in the corn puree. Rinse the rest of the corn under hot water, drain it, and add it to the pan. Pour in the cream and water, season with salt and white pepper, and bring to a simmer. Reduce the heat to low and cook the corn, stirring and scraping the bottom of the pan occasionally, for 30 minutes, or until you have a thick and creamy porridge.

You can serve this right away or cover it and leave on the stove for an hour, then reheat it.

corn custard SERVES 4 TO 6

Serve this soft, savory custard with fried chicken, with simple pork dishes, with hamburgers. Think of it as nursery food for grown-ups.

4 ears corn, shucked

2 cups milk

2 tablespoons unsalted butter

1 teaspoon sugar

Coarse salt and freshly ground white pepper

4 large eggs, lightly beaten

Heat the oven to 350 degrees, and butter a 1½-quart soufflé dish. Line a roasting pan with a few layers of paper towels or newspaper.

Cut the kernels from 3 ears of the corn into a bowl with a sharp knife, and scrape the cobs with the back of your knife to release any "milk." Grate the other ear on the coarse side of a box grater, and add it to the bowl.

Have ready a bowl filled with ice. Put the corn and its milk in a saucepan with the milk and butter, and bring to a simmer over medium heat. Reduce the heat and cook at a gentle simmer for 5 minutes. Set the saucepan of corn in the bowl of ice and stir to cool down to lukewarm.

Add the sugar, salt and white pepper to taste, and eggs and stir. You want this well combined, but you don't want it frothy. Pour the custard into the soufflé dish and set the dish in the roasting pan. Add about 2 inches of hot water to the roasting pan and slide it into the oven. Cook for 45 to 55 minutes, until the custard is almost set. When you shake the soufflé dish, the custard should jiggle in the center. The custard will continue to cook out of the oven, so if it's completely set in the center, you've got a tough custard.

Lift the soufflé dish out of the roasting pan, wipe it dry, and serve.

fried eggplant SERVES 4 TO 6

This is a versatile recipe. Make Eggplant Parmesan (see page 272) with it. Serve it by itself, hot or at room temperature. It makes great sandwiches, and, boy, is it good with the cod on page 130.

Try different colors of eggplant, like the violet or striated ones, which have the creamiest texture. I like them on the small side, and egg shaped. I always check the blossom end for the smallest dimple possible. When I was growing up, I was told that meant the eggplant had the least seeds. And, yes, sometimes it's true.

The photo is on page 71.

2 pounds eggplant

1 cup all-purpose flour

Coarse salt and freshly ground black pepper

2 large eggs

½ cup water

3 cups dried bread crumbs

Vegetable and olive oil, for frying

Set out some cooling racks over baking sheets.

Slice the eggplant into thin rounds, about ¼ inch thick. Put the flour into a bag and season it highly with salt and pepper. Crack the eggs into a shallow bowl and beat them lightly. Add the water and beat until they make a froth. Pour about a cup of the bread crumbs onto a plate. You're ready to bread.

Drop a handful of eggplant slices into the bag of flour. Close it up and shake it. Reach in and pull out the slices, shaking them off in the bag, and drop them in the eggs. Coat both sides, lift up, and hold them over the bowl until they stop dripping; then lay them on the crumbs and coat them well, pressing the crumbs onto both sides. Move them to the racks as you finish breading. Keep going with the rest of the eggplant, adding crumbs to the plate as you need them.

Heat a skillet over medium-high heat for a minute or two. Pour in about 1/3 inch of vegetable oil and a couple of tablespoons of olive oil for flavor. Heat until the oil is shimmering. Slip in slices of eggplant just to fill the pan without overlapping or crowding. Brown until golden on the first side, turn over, and brown the other side. Keep an eye on this; you may want to adjust the heat up or down a hair to keep the eggplant sizzling briskly but not burning. Lift the slices out with tongs and let them drain on the racks while you continue frying. You'll need to replenish the oil as you go; make sure it shimmers before you add any eggplant to it.

I serve these just as is, or with Peperonata (page 283). They are best hot.

eggplant parmesan doesn't have to be stodgy

Make a fresh tomato sauce by sizzling 1 minced garlic clove in 3 tablespoons of olive oil in a saucepan over medium heat. Add 1 1/2 pounds diced plum tomatoes—ripe summer ones—and a good pinch of salt. Let it come to an active simmer, then adjust the heat so it stays at that simmer and cook for about 15 minutes. You're looking for the tomatoes to release their juices and thicken slightly.

Make a mix of chopped fresh basil, parsley, and mint; you want about 1 cup.

Spoon about 1/2 cup of the tomato sauce into the bottom of an oiled casserole, one about 8 by 10 inches. Spread out a third of the fried eggplant in the casserole. Top with a third of the remaining sauce, half the herbs, and 1/4 cup grated Parmesan. Repeat. Your top layer will be eggplant, sauce, and 1/4 cup Parmesan. You could top it with some grated fresh mozzarella if you want, but it is eggplant *Parmesan*, right?

Bake in a preheated 350-degree oven for 30 to 40 minutes, until piping hot. Let it rest for 10 minutes before serving. It's enough for 4 to 6.

chinois noodles (page 310)

homemade ricotta cavatelli (page 242)

opposite: broiled rib-eye steaks
with gorgonzola butter (page 134)

pancetta and lettuce sandwich (page 53)

quick onion pickles (page 386)

oil-poached tuna (page 190)

bread-and-butter pickles (page 384)

sicilian spinach pies (page 76)

chicken milanese (page 118)

beef and carrot stew (page 204)

sumac chicken with bread salad (page 122)

fennel à la grecque SERVES 4 TO 6

Fennel perfumed with lemon and cooked long and slow is a great thing to have on hand in the refrigerator. Make a batch on the weekend, so you can have it all ready during the week.

3 large fennel bulbs

1 cup dry vermouth or dry white wine

$^1/_2$ cup fruity olive oil

Grated zest and juice of 1 lemon (a Meyer lemon, if you have one)

1 teaspoon fennel seeds, crushed

Coarse salt and freshly ground white pepper

Cut the stems off the fennel, and reserve some of the fronds for serving. Slice off the bottom of the bulbs and slice the bulbs about $^1/_2$ inch thick. Some of the slices will fall apart; this isn't a problem. Spread the fennel out in a very large deep skillet, in as close to one layer as possible.

Pour in the vermouth and oil, add the lemon zest and juice, and season with the fennel seeds and salt and white pepper. Bring to a boil over medium-high heat, then reduce the heat to low, cover the skillet, and simmer the fennel for $1^1/_4$ to $1^1/_2$ hours, giving it a gentle stir once in a while. It should be meltingly tender when done.

Serve this at room temperature.

grandma's greens SERVES 4

Here bitter greens are slow-cooked and tempered with some spinach to take the edge off the bitterness. Either escarole, chicory, dandelion, chard leaves, or mustard is a good choice, but then, so is a combination. Double the recipe, so you'll have leftovers.

2 garlic cloves, chopped

1/4 cup olive oil

1 cup water

Coarse salt and freshly ground black pepper

1 pound greens (see headnote), torn into pieces

1/2 pound spinach, stemmed

Put the garlic and oil in a wide saucepan over medium-low heat. Cook gently until the garlic sizzles and turns golden. Pour in the water, season with salt and lots of pepper, and bring to a boil over medium-high heat. Add the greens and spinach and stir. Once the greens have wilted, reduce the heat to low, cover, and simmer for 30 minutes.

Serve these hot or at room temperature. Save all the juices in the pot to pour over leftover greens so you can reheat them. And you'll also want those juices for Gorgonzola and Greens (page 79).

the simplest cooked greens

Whenever I serve this to someone new, there's a purr of surprise. The only secret is that I cook the greens until they're done. Tender, not crisp.

Bring a large pot of water to a boil. Wash about 2 pounds of greens well and rip into big pieces. Salt the water and add the greens. Boil, stirring a few times, until the greens are completely tender, at least 10 minutes but maybe 15. Taste and cook longer if they still have a bit of tooth to them. Drain (a little cooking water still clinging is fine) and spread out on a platter. Drizzle with 1/4 cup of extra-virgin olive oil and sprinkle with sea salt. They can sit for a couple of hours. Serves 4 to 6.

peperonata SERVES 4 TO 6

Peperonata is a fine accompaniment to steak or chicken. It also makes a great sauce for a sturdy pasta like penne. This dish is often made with green and red bell peppers, but green peppers turn a gloomy gray green while they cook, and it's an unfortunate color for a dish that's so lively. So go with red and yellow, or red and orange peppers.

2 largish red onions, sliced into thin half-moons
1/4 cup olive oil
Coarse salt
3 garlic cloves, smashed
6 anchovy fillets, chopped
3 red bell peppers, cut into 1/2-inch-wide slices
3 yellow bell peppers, cut into 1/2-inch-wide slices
4 plum tomatoes, chopped
1/2–3/4 teaspoon dried oregano, crumbled
Freshly ground black pepper

Put the onions and oil in a large saucepan over medium heat. Add a pinch of salt and cook until the onions soften, about 5 minutes. Add the garlic and anchovies and cook for a minute or two, stirring, until the anchovies melt into the oil. Add the peppers and tomatoes, season with the oregano and pepper, and lower the heat to medium-low. Cover and cook, stirring once in a while, for about 30 minutes, until the peppers are tender but not mushy. Taste for salt and pepper.

Let the peperonata sit for about 30 minutes before serving.

olive oil mashed potatoes SERVES 4 TO 6

This mash is a great foil for stews. As with Company Mashed Potatoes (page 286), these can be kept warm, covered, over a pot of simmering water for 20 minutes or so before serving.

1½–1¾ pounds yellow-fleshed potatoes or russets, peeled and cut into chunks

1 garlic clove, peeled

Coarse salt

¼ cup fruity olive oil

Freshly ground white pepper

Put the potatoes and garlic in a pot, cover with cold water by at least an inch, add a good pinch of salt, and bring to a boil. Cover partway, reduce the heat to medium, and cook until the potatoes are tender. Scoop out about 1 cup of the cooking water.

Drain the potatoes, return them with the garlic to the pot, and put them back over the heat to dry. Shake the pan and stir until the potatoes are floury and have made a film on the bottom of the pan.

Put the potatoes through a ricer or mash them with a hand masher until perfectly smooth. If you're using a ricer, rice them into a bowl, then return the potatoes to the pot. Either way, keep the pot over low heat while you finish the mash.

Beat the olive oil into the potatoes with a sturdy wooden spoon. Add the reserved potato water in small additions, about ¼ cup at a time, stirring first, then beating vigorously each time once the water has been absorbed. You may not need all of it. It depends on how thirsty the potatoes are and how loose you like your mash. Season with salt and white pepper. Serve hot.

variations

Think about adding some root vegetables to this mash. A few carrots, peeled, sliced, and cooked along with the potatoes, are particularly nice. So is a big parsnip or some small golden turnips. Best of all may be cauliflower, broken into small florets; I'd use about 1½ cups.

You could forgo the garlic clove with the potatoes, and beat in 1 head of Roasted Garlic (page 137) with the olive oil. Season with some thyme leaves.

company mashed potatoes SERVES 4 TO 6

Why "company"? Well, this mash is on the rich side—on the very rich side—just the kind of richness you want when you're sharing a special meal with friends. See the variations below for some more everyday versions. And one even more lush.

You really should eat these right when you make them, though in a pinch you can keep them warm over a pot of simmering water, but you know that. You know it as well as you know not to use your hand mixer or food processor when you mash potatoes—unless you like library paste.

1½–1¾ pounds russet potatoes, peeled and cut into chunks

Coarse salt

6 tablespoons (¾ stick) unsalted butter, softened

¾–1 cup heavy cream, heated

Freshly ground white pepper

Put the potatoes in a pot, cover with cold water by at least an inch, add a good pinch of salt, and bring to a boil. Cover partway, reduce the heat to medium, and cook until the potatoes are tender.

Drain the potatoes, return them to the pot, and put them back over the heat to dry. Shake the pan and stir until the potatoes are floury and have made a film on the bottom of the pan.

Put the potatoes through a ricer or mash them with a hand masher until perfectly smooth. If you're using a ricer, rice them into a bowl, then return the potatoes to the pot. Either way, keep the pot over low heat while you finish the mash.

Beat the butter into the potatoes with a sturdy wooden spoon. Add the cream in small additions, about ¼ cup at a time, stirring first until the potatoes absorb the cream, then beating vigorously. You may not need all of it, depending on how thirsty the potatoes are and how loose you like your mash. Season with salt and white pepper. Serve hot.

variations

For a trimmer version, use 4 tablespoons (1/2 stick) butter and replace the cream with heated half-and-half or milk.

For even trimmer mashed potatoes, replace the russets with yellow-fleshed potatoes, use 3 tablespoons butter, and beat in heated buttermilk as the liquid.

For steak night, follow the master recipe, and then fold in about 1/4 pound of Gorgonzola dolce (not the sharp, aged naturale), crumbled, or, in a pinch, Roquefort, and 2 tablespoons minced fresh chives.

potato tiello SERVES 6 TO 8

This is a version of a casserole you'd find in southern Italy, where starches are often combined to great effect. Here potatoes marry rice. It's a handsome thing, and rather tasty. Try it with meat loaf, or chicken.

8 sun-dried tomato halves (*not* oil-packed)
1 cup hot water
Coarse salt
1/2 cup Arborio rice
1 cup freshly grated Pecorino
1/2 cup chopped fresh flat-leaf parsley
2 garlic cloves, minced to a paste
2 pounds yellow-fleshed potatoes
Freshly ground black pepper
3 tablespoons olive oil
2 slices farm bread, lightly toasted
2 cups chicken stock (page 20, or canned)

Heat the oven to 350 degrees. Oil a large casserole.

Cover the tomatoes with the hot water and let them soak and reconstitute while you do the rest of the prep.

Bring a few cups of water to a boil. Salt it, and then pour in the rice. Cook, stirring once or twice, for 8 minutes. Drain.

Put the cheese, parsley, and garlic in a bowl and mix well with your fingers, making sure you get the garlic distributed.

Peel the potatoes and slice very thin on a mandoline.

Fish the tomatoes out of the water and chop them. Don't discard the soaking water.

Put a layer of about half the potatoes in the casserole. Season with salt and pepper and strew with about a third of the cheese mix.

Spread the rice on top of this, and scatter on the tomatoes. Drizzle with 1 tablespoon oil, and strew with another third of the cheese. Cover with the rest of the potatoes and season them with salt and pepper.

Crumble the bread into the bowl with the rest of the cheese and mix it up with your fingers, breaking the bigger pieces of bread as you mix. You want to end up with coarse seasoned crumbs. Scatter the crumbs over the casserole. Pour in the tomato water and the stock, and drizzle with the remaining 2 tablespoons oil.

Cover the tiello snugly with aluminum foil and bake for 1 hour. Take off the foil and bake for another 20 minutes. The liquid will be just about absorbed, the potatoes tender, and the crumbs golden.

Let this sit for 10 minutes or so before serving.

lemon potatoes SERVES 4 TO 6

Get a good crust on these when you roast them. The little bits of chopped roasted lemons are a surprising bright note.

If you can't find fingerlings, substitute creamer potatoes or tiny Yukon Golds.

- 2 lemons, scrubbed
- 1 garlic clove, chopped
- 1 1/2 pounds fingerling potatoes, scrubbed and halved lengthwise
- 1/4 cup olive oil
- 2 teaspoons fresh thyme leaves
- 1/2 teaspoon dried oregano, crumbled
- Coarse salt and freshly ground black pepper

Heat the oven to 350 degrees.

Slice off the ends of the lemons and discard. Cut each lemon in quarters lengthwise. Cut off the membrane on the inner edge of the lemon wedges, and nudge out the seeds. Slice the lemons, and put them in a food processor with the garlic. Hit the pulse button a few times to chop the lemons coarse.

Toss the potatoes with the lemons and garlic, oil, herbs, and salt and pepper to taste. You can do this in a bowl if you don't mind dirtying a dish, or just do it on the baking sheet you'll be roasting the potatoes on.

Roast for 30 minutes. Stir and flip the potatoes over, and roast for another 30 minutes. Taste one for salt (these are nice with a bit more salt sprinkled on once they're cooked), and serve.

roast pumpkin with sage SERVES 8

Yes, yes, you can do more than bake a pie with a pumpkin. The roasted cubes will be tender, soft, with crispy corners.

1 (5-pound) pumpkin

15–20 sage leaves (depending on their size)

Coarse salt and freshly ground black pepper

1/3 cup olive oil

1 tablespoon balsamic vinegar

Heat the oven to 450 degrees.

Cut the pumpkin into wedges. Scrape out the seeds and peel the wedges. Cut the flesh into 1-inch cubes.

Put the pumpkin on a baking sheet with the sage. Season well with salt and pepper and pour on the oil. Toss well, then spread the pumpkin out. Check to make sure that the sage is evenly distributed.

Slide the baking sheet into the oven and roast for about 30 minutes, until the pumpkin is tender and browned on the edges. Turn the pieces over about halfway through with a spatula.

When the pumpkin's done, transfer it to a platter. Sprinkle with the balsamic vinegar. You can serve this right away or leave it on the counter and serve at room temperature.

creamy spinach SERVES 4

There are certain sides that should never go out of fashion. Here's one of them.

2 pounds spinach, stemmed

2 tablespoons unsalted butter

1/2 cup chopped shallots or scallions

Coarse salt

3/4 cup heavy cream

Freshly ground black pepper

Freshly grated nutmeg

Bring a large pot of water to a boil. Add the spinach and boil for 4 to 5 minutes, until very tender. Drain, refresh in cold water, and drain again. Squeeze out the excess water and chop the spinach. You can do this well in advance.

Come dinnertime, melt the butter in a large skillet over medium heat. Add the shallots and a pinch of salt and cook, stirring, until the shallots soften, 2 to 3 minutes. Pour in the cream, season with salt, pepper, and some nutmeg, and bring to a full boil.

Crumble in the spinach and cook, stirring often, for about 5 minutes, until the spinach is very hot and the cream has reduced. Serve right away.

broiled tomatoes SERVES 2 TO 4

These are so easy that you should be making them to go along with lots of things: with scrambled eggs for breakfast, next to a quick steak, and, surely, with Welsh Rabbit (page 75).

4 plum tomatoes

Coarse salt and freshly ground black pepper

1 teaspoon dried sage

2 teaspoons fresh thyme leaves

1 teaspoon sugar

1 teaspoon olive oil

Slide an oven rack into the top position, and turn on the broiler to heat it. Oil a baking pan. It could be a small baking sheet, or a gratin dish—something that will hold the tomatoes.

Halve the tomatoes the long way and cut out the cores. Put the halves cut side up on your pan and season with salt and pepper. Combine the sage, thyme, and sugar and sprinkle over the tomatoes. Drizzle with the oil.

Broil the tomatoes for 2 to 3 minutes, until they are sizzling and just softened. No more—you don't want them to get mushy. Serve them hot.

variation

Nudge the seeds out of the tomatoes and drizzle with about 1 tablespoon honey instead of the sugar. Combine the herbs with 1 tablespoon fresh or dried bread crumbs.

roast tomatoes SERVES 4

This dish is best with ripe summer tomatoes, particularly heirlooms, but it also transforms winter plum tomatoes into something quite nice.

8 small ripe tomatoes
1 garlic clove, peeled
1 anchovy fillet
1/4 cup fresh flat-leaf parsley leaves
Coarse salt and freshly ground black pepper
1 heaped tablespoon freshly grated Parmesan
1 tablespoon olive oil

Heat the oven to 400 degrees, and oil a casserole with low sides.

Cut the tomatoes in half through the core and trim out the cores. Set the tomatoes cut side up in the casserole, pretty snugly together.

Mince the garlic, then pile on the anchovy and parsley and chop until you make a paste (or pound in a mortar and pestle instead, if you have one).

Season the tomatoes with salt and pepper and smear them with the paste. Sprinkle with the cheese, drizzle with the olive oil, and bake for 20 minutes. Serve hot or warm.

tiny tomatoes on the grill SERVES 4

Double this, triple this. Leftovers are great on sandwiches. Make it when you have the grill fired up for something else (like the Beer and Molasses Flank Steak, page 140).

1 pint cherry tomatoes
2 tablespoons olive oil
1 garlic clove, smashed to a paste
1 tablespoon herbes de Provence, crumbled
Coarse salt and freshly ground pepper

Put the tomatoes in a bowl and add the rest of the ingredients. Stir. Let marinate for an hour or so.

This is a good time to pull out the grill basket. If you don't have one, thread the tomatoes on skewers.

Grill the tomatoes for 5 to 10 minutes, shaking the basket or turning the skewers, until they are just starting to burst. Turn them out into a bowl, or slide them off the skewers. If you've used small bamboo skewers, you might instead just line them up on a serving plate.

grilling vegetables and fruit

If you've fired up the grill, you should be grilling some vegetables too, right? And maybe some fruit, as another side dish or for dessert. The process is almost instinctive, but here are some ideas that should make it even easier and lead to a tastier dish.

Start by going for variety.

Large pieces are easier to grill than small ones. There's less of a chance that they'll slip through the grill. Once you have all your vegetables grilled, you can cut them into smaller pieces for serving.

A medium-hot fire (you can hold your hand 5 inches from the grill for 7 seconds) will give you vegetables that are cooked through and lightly browned. Use a hot fire when you're grilling fruit. You want to get a good quick char before the fruit gets mushy.

Except for eggplant and squashes, save the salt and pepper until after you've grilled. If you've made Herbed Salt (page 19), now's a good time to use it.

Oil the vegetables well before grilling. If you want, you can dress the vegetables after grilling with some more oil and a splash of vinegar.

Onions I like grilling red onions rather than yellow, more for the color than anything else. Cut into 1/3-inch-thick slices, and secure the onion rings with three toothpicks stuck into each slice to make a peace sign.

Squash All the summer squashes are great candidates for grilling. Cut them into 1/3-inch-thick slabs (lengthwise will be easier to grill) and toss the slices with salt (Herbed Salt, if you have it) about an hour before grilling. Blot dry before coating with oil.

Eggplant Cut lengthwise into ⅓-inch-thick slices. Use a vegetable peeler on the first and last slices so you don't have one side that's all skin. Salt the eggplant about an hour before grilling, and blot it dry before brushing the slices with oil.

Baby fennel Blanch the fennel for 5 minutes. Blot dry before coating with oil.

Bell peppers Cut a slice off the top and bottom of each pepper before halving and seeding. The pepper halves will be easier to grill evenly if they aren't shaped like a cup.

Scallions Leave them whole—just trim off the root.

Tomatoes See page 294.

Apricots Halve and pit them and wrap in foil with a bit of butter, a pinch of sugar, and some lavender. Put on the grill for about 10 minutes. Leave them wrapped in the foil until dessert, then serve over ice cream.

Peaches Peel them or not. Halve them, pit, and grill the cut sides first. Grill on the rounded sides just long enough to heat the fruit all the way through.

Nectarines Same deal as peaches.

Pineapple Cut slices that are about ½ inch thick. Cut the slices into quarters and trim out the core after grilling.

honey-glazed turnips and pears SERVES 4 TO 6

These are sharp and sweet and nicely browned. Serve with pork or chicken.

3 Bosc pears

1 1/2 pounds turnips

Coarse salt and freshly ground white pepper

Juice of 1/2 lemon

1/4 cup olive oil

3 tablespoons honey

Heat the oven to 350 degrees.

Peel and quarter the pears lengthwise. Cut out the cores. Peel the turnips, halve them crosswise, and cut into wedges about 1/2 inch thick. Season the pears and turnips well with salt and white pepper and toss with the lemon juice and olive oil—in a bowl or on the baking sheet.

Roast for 30 minutes, then turn the turnips and pears over with a spatula. Roast for another 30 minutes, until browned and tender.

Turn the heat up to 400 degrees. Drizzle the honey over the turnips and pears and roast for 10 minutes more to glaze. Serve hot.

mashed turnips with pears

If I don't roast turnips, I may make a mash of them with pears. For that, boil 4 big turnips (peeled and chunked) until they're not quite tender, then add 2 big pears—peeled and cored and cut up into small pieces—to the pot and cook them together until very tender. Drain, put in a food processor with a knob of butter, and process until silky smooth. Add a few tablespoons of heavy cream and salt and pepper. This mash is always pretty loose. If you make it ahead, you can just reheat it in the pot you cooked it in.

oniony orzo SERVES 4 TO 6

This is a great side for when you're serving something juicy in wide shallow bowls (like the cod on page 130). But it's also just wonderful with simple lamb chops. If you ever find porcini bouillon cubes (I have friends bring them back when they travel to Italy), try adding one here.

1 large onion, chopped

4 tablespoons unsalted butter

Coarse salt and freshly ground black pepper

2 cups orzo

1 bouillon cube (optional)

Put the onion and 3 tablespoons butter in a saucepan over medium-low heat, season with salt and pepper, and cook gently until the onion is soft and golden. This should take 20 to 25 minutes, and you can do this well in advance.

Put a pot of water on to boil over high heat. Once it's boiling, salt the water and add the orzo and the bouillon cube, if you're using it. Cook until the orzo is just tender, a few moments past al dente. Drain, toss with the onion and 1 tablespoon butter, and serve.

variations

You can add a handful of chopped fresh parsley to this if you want, or some chopped oil-cured black olives and a little bit of fresh thyme. Or you could cook some mushrooms (sliced or whole) with the onion too.

mushroom pilaf SERVES 4 TO 6

There are times when you just want to fancy up your rice. This pilaf has lots of mushroom flavor, and it's an elegant accompaniment to a pork roast or a chicken.

1 ounce (about 1 cup) dried mushrooms (porcini preferred, but it's your choice)

2 cups chicken or vegetable stock (page 20 or 21, or canned), brought to a boil

1 cup basmati rice

1/3 cup minced shallots

2 tablespoons unsalted butter

Pinch of saffron threads

Coarse salt

2 scallions, chopped, for garnish (optional)

Cover the mushrooms with the boiling stock and leave them for 30 minutes to reconstitute.

Put the rice in a bowl and fill it with cold water. Swirl the rice around with your hand, then pour off the water. Repeat 3 or 4 times, until the water is clear after you swirl it. Drain the rice.

Lift the mushrooms out of the stock (save the stock) and rinse them well. Squeeze dry, and chop them up.

Put the shallots and butter in a saucepan over medium heat, and cook until the shallots are soft, 4 to 5 minutes. Add the rice and cook, stirring, until the rice starts to crackle. Carefully pour in the stock, leaving behind any grit. Add the mushrooms, saffron, and salt to taste. Stir, and bring to a simmer; then cover the pan, reduce the heat to very low, and cook for 15 minutes. Turn off the heat.

Cover the rice with a clean kitchen towel, put the lid back on the pan, and let sit for 5 minutes.

Fluff the rice with a fork and pile into a serving dish. Scatter the scallions on top, if you're using them.

rice and the clean kitchen towel

Letting rice rest for a few minutes after cooking gives the grains the time they want to finish absorbing the liquid, separating, and fluffing up. The towel ensures that moisture doesn't condense on the underside of the lid and drip back onto the rice.

riso SERVES 4

The trick here is cooking Arborio rice as you would pasta: in abundant boiling salted water. In its simplest form, dressed with lemon, egg, and cheese, it's like the easiest "risotto" imaginable. Like risotto—and like pasta, for that matter—it is incredibly adaptable, as you'll see from the variations.

The photo is on page 156.

Coarse salt

1 cup Arborio rice

Grated zest and juice of 1 lemon

1 large egg

4 tablespoons (1/2 stick) unsalted butter, very soft but not at all oily

1/2 cup freshly grated Parmesan

Bring a large saucepan of water to a boil. Salt the water well and pour in the rice in a slow, steady stream; you want the water to stay at the boil. Stir, and boil the rice for 17 minutes, or until just al dente.

Meanwhile, combine the lemon zest and juice in a small bowl. Add the egg and beat well with a fork.

When the rice is cooked, scoop out about a cup of the cooking water. Drain the rice—quickly and not too thoroughly—and immediately return it to the pan, while it's still rather wet. Stir in the lemon and egg, which will cook from the heat of the rice, then stir in the butter. Once the butter is incorporated and melted, stir in the cheese. Add enough of the cooking water to make the rice moist but not soupy. Work quickly—this process shouldn't take more than a minute or so.

Serve right away.

variations

riso with parsley

Replace the Parmesan with 1/3 cup grated Pecorino, and stir in 1/3 cup chopped fresh flat-leaf parsley with the cheese.

riso with peas

Empty a 10-ounce package of frozen peas into the strainer you'll be using for the rice. Run the peas under hot water for a minute or so to defrost them.

Follow the master recipe, draining the rice over the peas, and returning it all to the pan to finish with the lemon, egg, and cheese.

riso with asparagus

Break the tough stems off 1 pound asparagus and discard. Trim off and reserve the tips. Cut the stems in half.

When the pan of water comes to a boil, salt it and add the asparagus stems. Cook them for 6 minutes or so, until very tender. Scoop out the asparagus with a slotted spoon and drop it into a blender. Ladle about 1/4 cup of the cooking water into the blender and blend the asparagus to a smooth puree.

Proceed with the master recipe. Drop the asparagus tips into the saucepan of rice just before you drain it (the tips will cook very quickly, and you don't want them mushy). Drain and return to the pan.

Stir in the lemon and egg, then the butter, then the pureed asparagus. Rinse out the blender with the reserved cooking water and stir that liquid in as needed to keep the riso moist. Stir in the cheese.

riso with avocado squash

Cut about 1 pound avocado squash or pattypan squash into 1/3-inch dice, and steam it to crisp-tender while the rice is cooking. Proceed with the master recipe, adding the squash before you stir in the lemon and egg.

riso with tomato and zucchini

While the water for the rice is coming to a boil, seed a large ripe tomato and cut it into small dice. Put it into the strainer you'll be using for the rice. Scrub a small zucchini and cut into very small (1/4 inch) dice. Add the zucchini to the tomato, sprinkle in some coarse salt, and toss. Leave the strainer in the sink while the rice cooks.

Follow the master recipe, draining the rice over the tomato and zucchini and returning it all to the pan. If you'd like, stir in 2 tablespoons chopped fresh mint or basil with the cheese.

riso with bitter greens SERVES 4

This version, which I've adapted from one by cookbook author Viana La Place, is riso at its purest. No egg, no butter, no cheese—just the rice with peppery greens and fruity olive oil. Viana calls it a tonic.

Coarse salt

3/4 pound arugula or dandelion greens

1 cup Arborio rice

1/4 cup extra-virgin olive oil

Juice of 1/2 lemon

Freshly ground black pepper

Bring a large saucepan of water to a boil. Salt it well and add the arugula. Boil the greens for about 5 minutes, until tender. Scoop them out with a small strainer or a slotted spoon, drain them, and then chop them.

Meanwhile, cook the rice in the boiling water. When it's al dente, about 17 minutes, scoop out some cooking water and drain the rice. Return it to the pan still rather wet, then stir in the greens, oil, and lemon juice. Season with pepper, and add enough of the cooking water to make the riso moist but not soupy.

Serve immediately.

toasted israeli couscous with red pepper and saffron SERVES 6

There's no reason for couscous to be bland, and you don't need fancy equipment to make it either. A big wide saucepan, some bell pepper and saffron—and you've got something special. Quick, too.

I find the larger Israeli couscous a bit more satisfying than the smaller conventional type. Both are meant to be served as a foil for something good and saucy, though.

8 cups chicken stock (page 20, or canned)

Pinch of saffron threads

Coarse salt

1 largish (about 8 ounces) onion, chopped

¼ cup olive oil

1 red bell pepper, chopped fine

1 pound (3 cups) toasted Israeli couscous (see Note)

Pour the stock into a saucepan and crumble in the saffron. Bring it to a simmer over medium heat; when you reach a simmer, turn the heat to very low. Check to make sure your stock is well salted.

Meanwhile, put the onion and oil in a large wide saucepan (or a large deep skillet) and turn the heat to medium. Add a pinch of salt and cook until the onion is starting to soften, just a few minutes. Give a stir once or twice. Stir in the bell pepper and cook until the onion is golden (not browned, though it'll pick up some color from the pepper) and soft and the pepper is tender. This should take 5 or 6 minutes.

Pour in the couscous and cook, stirring and scraping from the bottom all the while to coat all the couscous with the oil. After a couple of minutes, you'll notice a new sound in the pan, a sizzle, and it will sound as if you're stirring tiny pebbles. You won't see any more oil in the bottom of the pan.

Ladle in about 3 cups of the simmering stock, stir, and reduce the heat to low. Cook, stirring often, until the stock is just about absorbed. Ladle in another cup of stock. Again, cook and stir until the stock is absorbed. Continue cooking and adding stock by the cupful, until you've added 7 cups. Take a taste; if the couscous is tender enough for you (and it will soften a bit more as it stands), stop adding stock. If it's still a bit too firm in the center for your taste, add the last cup of stock and cook until it's absorbed.

Turn off the heat and cover the pan with a kitchen towel, then put the lid on. Let the couscous sit to steam for 10 minutes.

Fluff the couscous up with a fork, transfer it to a bowl, and serve.

Note: You can get Israeli couscous already toasted from Kalustyan's (www.kalustyans.com), or you can toast the couscous yourself. Heat a large skillet over medium heat, add the couscous, and keep stirring until the rounds are all lightly colored and aromatic.

mac and cheese SERVES 6 TO 8

This is something I'll make when kids are coming over for dinner. That way, I can pretend it's for the kids, and I'm just having a taste.

The debate is over what kind of dish to make this in. Should it be something wide and low, so there's lots of crust to share? Or something deep, to keep it all pretty creamy? You decide.

FOR THE CHEESE SAUCE

- 2 tablespoons unsalted butter
- 2 tablespoons all-purpose flour
- 4 cups milk, warmed
- 1 pound best cheddar, shredded
- ½ cup freshly grated Parmesan
- 1 tablespoon Worcestershire sauce
- Freshly grated nutmeg
- Coarse salt and freshly ground black pepper

- Coarse salt
- ¾ pound small shells, farfalle, mini penne, or other small pasta

FOR THE BUTTERED CRUMBS

- 3 slices close-textured white bread (like Pepperidge Farm)
- 2 tablespoons unsalted butter

Heat the oven to 350 degrees. Butter the casserole of your choice (see headnote); you'll need one that holds 2½ quarts. Bring a large pot of water to a boil.

FOR THE CHEESE SAUCE

Melt the butter in a large saucepan over medium heat. Once it's bubbling, add the flour and cook, stirring, for about 2 minutes. No browning of the flour, you want a white roux. Pour in about half the milk and whisk with vigor to dissolve the roux, then whisk in the rest of the milk. Cook, stirring often, until the sauce thickens.

Add the cheeses and turn off the heat. Stir to melt the cheddar (don't fret if it doesn't all melt), and season with the Worcestershire, a few gratings of nutmeg, and salt and pepper.

By now, the water should have boiled, so salt it and cook the pasta to al dente.

MEANWHILE, FOR THE BUTTERED CRUMBS

Break the bread into pieces and drop them into a food processor. Process until you have fine crumbs. Heat the butter in a skillet over medium heat, and when it stops bubbling, add the crumbs. Cook, stirring, until the crumbs are lightly browned. Scrape the crumbs onto a plate (they'll keep browning if you leave them in the skillet).

Drain the pasta and put it back into the pot. Pour in the sauce, stir, and then scrape the pasta into your casserole. Top with the crumbs. Slide it into the oven and bake until the top is browned and the sauce is bubbling. Timing, of course, will depend on the size of the casserole, but start checking after 25 minutes.

Serve hot.

variations

Mess around with the cheeses. One possible combination is half a pound of best cheddar, half a pound of Gouda, and a quarter pound of smoked cheddar.

You can substitute Pickapeppa sauce for the Worcestershire.

FRIED GREEN TOMATOES

Fried green tomatoes belong on your plate with mac and cheese, and they're really easy to do. Core the tomatoes and cut a thin slice off the top and bottom of each one, so the slices you're going to fry have peel only on the perimeter. Cut the tomatoes into 1/3-inch-thick slices. Flour lightly, dip into beaten egg, and then coat in cornmeal. Fry in about 1/3 inch of hot peanut oil, turning once, just long enough to brown the coating; you don't want to overcook the tomatoes and get them soft. They deserve to be served with Tabasco sauce.

And if you think green tomatoes are a hard-to-find ingredient, head to the grocery and take a good look at those hard pink things in the produce section. Green tomatoes, just waiting for you. Pick ones that are very firm.

chinois noodles SERVES 4

What's nice about this light pasta dish—aside from its being quick as a flash to make—is that it can sit for a bit, equally good warm or hot. So it's a smart dish to make when you have something else to finish at the last minute.

If you have both spinach and egg linguine in the cupboard, use a combination.

Serve this with steaks, or chops, or fish.

The photo is on page 273.

2 tablespoons peanut oil

2 tablespoons roasted sesame oil

2 tablespoons soy sauce

2 tablespoons oyster-flavored sauce

1 teaspoon sambal oelek (chili paste)

2 tablespoons cold water

Coarse salt

10 ounces spinach linguine

3 scallions

2 tablespoons roasted peanuts (optional)

Put a large pot of water on to boil.

Combine the peanut and sesame oils, soy and oyster sauces, chili paste, and cold water in a serving bowl. Whisk.

When the water boils, salt it well and add the linguine. Cook it until al dente. While the noodles are cooking, trim the scallions and cut into fine julienne, with the pieces about 3 inches long.

Drain the noodles, dump them into the sauce, and toss. You can serve this now or leave it on the counter for a while.

Right before serving, toss again, strew with the scallions, and scatter with the peanuts, if you're using them.

polenta SERVES 4

I don't know of anything that compares to the flavor and texture of real slow-cooked polenta. Just cornmeal and water and salt go into the pot, but the result is a satisfying, warming porridge with a rich taste of corn.

I've tried the other methods—microwave, oven—I'm not convinced they're better. Polenta takes time to cook and it wants watching, so I make it when I've got other things going on in the kitchen and I'll be there anyway. Or I make it when there's something stewy for dinner, and polenta will be the only last-minute thing on the menu. And I set up drinks in the kitchen so I'll have company while I stir.

Get the best stone-ground polenta you can find when you make this.

5 cups water

Coarse salt

1 cup stone-ground polenta

4 tablespoons (1/2 stick) unsalted butter (optional)

Bring the water to a boil in a heavy saucepan over medium heat. Add a good pinch of salt. Pick up a whisk and a fistful of the polenta, hold your fist over the boiling water, and let the polenta rain down into the water while you whisk. Repeat until you've added all the polenta, then reduce the heat to low and stir just about constantly. The polenta will become porridgelike and will erupt with volcanic bubbles.

Lower the heat a bit more so you get regular bubbles, and cook the polenta for 45 minutes. Stir every few minutes, scraping the sides and the bottom—make sure you get into the corners of the pot. The polenta is done when it's creamy, with no hint of graininess.

Check for salt, and stir in the butter if you want it. You can serve this in a bowl, or you can do what my grandmother used to do: turn it out onto a big wooden board and spoon a stew into the center.

salads

salads

Salads are handy things.

Salad is an umbrella category, covering the raw and the cooked, the savory and the sweet, with just some dressing tying them all together.

The salads I'm including here go into all parts of the meal. Some combine a savory cooked thing like a fritter or bread pudding with a bit of green on the side. These can clearly be first courses—but who's to say they couldn't be the center of a very light lunch?

The classic salad—those greens with a dressing—I think belongs after a main course. Maybe on a plate all its own, or maybe on the dinner plate. It all depends on how formal the meal, and also what was on that plate and what's in the salad. Alchemy happens when you've got meat juices mixing up with a salad. You will, of course, suit yourself. If you were brought up to believe that salad is a first course, there's nothing I can really say to change your mind.

A lot of the recipes here fall into the category of what Italians call *insalate*. Here you're on your own. I'd serve most of them as an antipasto—first course. A small plate of Eggplant and Mint or of Roast Peppers with Capers and Anchovies is an elegant start to a meal. However, they are also pretty wonderful as side dishes.

The starchy salads—rice and potato—are sides, of course, but with a little zing to them, so they're not the same old, same old.

Something I find particularly refreshing in salads is fruit. I'm especially fond of salad dressings made with oranges, and I make them all winter. Should you want to try, cut the peel and pith off some oranges—blood oranges if you can find them—and then cut out the segments. Drop the segments into the salad bowl and squeeze out the juice from the membranes into the bowl too. Add a very thinly sliced red onion, some lemon juice and balsamic vinegar, and some olive oil. The seasoning is salt and pepper, with a pinch of cayenne and some crumbled dried oregano. You could also use a grapefruit if you want, or segments of Meyer lemon; add some chopped black olives.

Let the dressing sit for about half an hour before tossing the lettuces into it, then taste as you fiddle with the proportions of vinegar and oil. And the best way to taste a salad dressing is by dipping a piece of lettuce into it.

The thing that's most important about these dishes is seasonality. Please don't make any of these tomato salads with anything other than the ripest summer tomatoes. That also goes for sliced tomatoes and mozzarella. When I go into a restaurant and find this dish in January, that's a warning sign for me. If you're desperate for a salad with mozzarella, you can make it with roast peppers—or even with sun-dried tomatoes that have been marinated in oil, and then you've got the tomato oil to drizzle. And while you'll find zucchini and eggplant in the store year-round, when you buy them in season from a local farmer, you'll find that they have extraordinary flavor. That's what you want in your salad.

bitter greens with mustard cream SERVES 6

Here's a great salad for the winter months, when tender lettuces may not be great but there's escarole and chicory in the market. Other choices for greens are watercress and arugula and dandelion. All of these greens are tamed by the creamy dressing, which I just make in the salad bowl.

1/2 cup heavy cream

3 tablespoons Dijon mustard

Juice of 1/2 lemon

Coarse salt and freshly ground black pepper

6 big handfuls sturdy bitter greens (see headnote), torn into pieces

Whisk the cream and mustard to soft peaks. Squeeze in the lemon juice, season well with salt and pepper, and whisk again.

Toss the mustard cream with the greens and serve.

mixed greens with buttermilk and sun-dried tomato dressing SERVES 4

This salad is cool, creamy, and tangy, with a soft rose hue. The dressing belongs on a summer table.

FOR THE DRESSING

5 sun-dried tomato halves (*not* oil-packed)

½ cup hot water

½ cup buttermilk (or plain yogurt)

3 tablespoons olive oil

1 tablespoon red wine vinegar

Coarse salt and freshly ground black pepper

FOR THE SALAD

4 big handfuls mixed greens, torn into large pieces

5 or 6 radishes, trimmed and sliced thin

2 carrots, grated

FOR THE DRESSING

Cover the tomatoes with the hot water and let them sit for about 30 minutes to reconstitute.

Fish the tomatoes out of the water (save the soaking water), chop them, and put them in a blender with the buttermilk. Whir them around until the tomatoes are pureed. Add the oil, vinegar, 2 tablespoons of the soaking water, and salt and pepper to taste. Whir to combine into a creamy dressing. Taste the dressing with a piece of lettuce, and adjust the salt and pepper. Pour it out into a jar. Makes about ¾ cup.

FOR THE SALAD

Pile the lettuces, radishes, and carrots in a salad bowl. Spoon in about ⅓ cup of the dressing, toss well, and serve. The extra dressing will keep in the refrigerator for about a week.

dandelion salad SERVES 4

We're lucky in New York City to have farmers' markets year-round, though in the late winter and early spring months, when all you find are storage vegetables, they can seem a little tired. Still, I'd rather buy from a farmer than a grocery. But then you get a hint of the new season to come, with bunches of wild dandelion. Spring is the best time for this green, since it's not very bitter then.

You could also make this salad with curly endive or frisée or even leaf lettuce. Turn it into a lunch by serving it with a poached egg.

2 slices thick-cut bacon, cut into matchsticks

1 teaspoon olive oil, or as needed

1 small head green garlic, or 1 small garlic clove, minced to a paste

2 tablespoons white wine vinegar

1 teaspoon Dijon mustard

Coarse salt and freshly ground black pepper

4 handfuls dandelion greens, torn into smallish pieces

Put the bacon in a cold skillet with the oil. Turn the heat to medium and cook the bacon until it's browned and crisp. Take the bacon out of the skillet with a slotted spoon and drain it on paper towels. Save the fat.

Peel the green garlic, if using, smash it with the flat of your knife, and chop it. Scrape the garlic into a salad bowl and add the vinegar, mustard, and salt and pepper to taste. Whisk. Add 2 tablespoons of the bacon fat (add some olive oil if there isn't enough fat in the pan), and whisk again. Add the dandelion greens and toss. Scatter the bacon over the salad and serve.

green garlic

This is a reason in itself to go to farmers' markets, since you'll never find green garlic in the grocery. These immature bulbs have a much milder flavor than they would later, when dried, and you'll have the pleasant surprise of finding out that the head hasn't yet divided into cloves; it's just one big nugget of nutty garlic. Trim off the root and the outer layer just as you would a scallion, and, just as you would with a scallion, use the greens too.

tender greens with strawberry vinaigrette SERVES 4

This is certainly best when you make it with real strawberries, garnet red and juicy throughout, but you can make do with the woody stand-ins you often find in the grocery.

1 cup strawberries, hulled and sliced
1 small red onion, sliced very thin
2 tablespoons extra-virgin olive oil
1 tablespoon red wine vinegar
1 tablespoon balsamic vinegar
Coarse salt and freshly ground black pepper
4 big handfuls tender mixed greens, torn into large pieces

Combine the strawberries, onion, oil, vinegars, and salt and pepper to taste in a salad bowl and give the dressing a stir. Let it sit on the counter for at least 30 minutes for the berries and onion to marinate.

Right before you're ready to serve the salad, dip a piece of lettuce into the dressing and taste. Adjust the salt and pepper if you need to. Then add the greens, toss, and serve.

iceberg wedges with blue cheese dressing SERVES 6

Call it retro, if you're a name-calling type, but there are some salads that are just too good to be pushed out of fashion. Wedges of very cold iceberg lettuce with a stripe of blue cheese dressing is one of those.

$^3/_4$ cup sour cream

$^1/_2$ cup mayonnaise

$^1/_4$ cup olive oil

1 tablespoon red wine vinegar

1 teaspoon Worcestershire sauce

1 garlic clove, minced to a paste or put through a press

$^1/_2$ pound crumbly blue cheese

1 head iceberg lettuce

Combine the sour cream, mayo, oil, vinegar, Worcestershire, and garlic in a food processor. Crumble in the cheese and process until combined; the dressing should still have some small lumps of cheese visible. Transfer to a plastic container and refrigerate.

Whack the lettuce on the counter, core down, then turn it over and twist out the core. Cut the lettuce in half, then into 6 wedges. Put a wedge on each of 6 salad plates—standing up, like a smile—and refrigerate until you're ready to serve.

Spoon a couple of tablespoons of the dressing onto each wedge of lettuce and bring the plates to the table.

fennel slaw MAKES ABOUT 10 CUPS

Crisp coleslaw is pretty much mandatory when you serve Piggy (page 221) or fried chicken. This version is good and crisp.

You'll need to put this together early in the day you plan to serve it, since it needs time in the refrigerator.

1 ($1\frac{1}{2}$-pound) green cabbage

3 fennel bulbs, trimmed

2 tart green apples

2 tablespoons minced ginger

$1\frac{1}{2}$ teaspoons coarse salt

$\frac{1}{2}$ teaspoon fennel seeds, crushed

$\frac{1}{2}$ cup sour cream

$\frac{1}{2}$ cup mayonnaise

2 tablespoons sherry vinegar

Quarter the cabbage, cut out the core, and shred the cabbage fine. Use a knife, use a mandoline—your choice. Repeat for the fennel: quarter, core, and shred. Peel and core the apples and slice them as thin as possible.

Combine the cabbage, fennel, and apples in a big bowl. Add the ginger, salt, and fennel seeds and toss it all with your hands.

Whisk the sour cream, mayonnaise, and vinegar together in a small bowl. Scrape into the slaw and mix very well (hands are best). The slaw may seem dry when you first mix it; not to worry. Cover and refrigerate for at least 2 hours before serving.

the magic mandoline

Time was when I looked with scorn at this piece of equipment. Martha Stewart converted me, and I made the investment in a fancy, and expensive, French mandoline. I couldn't figure out how anyone could do without it. Then I started working with Rick Moonen, a New York chef with serious French training.

We were cooking together, and Rick pulled out a Japanese slicer. *Ppfhh,* I said. Why no French mandoline, Mr. Chef? Rick had no use for the fancy, expensive machine. He waxed poetic about the angled blade of the Japanese slicer, how it was so much easier to use, such a smarter design. I tried it and was converted yet again.

So here's the moral: you need something in your cabinet that will let you make impossibly thin slices, but you need not go into hock. Get yourself an inexpensive one, with a plastic frame and the angled blade. It should set you back around $50—a far cry from the $150 a "professional" French one will cost.

apples and arugula SERVES 4

It's as simple as it sounds—and as pure in flavor. Adjust this salad up or down, depending on how many you have sitting at the table.

I use a combination of apples: something sweet and something tart. Find what you like.

3 apples (like a Macoun, a Granny Smith, and a Golden Delicious)
Grated zest and juice of 1 lemon
Pinch of cayenne
1 bunch arugula
Coarse salt
4 tablespoons extra-virgin olive oil

Peel and core the apples, and cut them into impossibly thin slices—a mandoline is a help here. Toss them with the lemon zest and juice and the cayenne (if you're adventurous, use a big pinch).

Tear the arugula into smallish pieces and put it into a salad bowl. Salt it and then toss with 3 tablespoons olive oil. Pile the apples on top and drizzle with the last tablespoon of oil. This can sit while you finish the rest of dinner, but don't leave it so long that the apples start turning brown.

tomatoes and lemon SERVES 4

I learned this simple and delicious way of serving summer tomatoes from Lee Bailey, cookbook author and consummate style maker. It's such a fresh, clean salad. Make it with the ripest summer tomatoes, and bring out your best sea salt. Eat the lemons if you want, or just enjoy the flavor they lend the tomatoes.

The photo is on page 70.

3 or 4 ripe tomatoes
1 or 2 lemons, scrubbed
Coarse sea salt
Extra-virgin olive oil—a good, fruity one

Core and slice the tomatoes, setting the first and last slices aside. Slice the lemons as thin as you can.

Shingle the tomatoes and lemons in two rows down a platter, alternating them. Chop the reserved tomato slices and scatter them down the center, between the two rows. Let the tomatoes and lemons sit at room temperature for at least 30 minutes.

Right before serving, season with sea salt and drizzle—very lightly—with olive oil.

tomato tomato salad SERVES 4 TO 6

This salad—sliced tomatoes dressed with fresh tomato sauce—is most beautiful when you make it with a mix of different-colored heirlooms: yellow, orange, and green. This is not to say that you shouldn't make it when all you can find are perfectly ripe Brandywines, or even beefsteak tomatoes. If you find some tiny currant tomatoes, scatter them over the salad.

You'll be making twice as much sauce as you need for this amount of sliced tomatoes, but it's just not worth making less. The sauce will keep for a few days in the fridge, so make the salad again or use the leftovers for pasta.

1½ pounds plum tomatoes
Coarse salt
2 tablespoons chopped fresh basil
3 tablespoons extra-virgin olive oil
Freshly ground black pepper
1½ pounds heirloom tomatoes

Cut or break the plum tomatoes in half and put them in a saucepan with a big pinch of salt. Cover and cook over medium-high heat, stirring once in a while, until the tomatoes are very soft and juicy. This will take 15 to 20 minutes.

Put the cooked tomatoes through a food mill fitted with the medium disk and return the puree to the saucepan. Cook over high heat for about 5 minutes to thicken the sauce. Season with the basil, 2 tablespoons olive oil, and salt and pepper. Transfer to a bowl and let cool to room temperature.

When you're ready to serve, slice the heirloom tomatoes and arrange them nicely on a platter. Spoon half the sauce over the tomatoes and drizzle with the remaining 1 tablespoon olive oil.

tomatoes, kirby cucumbers, and feta

It's August. You don't want to cook—you almost don't want to eat, but you're hungry. And since it's August, you can get real tomatoes.

Gear your amounts to the number of people who will be sitting at the table. And think about a bright and pretty chilled white wine, or even better, a cold primitive Sicilian red.

You want a good crusty bread on the table.

The ripest tomatoes you can find

Kirby cucumbers or English (seedless) cucumbers

Feta

Coarse sea salt and freshly ground black pepper

Cayenne, if you want

Extra-virgin olive oil

Halve the tomatoes through the stem, cut out the core, and slice into pretty thick slabs. Scrub the Kirbys and cut into thinnish slices. Combine the tomatoes and Kirbys on a platter (or on a plate if you're doing this for yourself) and crumble as much feta as you want over the top.

Season the salad well with salt, grind some pepper over the top, and add some cayenne if you like. Drizzle well with oil. Don't be stingy.

If you have the time and inclination, let this sit for 20 minutes to half an hour. Or eat it right away. If you let it sit, you'll have more juices to sop up with that crusty bread.

beets, tomatoes, and peaches SERVES 6

This may just be my favorite summer salad. Make it only with the ripest, slurpiest peaches and the juiciest farmer tomatoes.

I try not to dirty too many dishes when I cook, but here's a case where I'll make the salad in a mixing bowl and then transfer it to a platter. The beets will throw off their juices, and the salad gets messy when you toss it. Using the bowl means you'll end up with a better-looking platter.

The photo is on page 72.

1 bunch (4 medium) beets, roasted (see page 257)

3 ripe tomatoes

3 ripe peaches

3–4 tablespoons extra-virgin olive oil

Coarse salt and freshly ground black pepper

Slip the skins off the beets, halve them, and slice them. Drop the slices into a mixing bowl. Core the tomatoes and cut them into wedges. Add to the beets. Wash the fuzz off the peaches—you shouldn't need to peel them if you've got ripe peaches from the farm; they'll have tender skin. Cut the peaches into wedges, thinner than the tomatoes, and add them to the bowl. Drizzle in the oil, season with salt and pepper, and toss.

Transfer to a platter or salad bowl, and serve this when you're ready. It can sit a while.

eggplant and mint SERVES 4 TO 6

Make this salad early in the day and leave on the counter to wait for dinnertime. Try to find black mint or peppermint for the best flavor.

4 small eggplant (about 1½ pounds)
Coarse salt
Olive oil, for frying
10–12 fresh mint leaves, torn
1 tablespoon salted capers, rinsed
Freshly ground black pepper
1–2 tablespoons red wine vinegar

Cut 4 lengthwise strips of skin from each eggplant, spacing them evenly. Cut the eggplant into ¼-inch slices, dropping them into a colander and salting them as you go. Put a paper towel or two on top, weight the eggplant down with a can of something, and let sit for about an hour.

Pat the eggplant dry with paper towels.

Heat ⅛ to ¼ inch of oil in a skillet over medium heat until it shimmers. Fry the eggplant in batches until well browned. Drain the eggplant on a rack set on a baking sheet, and replenish the oil as needed while you're frying—just make sure it's shimmering before you add more eggplant.

Toss the eggplant with the mint and capers in a shallow bowl. Grind on some pepper, drizzle with vinegar to taste, and let sit for at least 20 minutes before serving.

variation

Lemony ground sumac (see page 123) counters the richness of fried eggplant. Forget the mint, capers, and vinegar, and sprinkle the eggplant with about 2 teaspoons ground sumac. Let sit for 20 minutes.

little fava salad SERVES 4

You really don't need much to turn fava beans into a salad, which balances out the time you'll take to remove their skins. Ah, but that prep is so worth it.

2 pounds fava beans, shelled and peeled

1/4 cup sliced radishes

Coarse salt and freshly ground black pepper

Extra-virgin olive oil

Pecorino, for shaving

Combine the favas with the radishes in a bowl, season with salt and pepper, and drizzle with olive oil. Toss well and check the seasoning. You can leave this at room temperature for a few hours, or serve it immediately.

Right before serving, use a vegetable peeler to shave some Pecorino over the top of the salad.

prepping fava beans

This is for your afternoon quiet time, or the chore you share with a friend. It's a two-step process, and you might as well be comfortable, so set yourself up on the porch with a bowl in your lap or at a corner of the kitchen table.

Crack open the pods and nudge the beans out from the cottony lining into a heatproof bowl.

Bring a pot of water to a boil. Pour the boiling water over the favas, enough to cover them, and let sit until the water cools.

You could also put the shelled beans into a saucepan, cover with cold water, and bring to a boil. Boil for a minute or two, then drain and refresh the beans in cold water.

Step two is peeling, to release the tender, bright green beans from their skin. Make a nick in one end of the peel with your thumbnail and then pinch the peel to squeeze the bean out. Separate the halves of the bean and drop them into a bowl.

roast peppers with capers and anchovies SERVES 4

The saltiness of capers and anchovies is a great foil for the silky sweetness of red bell peppers.

Now, about electric stovetops: they're not an option. Yes, you can roast peppers in an oven (see the box), but you don't get the char flavor that's so distinctive and essential here. If your heat is electric, try to make these only when you've got the outdoor grill fired up.

Look for peppers that have smooth surfaces; the ones with a lot of crevices lead only to tears when you're roasting.

When you pile these on crusty Crostini (page 16), you've got a great nibble.

4 large red bell peppers

12 anchovy fillets, halved

2 garlic cloves, sliced as thin as possible

1/4 cup extra-virgin olive oil

1/4 cup salted capers, rinsed well (capers in brine are fine too, but use fat ones and rinse them)

2 teaspoons balsamic vinegar

Turn two burners up to high and set the peppers over the flames. Char them thoroughly, getting the skin good and black all over. You'll find that tongs are a helpful tool for turning them. When the peppers are blackened all over—all over—put them in a paper or plastic bag and close the bag, or put in a bowl and cover tightly with plastic wrap, and let them steam for 10 minutes. Yes, you can let them steam until they are completely cool, but the peppers will get very limp. I like them to have some tooth to them, like pasta cooked al dente.

Rub the blackened skin off the peppers (have paper towels handy for wiping your hands). Don't obsess over every little bit of charred skin, but if you haven't been thorough in charring, make sure you remove the bits of uncharred skin. Never rinse roasted peppers. Split each pepper open over a mixing bowl to catch any of the juices inside, then remove the seeds and veins. Cut the peppers into ⅓-inch-wide slices—halve the slices if your peppers are very long—and drop them into the mixing bowl.

Add the anchovies, garlic, and olive oil and toss.

Arrange the peppers on a platter and scatter the capers on top. Try to dress the peppers at least 30 minutes before serving to give the garlic a chance to work its magic. You can let this sit on the counter for a couple of hours.

Right before serving, sprinkle with the balsamic vinegar.

roasted italian peppers

These long, skinny peppers that are usually light green come with a lot of names: Italian peppers, frying peppers, Cubanelles. Traditionally they're fried, but I like them roasted, and this time I do use the oven. I also don't worry about removing the skin and seeds.

Put 8 Italian peppers onto a baking sheet and slide them into a preheated 350-degree oven. Roast, turning once, for 25 to 30 minutes. The peppers should be puffed up and browned in spots. (No char here.)

Arrange the peppers on a platter, drizzle them with your best extra-virgin olive oil, and sprinkle with coarse sea salt. Serve as a side dish, either right away or after letting them sit for a couple of hours; they're great at room temperature.

grilled squash with onion and mint SERVES 4 TO 6

This is one of those handy room-temperature salad/side dishes. If you can't find avocado squash in your farmers' market, substitute other summer squash.

Make this early in the day so the flavors combine. Or prepare the onion early and grill the squash at the last minute.

The photo is on page 156.

1 large red onion, sliced thin

2 tablespoons olive oil, plus more for brushing

Coarse salt

1/4 cup water

3 tablespoons red wine vinegar

1 tablespoon chopped fresh mint

Freshly ground black pepper

2 avocado squash (1 1/4–1 1/2 pounds), cut into half-moons about 1/3 inch thick

Put the onion and oil in a skillet with a pinch of salt and cook over medium heat until the onion has softened but not browned, 5 to 6 minutes. Pour in the water, cover, and reduce the heat to medium-low. Cook for another 8 to 10 minutes, until the onion is very soft and most of the water is gone. Stir in the vinegar and mint, and season with salt and pepper. Leave the onion in the skillet, out of the way.

Prepare an outdoor grill or heat a ridged grill pan over high heat.

Brush the squash with oil and season with salt and pepper. Grill the squash for about 3 minutes a side, until tender and nicely marked. As you finish grilling, arrange the slices in a shallow bowl or platter. When you have half the squash in, top with half the onion. Layer on the rest of the squash and top with the remaining onion.

You could serve this right away, but it's really better when it's had a chance to sit for at least an hour.

zucchini all'insalata SERVES 4

Here's a nice addition to summer meals. The zucchini you get from a farmer will be tastier than the ones from the grocery. And use the fruitiest olive oil you have in the pantry.

Try this with other varieties of squash too, like avocado or Leida.

1 cup water

1 small garlic clove, peeled

1 fresh cayenne pepper (or other red hot pepper), split lengthwise

6–8 cherry tomatoes, halved

Coarse salt

1½ pounds small zucchini, scrubbed

½ teaspoon grated lemon zest

2–3 tablespoons extra-virgin olive oil

Juice of ½ lemon

Combine the water, garlic, hot pepper, and cherry tomatoes in a large skillet over low heat. Add a big pinch of salt. Cover partway, bring to a simmer, and cook for 15 minutes; the water should be reduced by half.

Meanwhile, cut the zucchini lengthwise into long strips about ⅓ inch thick. Cut the strips in half both ways; all the pieces will have skin on them.

Add the zucchini to the skillet and toss with tongs. Cover partway and cook, tossing once or twice, until the zucchini is just tender, 8 to 10 minutes.

Fish out the zucchini with tongs and arrange on a serving dish. Turn the heat under the skillet to high and reduce the juices by half. Stir the lemon zest into the juices and spoon over the zucchini. Drizzle on the olive oil and lemon juice.

Sprinkle with a bit more salt if you want, and serve at room temperature.

cucumber and pineapple salad with mint

SERVES 6 TO 8

Great for a hot summer's day, or when there's something very spicy on the table, this salad is cool and cleansing.

1 small pineapple (or half a large one)

4 large Kirby cucumbers (about 1¼ pounds) or 2 English (seedless) cucumbers

1 red onion

¼ cup chopped fresh mint

2 tablespoons extra-virgin olive oil

Coarse salt and freshly ground black pepper

Slice the top and bottom off the pineapple, stand the pineapple on your cutting board, and slice off the peel with a sharp knife. Now lay the pineapple on its side and cut out the eyes. Cut the pineapple in half the long way, cut each half in half again, and cut out the core. Cut each quarter into bite-sized pieces and drop into a wide salad bowl.

Cut off the ends of the cucumbers and toss them out. Slice the cucumbers into ¼-inch-thick rounds and add to the pineapple. Slice the onion into thin half-moons and add to the salad.

Add the mint, drizzle in the oil, and season with salt and pepper. Toss. Serve right away, or cover and chill in the refrigerator for a few hours.

spicy watermelon salad SERVES 4 TO 6

This gin-soaked salad is definitely for grown-ups.

1 (4-pound) watermelon

2 serrano chilies (or 1 jalapeño), minced

$^{3}/_{4}$ cup gin

1 red onion, sliced very thin

2 tablespoons extra-virgin olive oil

Coarse salt and freshly ground black pepper

Slice the watermelon, cut the flesh into bite-sized chunks, and ease out the seeds with the tip of a paring knife.

Combine the watermelon, chilies, and gin in a large sealable plastic bag. Refrigerate for 2 to 3 hours, turning the bag a few times so the watermelon will macerate evenly in the gin.

When you're ready to serve the salad, drain the melon in a sieve, and combine it with the onion and olive oil in a mixing bowl. Season with salt and pepper, toss, and transfer to a platter or salad bowl.

This is best served very cold.

smashed potato salad SERVES 4 TO 6

This zesty Southern-style potato salad is just what you want on your plate with fried chicken, with stuffed beef tenderloin, or with a chili dog or hamburger.

If you haven't made your own pickles, you can use a commercial hot mixed pickle.

1½ pounds yellow-fleshed potatoes, scrubbed

Coarse salt

1 celery stalk, minced

2 scallions, chopped

⅓ cup chopped Hot Mustard Pickles (page 388)

2 or 3 large eggs, hard-cooked (see page 59) and mashed thoroughly with a fork

½ cup mayonnaise

2 tablespoons brown mustard

2 tablespoons chopped fresh flat-leaf parsley

1½ teaspoons chopped fresh dill

Freshly ground black pepper

Put the potatoes in a saucepan, cover with cold water by at least an inch, add a good pinch of salt, and bring to a boil over high heat. When you have the potatoes boiling, cover the pan partway and reduce the heat to medium. You want the water bubbling, but not violently. Cook until the potatoes are tender, about 20 minutes. Drain the potatoes on a rack set in the sink (that way the potatoes are in a single layer and don't steam as they cool).

Meanwhile, combine the celery, scallions, chopped pickles, eggs, mayonnaise, mustard, parsley, and dill in a mixing bowl. Season with salt and pepper.

As soon as the potatoes are cool enough to handle—still pretty warm, please—peel them, cut them into chunks, and drop the chunks into the bowl with the dressing. Use a heavy metal spoon to chop and smash the potatoes into the dressing: use the side of the spoon to chop up the potato chunks, then fold and push down with the back of the spoon. You're going for the texture of very lumpy mashed potatoes.

Cover with plastic wrap and chill the salad for at least 2 hours before serving.

two-rice salad SERVES 4

Red rice adds a nutty taste to this salad. If you've never had it, you should.

$^1/_2$ cup red rice

Coarse salt

$^1/_2$ cup long-grain white rice

$1^1/_2$ cups frozen petite peas

2 tablespoons unsalted butter

$^1/_4$ cup sliced almonds

$^1/_2$ pound feta cheese

$^1/_4$ cup chopped fresh mint

Grated zest of 1 lemon

Rinse the red rice in several changes of cold water. Do this in a bowl: Put in the rice, run in water, and swirl the rice around; drain. Repeat until the water in the bowl is clear.

Put the rice in a small saucepan with $^3/_4$ cup cold water and a good pinch of salt and bring it to a boil. Turn to the lowest possible heat, cover, and cook undisturbed for 30 minutes. Take the pan off the heat, cover the rice with a kitchen towel, put the lid back on the pan, and let rest for 15 minutes.

Meanwhile, put the white rice in another small saucepan with $^3/_4$ cup cold water and a pinch of salt. Bring to a boil, turn to the lowest possible heat, cover, and cook undisturbed for 15 minutes. Take the pan off the heat and put a kitchen towel over the rice. Cover the pan again and let rest for 10 minutes.

Scrape both rices out into a mixing bowl and fluff them up with a fork.

Put the peas in a strainer and run hot water over them to defrost. Taste one to make sure. Drain well and add to the rice.

Melt the butter in a small skillet and add the almonds. Cook, stirring, for a few minutes, until the almonds are lightly browned. Add to the rice.

Crumble in the feta—big and little chunks are nice. Add the mint and zest and toss well. Taste for salt. Transfer to a serving bowl.

You can leave this out for a few hours before serving. Just keep it covered with damp paper towels.

Note: Red rice is available in many markets like Whole Foods, or you can order it from Kalustyan's (www.kalustyans.com).

celery salad with ricotta fritters SERVES 6

This is a first-course salad, for when you want to be fancy. The rich little fritters are set off by a very clean and refreshing salad.

If you don't have access to fresh ricotta, you should plan ahead, since the grocery stuff is much wetter. The night before (or the morning of the dinner), line a strainer with a dampened paper towel, scrape in the grocery-store ricotta, set the strainer in a bowl, and leave it in the refrigerator to drain until it's time to start cooking.

The photo is on page 71.

FOR THE FRITTERS

1 pound ricotta (see headnote)

2 tablespoons fresh goat cheese (optional)

1/2 cup freshly grated Pecorino

1 large egg

1/4 cup all-purpose flour

Coarse salt and freshly ground black pepper

Olive oil, for frying

About 1 1/2 cups dried bread crumbs

FOR THE SALAD

4 celery stalks, sliced very thin on the bias

All the tender leaves from inside the heart of celery

1/2 cup fresh flat-leaf parsley leaves

3 tablespoons extra-virgin olive oil (something very fruity, if you have it)

Coarse sea salt

FOR THE FRITTERS

Whisk the ricotta, goat cheese (if using), Pecorino, egg, and flour together in a mixing bowl. Season with salt and pepper and whisk again.

FOR THE SALAD

Toss the celery, celery leaves, parsley, and oil together with salt to taste. Distribute among six salad plates. You can do both these steps about 30 minutes ahead.

When you're ready to serve, heat ¼ inch of olive oil in a large skillet over medium-high heat. While the oil heats, form the fritters, using about 2 tablespoons of the batter for each, and coat them well in the bread crumbs. When the oil is just about to smoke, start frying the fritters, turning them when they are golden, and draining them on paper towels (these are too delicate to drain on a rack).

Once all the fritters are fried and drained, divide them among the salad plates and serve.

tangy greens with cheddar bread puddings

SERVES 6

Use the best country bread you can find for these little puddings, and a nice sharp cheddar, maybe one from Vermont.

FOR THE PUDDINGS

3 ounces cheddar, cut into small cubes

1 cup cubed white country bread (about 1 slice)

6 large eggs

1 1/4 cups milk

1/2 teaspoon dry mustard

Coarse salt and freshly ground black pepper

Freshly grated nutmeg

Tabasco sauce

FOR THE SALAD

1 small shallot, minced

2 teaspoons Dijon mustard

2 tablespoons sherry vinegar

Coarse salt and freshly ground black pepper

1/4 cup olive oil

6 handfuls mixed greens

FOR THE PUDDINGS

Heat the oven to 350 degrees.

Line a baking dish with a few layers of newspaper or paper towels and set six custard cups in the dish. Divide the cheese among the custard cups, and then the cubed bread.

Crack the eggs into a large measuring cup (a 4-cup capacity is good for this) or a bowl with a spout and beat them lightly. Pour in the milk, and add the mustard, salt and pepper to taste, a few gratings of nutmeg, and 3 or 4 shots of Tabasco. Beat lightly to combine. You don't want this getting frothy, or you'll end up with bubbles on top of, and inside, your puddings.

Pour the custard over the bread and cheese. You'll fill 4-ounce cups to the brim; 6-ounce cups will be about two-thirds full. Pour enough hot—not boiling—water into the baking dish to come about halfway up the sides of the custard cups, and slide the dish into the oven. Bake for 45 minutes, or until the puddings are set.

Lift the puddings out of the water bath and let them cool on a rack. You can serve them warm or at room temperature.

FOR THE SALAD

At serving time, combine the shallot, mustard, vinegar, and salt and pepper to taste in a big bowl and whisk together. Drizzle in the oil, whisking until you have an emulsion. Add the lettuce and toss well.

Nudge the puddings out of the cups and set one on each of six salad plates. Divide the salad among the plates and serve.

nibbles

nibbles

Civilization began with the invention of the cocktail hour.

That quiet hour when adults gather for a drink, a visit, and conversation makes the slow transition from whatever's been going on during the day to the main event of the evening: gathering around the table for a shared meal. Central to this is that little bite of something salty, something savory, something that gets your mouth ready for dinner. Of course, the other role of the cocktail hour is to keep everyone occupied while you get dinner ready.

The late cookbook author Lee Bailey was a superb host and a great believer in cocktails. But Lee's idea of a nibble was a bowl of pecans; he never put out anything more than that. And his cocktail hour did have a tendency to last rather more than an hour, so by the time dinner made its appearance on the table, everyone was, well, let's say *very* relaxed. My cocktail hour, particularly when I'm in Virginia at my friends Tom and Marian's house in the summer, is pretty extended too. There I can make the excuse that we can't eat before 8:30, since the sun in the dining room is blinding while it sets. That sounds reasonable, doesn't it? But I do make sure there's a lot more out to pick at than just a bowl of pecans (good as those can be).

One of the simplest things to put out is a bowl of radishes. Mix them up—sharp, round, bright red radishes; long, milder breakfast radishes; white icicle radishes—and have some soft butter and coarse salt next to them so you can swipe a radish through the butter and dip it in the salt before devouring. British chef Fergus Henderson puts his radishes out with all their greens attached, and guests are charged with filling the salad bowl with them as they eat the radishes. He keeps vinaigrette at hand to dress the radish greens when it comes time for dinner.

Salsas and guacamole are easy dishes to make, and they do spark appetites. There's something about bowls of salsa and chips that says party, and they are amiable recipes that adapt to different tastes, to what's in season, to what you have on hand.

Cheese platters are certainly easy enough to put out with drinks, and it keeps getting easier to find better cheeses in grocery stores. But I have to tell you that putting out a dish of Homemade Ricotta—still slightly warm, since you prepared it right before your guests arrived—is a pretty spectacular treat. Try it, and remember that you don't have to tell anyone how quick it was. Or you could also follow the lead of my friend Rori Trovato, one of the best food stylists in the business. Inspired by bocconcini, those little marinated nuggets of fresh mozzarella, Rori makes balls of cream cheese, marinates them in olive oil with roasted garlic, toasted cumin seeds, peppercorns, and lots of cilantro, and serves them with flatbreads.

If dinner's under control, I'll fry something to have with drinks: oysters, maybe. (Fat and juicy shucked oysters are available in jars almost everywhere.) Soaked in a little milk, or some beaten egg, coated in panko or flour or cornmeal, and deep-fried—there's just nothing like them. Or I might hide anchovies in little pieces of pizza dough, which you can buy from a pizzeria if you don't want to make your own, and fry those. I really love fried string beans; that's the recipe I'm giving you in this chapter.

artichoke and crab dip MAKES ABOUT 4 1/2 CUPS

This is one of those sinfully rich hot dips that you serve when you're feeling retro. If you can find fresh crabmeat, go ahead and use it. But I have to tell you that canned is fine for this.

And what crackers? Ritz, of course.

1 cup mayonnaise

1 cup sour cream

3/4 teaspoon curry powder

1 teaspoon dill weed

2 (6-ounce) cans crabmeat, drained and picked over

1 (14-ounce) can artichoke bottoms, drained and chopped

1/3 cup sliced almonds

Crackers, for serving

Heat the oven to 350 degrees, and butter a 12-inch gratin dish or a low-sided casserole.

Stir the mayo, sour cream, curry powder, and dill together in a medium bowl. Add the crabmeat and artichokes and mix thoroughly. Scrape into the gratin dish and smooth the top. Strew with the almonds. You can prep this early in the day and keep the dip covered in the refrigerator.

Bake the dip for about 20 minutes (longer if it's been refrigerated), until hot and bubbling around the edges. Serve it right away, with a stack of crackers and a spoon.

smoked trout pâté MAKES ABOUT 2 1/2 CUPS

Here's a quick party spread, as easy as it is delicious. Put it out in a bowl with some crackers. Or spread on Crostini (page 16), top each with a caper or a parsley leaf, and have Mimsy pass them.

Chances are that when you buy the trout, you'll get four fillets. I think that's too much for the pâté, but you could add the other fillet if you want. Or, if you're going the Mimsy route, top the crostini with flakes of trout. Remember too that trout fillet is a pretty nice addition to a salad.

3/4 pound smoked trout fillets

4 tablespoons (1/2 stick) unsalted butter, softened

8 ounces cream cheese, at room temperature

1 tablespoon prepared horseradish

Grated zest and juice of 1 lemon

Slip the skins off the trout and toss them out. Break the fish into pieces and drop into a food processor. Pulse until you have small flakes.

Cut the butter and cream cheese into pieces and add to the processor, along with the horseradish and lemon zest and juice. Process until well combined, smooth, and fluffy. You'll need to scrape down the bowl once.

Scrape the pâté out into a nice bowl for serving, or into another bowl if you're making canapés. Yes, you can make this way in advance and refrigerate it. Just make sure to take it out at least 30 minutes before serving, so it will be easy to spread.

homemade ricotta MAKES ABOUT 1½ CUPS

This is so creamy and so good.

Truth to tell, it's not ricotta. Real ricotta is made with whey, and the best ricotta is made with the whey from sheep's milk, the leftovers in the Pecorino process. Hence *ricotta,* which means twice cooked. The milk is heated for the Pecorino, and then the whey is heated for the ricotta. But are you going to be making Pecorino? I don't think so, and this is a pretty terrific way to get to the tender curds of ricotta. Fast, too.

You've got options for serving this. See the box.

The photo is on page 68.

1 quart whole milk

1 cup heavy cream

1 scant teaspoon coarse salt

2 tablespoons white vinegar

Line a strainer with a double layer of dampened cheesecloth and set it in a bowl (deep enough so the strainer doesn't sit on the bottom of the bowl).

Rinse a large saucepan with cold water (for easier cleanup). Pour the milk and cream into the saucepan. Add the salt. Bring to a simmer over medium heat; a skin may form on the surface. Continue to cook until you see bubbles all over the surface.

When the milk is simmering, turn off the heat and pour in the vinegar. Leave it alone for about 1 minute, then stir slowly and gently. The milk will start separating into curds and whey (the liquid); you are looking for the whey to become clearish, which will take about 1 minute of gentle stirring.

Pour into the strainer. Lift the strainer out of the bowl and pour out the whey, then set the strainer back in the bowl and let the cheese drain for 15 minutes.

The ricotta is ready to serve now, and it will be soft and moist. Gather up the corners of the cheesecloth and lift. Set the cheese in your other palm and unfold the cloth. Invert a bowl or plate over the cheese in your hand, flip it over, and lift off the cheesecloth. You can also refrigerate it, covered, for later; it will be denser, more like cottage cheese.

serving homemade ricotta

At the cocktail hour, pile the ricotta in a bowl, drizzle it with extra-virgin olive oil—enough so you have a ring of oil around the cheese—and sprinkle it with coarse sea salt and coarsely ground black pepper. Or grains of paradise (crunchy seeds from West Africa, with a floral scent and the heat of black pepper). Set it out with slices of semolina bread.

This could also be lunch. You've made a big green salad or you have a platter of Roast Peppers with Capers and Anchovies (page 332). You have a great loaf of bread. You've got the ricotta in a bowl with the oil and salt and cracked pepper. You slather pieces of bread with the cheese and eat it with the salad.

Use this to make Ziti with Ricotta (page 162), making sure to add the goat cheese, since this ricotta is very sweet. It's enough for 1 pound of pasta. Or use it in a lasagne.

Ricotta can also be dessert or a sweet breakfast. Sprinkle it with a tiny bit of sugar and some cinnamon or drizzle it with tupelo honey and eat it with a spoon.

eggplant dip MAKES ABOUT 3 CUPS

Charring the eggplant under a broiler gives it a rich, smoky flavor, but if you've got the outdoor grill going, by all means char the eggplant there. My eggplant of choice for the dip is the long, narrow Asian variety, for its taste. But any eggplant will be fine. Look for a small dimple on the blossom end; that would mean fewer seeds.

1½ pounds eggplant, preferably 3 or 4 small ones (see headnote)
Olive or vegetable oil
1 small red onion, minced
1 garlic clove, minced to a paste or put through a press
1 large ripe tomato, seeded and chopped
¼ cup chopped pitted Kalamata or other black olives
½ cup chopped fresh flat-leaf parsley
¼ cup plain yogurt
2 tablespoons extra-virgin olive oil (something fruity)
Coarse salt and freshly ground black pepper
Toasted country bread or pita triangles (toasted or not), for serving

Heat the broiler. Crumple a large piece of aluminum foil and line a baking sheet (the crumpled foil keeps the eggplant from rolling around).

Rub the eggplant with olive or vegetable oil and broil them, turning frequently, until the skin is charred all over. This will take from 20 to 30 minutes, depending on the size of the eggplant.

When the eggplant is cool enough to handle, peel off the charred skin and let the flesh drain in a colander for about 20 minutes.

Chop the eggplant and stir it up with the onion, garlic, tomato, olives, parsley, yogurt, oil, and salt and pepper to taste.

Pile the dip into a serving bowl and set it out with the bread.

summer salsa MAKES ABOUT 3 CUPS

Ripe summer tomatoes are the rule.

1 white onion, minced

$^1/_2$ green bell pepper, minced

1 large ripe tomato, chopped

2 serrano chilies (or to taste), minced

Juice of 2 limes

$^1/_4$ cup chopped fresh cilantro

Coarse salt

Combine all the ingredients in a bowl, seasoning well with salt. Serve right away, or let it sit on the counter for a while.

roasted corn guacamole MAKES ABOUT 3 CUPS

The corn intensifies the flavor of the avocado somehow, making it even richer.

A molcajete, the Mexican lava rock mortar and pestle, is what you really want to use when you make this, but second best is a large garden-variety mortar with a pestle. Either way, you serve the guacamole in the vessel you make it in. Should you not find either of these in your kitchen, make a paste of the onion and chilies in a blender or food processor and mix the guacamole in a bowl with a fork.

The photo is on page 157.

- 2 ears corn
- Coarse salt
- 1 tablespoon olive oil
- 1/4 cup chopped white onion
- 2 or 3 serrano chilies, chopped fine
- 2 avocados
- 1/4 cup chopped fresh cilantro

Heat the oven to 400 degrees.

Husk the corn and cut the kernels from the ears. You can do this right on the baking sheet and avoid dirtying a bowl. Add a good pinch of salt and the olive oil. Toss well, breaking up any of the kernels that are attached to each other. Roast for 20 to 30 minutes, tossing with a spatula once in a while, until nicely browned. Let the corn cool.

Put the onion and chilies into a molcajete or other large mortar with a big pinch of salt. Reduce this to a paste with the pestle. Halve the avocados the long way, pop out the seeds, and squeeze the flesh on top of the paste. Use the pestle to combine, crushing the avocado as you go. Do leave some chunks of avocado, though; guacamole shouldn't be smooth. Stir in the corn and cilantro, and serve.

variations

You can certainly omit the corn, for a classic guacamole. Or you can make a fruit guacamole that Diana Kennedy discovered in Guanajuato, Mexico, by adding diced peaches or pears, halved green grapes, and pomegranate seeds. The fruit version does benefit from the juice of a lime too.

apricot salsa MAKES ABOUT 4 CUPS, WHICH SERVES A CROWD

A pretty mix of colors here and a satisfying mix of flavor. Go for two serranos for better zing.

The photo is on page 157.

2 large tomatoes (about 1$^1/_4$ pounds), chopped
1 yellow bell pepper, chopped fine
9 or 10 apricots, chopped
$^3/_4$ cup diced white onion
$^1/_3$ cup chopped fresh cilantro
1 or 2 serrano chilies, minced
Coarse salt
Juice of 1 orange

Slide the ingredients off your cutting board into a mixing bowl as you prep them. Add a good pinch of salt and the orange juice. Let it sit for a bit on the counter, or serve it right away.

variations

The moment for fresh apricots in the market is fleeting, but you could use other stone fruits like peaches or nectarines or plums.

spiced pecans MAKES ABOUT 2 CUPS

A little sticky, a little sweet, and a little spicy. Can you ask for more from a nut?

3 tablespoons unsalted butter

1 teaspoon coarse salt

1/2 teaspoon freshly ground black pepper

3/4 teaspoon cayenne (or less)

2 cups pecan halves

3 tablespoons sugar

3 tablespoons water

Melt the butter in a large skillet over medium heat. Once it stops sizzling, add the salt, pepper, and cayenne and cook for about a minute. Add the pecans. Cook, stirring often, until the nuts are fragrant and just starting to brown.

Sprinkle the sugar over the nuts and stir it in. The sugar will melt and caramelize as you cook and stir; you'll see small pools of caramel, each ringed with melted butter. Pour in the water all at once. It will sputter and steam, so be careful. And the caramel will seize up. Not to worry. Cook, stirring constantly, until the caramel melts and coats all the nuts.

Turn the nuts out onto a baking sheet and spread them with your spoon. Keep your hands off: they are blistering hot right now. Let cool completely, then break apart any nuts that have stuck together, and serve. They'll keep for a day or two in an airtight container.

deviled eggs MAKES 24 EGGS

I love making deviled eggs, I love eating them, I love experimenting with them. I'm giving you a basic recipe for a dozen eggs and variations for six, so you can mix and match if you want.

12 large eggs, hard-cooked (see page 59)

2 tablespoons tiny capers, rinsed

2 tablespoons Dijon mustard

6 tablespoons mayonnaise

Coarse salt and freshly ground black pepper

Shell the eggs, rinse them, and cut them lengthwise in half. Nudge out the yolks and push them through a sieve into a bowl. Add the capers, mustard, mayo, and salt and pepper to taste and beat until smooth. If you're the fancy type, you can fill a pastry bag with the yolks and pipe them into the whites. I just use a spoon.

variations

tarragon deviled eggs MAKES 12 EGGS

6 large eggs, hard-cooked

1/2 teaspoon dried tarragon (or 1 1/2 teaspoons chopped fresh)

1 teaspoon grainy mustard

1/4 cup mayonnaise

1/2 teaspoon white wine vinegar

Follow the master recipe.

anchovy deviled eggs MAKES 12 EGGS

6 large eggs, hard-cooked

2 tablespoons unsalted butter, softened

1 tablespoon anchovy paste

Freshly ground black pepper

Fresh parsley leaves, for garnish

Follow the master recipe, but beat the butter and anchovy paste together before adding to the yolks.

If your kitchen is on the cold side, your butter will be too. So, if the filling is very tight, loosen it with some mayonnaise. Garnish each egg with a parsley leaf.

mushroom deviled eggs MAKES 12 EGGS

6 large eggs, hard-cooked

6 tablespoons Mushroom Spread (page 181)

1 tablespoon mayonnaise

Coarse salt and freshly ground black pepper

Follow the master recipe.

string beans fritto SERVES 4

You can serve these addictive breaded beans as a side dish, but I love having them with drinks before dinner.

Look for the straightest beans: they'll be easier to fry and be prettier on the platter. This recipe is easily doubled.

$^{1}/_{2}$ pound green beans, trimmed
Coarse salt
$^{1}/_{2}$ cup all-purpose flour
1 large egg
$^{1}/_{3}$ cup freshly grated Pecorino
2 tablespoons water
Freshly ground black pepper
1 cup dried bread crumbs, plus more if needed
Olive oil, for frying
Coarse sea salt
1 lemon, cut into wedges

Bring a large saucepan of water to a boil. Add the beans and a good pinch of salt and cook for about 7 minutes, until the beans are tender. Not crisp-tender, please, but tender. Drain the beans, refresh them in a bowl of very cold water to stop the cooking, and drain them again. Dry the beans on paper towels.

Pour the flour into a paper bag. Crack the egg into a large shallow bowl and beat it with a fork. Add the Pecorino, water, and pepper and beat again. Pour about half the bread crumbs onto a plate. Have ready a rack set over a baking sheet.

Drop the beans into the bag of flour, close the top, and shake well to flour the beans. Shake the beans as you take them out of the bag to remove excess flour, and put them in the egg mixture. The best way to go here is to add all the beans to the egg and turn them around with your hands to make sure they're all coated. It's a thick egg mixture, and you won't have enough if you dip the beans one by one. Now coat the beans in the bread crumbs, adding more crumbs to the plate as you need them, and set the coated beans on the rack as you finish. You can prep through this step a few hours ahead and refrigerate the beans until you're ready to fry.

Heat about 1/4 inch of olive oil in a skillet set over medium heat, and set another rack over a baking sheet. When the oil is shimmering, add some of the breaded beans—don't crowd the skillet. Fry until the beans are golden brown, and remove them with tongs to the rack. Continue frying in batches.

Once you've fried all the beans, arrange them on a platter, sprinkle with coarse sea salt, and serve with the lemon wedges on the side.

olives with orange and thyme

Sure, you can buy olives that have already been seasoned, but it takes just a moment to do it yourself, and the results are so much more interesting. This is the kind of recipe you should play around with, finding what flavors you like to combine with olives or using what you have in the house. No orange? Try lemon. Don't care for thyme? What about rosemary or oregano?

The photo is on page 69.

Buy a pound of mixed olives—Kalamata, Sicilian green, Niçoise, whatever looks most appealing to you—and drop them into a bowl. Grate in the zest of 1 orange and add 2 to 3 teaspoons fresh thyme leaves, 1 tablespoon fresh flat-leaf parsley leaves (leave them whole, for looks), 1 smashed garlic clove, 2 tablespoons olive oil, and a few grinds of black pepper. If you like, add a pinch of crushed red pepper. Toss and let sit for an hour before serving.

cheese biscuits MAKES ABOUT 24 BISCUITS

Sara Ann Pearson, my friend Tom's mom, started me off on this recipe, which I tinkered with. It's a Southern classic—a crumbly, cheesy biscuit with a hint of heat from the cayenne. Mrs. P uses Cracker Barrel cheddar when she makes these addictive biscuits. You might too, or you might use a great farmhouse cheddar. The biscuits will look their best if you use an orange cheddar.

1/4 pound sharp cheddar, shredded

1/4 pound Parmesan, grated (1 cup packed)

12 tablespoons (1 1/2 sticks) unsalted butter, softened

2 cups all-purpose flour

1/4 teaspoon cayenne

Paprika, for dusting

Heat the oven to 450 degrees.

Combine the cheeses and butter in a mixing bowl, mixing well with your hands. Add the flour and cayenne and mix with your hands until you have a smooth and cohesive dough.

Turn the dough out onto a floured work surface and flatten it into a disk; pat in the edges so they won't be ragged. Roll the dough out about 1/3 inch thick, and cut out biscuits with a 2 1/2-inch cutter. Transfer to two ungreased cookie sheets, leaving the biscuits some room to spread. Gather the scraps together and continue cutting out biscuits. Dust the tops with paprika.

Slip the biscuits into the oven and bake for about 8 minutes, rotating the sheets top to bottom and front to back after 5 minutes, until the biscuits are very lightly browned. Cool on the sheets on a rack for a minute or two, then remove them from the sheets to the rack and cool completely.

Store any leftovers in an airtight container for a few days.

rosemary focaccia MAKES ONE 10-INCH FOCACCIA

This classic sandwich focaccia is very light and airy, perfect for splitting and filling with a slice or two of prosciutto, or for cutting into squares for nibbling. I'm also giving you two variations. The grapes and cherries sink down into the bread, so you can't really split these, but they're great for snacking.

The dough is too soft and sticky to knead by hand. It's best made in a standing mixer, but you can use a food processor.

The photo is on page 69.

1 (8-ounce) russet potato

Coarse salt

1 teaspoon active dry yeast

Pinch of sugar

2 1/2 cups all-purpose flour

3 tablespoons olive oil, plus more for the pan

Cornmeal, for sprinkling

2 tablespoons chopped fresh rosemary

Coarse sea salt

Peel the potato and cut it into large chunks. Put it in a small saucepan, cover with cold water by at least an inch, add a pinch of salt, and bring to a boil. Once it's boiling, reduce the heat to medium, cover the pot partway, and cook until the potato is very tender, just about falling apart. Drain, reserving 1 cup of the potato water, and return the potato to the pan.

Put the pan back on the heat for a minute or so, shaking the pan and stirring, to dry the potato. It's ready when you've got a film on the bottom of the pan. Put the potato through a ricer or work it through a strainer into the bowl of a standing mixer, and let it cool.

Once the potato water has cooled to lukewarm, stir in the yeast and pinch of sugar and let it stand for about 5 minutes, until creamy.

Add the flour, oil, and 1/2 teaspoon salt to the potato. Pour in the yeast and work the dough with the dough hook at medium speed until combined. Turn the speed up to medium-high and knead the dough with the hook for about 5 minutes. It will be very soft and sticky. Cover the bowl with plastic wrap and let the dough rise in a warm place until doubled, about 1 hour.

If you're going the food processor route, combine the potato, proofed yeast, flour, oil, and salt in the work bowl. Pulse to combine, then process for 90 seconds. Transfer to a large oiled bowl, cover with plastic, and set aside to rise.

Oil a 10-inch round cake pan and sprinkle the bottom with cornmeal. Scrape the dough out of the bowl into the pan—a dough scraper is handy here. Spread the dough out evenly with wet fingers, cover again with plastic, and let rise in a warm place until doubled. This second rise should take about 30 minutes.

About 10 minutes into the rising time, turn the oven on to 425 degrees, so it's hot when you're ready to bake.

When the dough has risen, sprinkle the top with the rosemary and coarse sea salt. Slide it into the oven and turn the heat down to 375 degrees. Bake the focaccia until golden, about 30 minutes. Let cool on a rack before turning the focaccia out of the pan.

variations

grape or sour cherry focaccia

About 20 minutes into the second rising, scatter over the dough 1/2 pound red or purple seedless grapes, tossed with 1 teaspoon olive oil; or 1 cup Sour Cherry Conserva (page 395), or commercial sour cherries in light syrup (available in many markets), drained. Sprinkle with 1 tablespoon chopped fresh rosemary and coarse sea salt if using grapes, or with 2 teaspoons fresh thyme leaves and coarse salt if using cherries. Let the dough finish rising and bake as above.

gougère "pizza" SERVES 6 TO 8

Inspiration here comes from Anne Willan, founder of École de Cuisine La Varenne, who is ever experimenting with gougères, those savory cream puffs. Instead of the fussier little puffs, the dough, packed with cheese and salami, is spread out on a baking sheet into a large "pizza," and topped with more cheese and herbs. The pizza is more dense than the standard cheese puff, more like a Yorkshire pudding, but, boy, is it good.

The photo is on page 158.

3/4 cup water

5 tablespoons unsalted butter, cut into 3 pieces

Coarse salt and freshly ground black pepper

Cayenne

1 cup all-purpose flour

5 large eggs

1/4 pound Gruyère, shredded

2 ounces sweet soppressata (or other salami) or prosciutto, chopped

1/4 pound Danish or Maytag blue cheese, crumbled

2 teaspoons minced fresh rosemary or sage

Heat the oven to 375 degrees.

Put the water and butter in a medium saucepan over medium-high heat. Season with salt, pepper, and a pinch of cayenne and bring to a boil. Once the butter's melted and the water's boiling, dump in the flour and stir vigorously with a sturdy wooden spoon. The dough will be kind of a mess, but it will quickly form a ball. Keep stirring over heat for about a minute to dry out the dough. When you have a smooth ball and a film on the bottom of the pan, take the pan off the heat. Let the dough cool for a minute or two.

Start beating 4 of the eggs into the dough, one by one. You can be traditional and do this by hand with a very sturdy wooden spoon, or just make life easier and use a hand mixer. As you work in each egg, the dough will seem to come apart, forming what look like big curds. Keep beating, and it will come back together. Beat the last egg in a small bowl and add enough of it to the batter so the batter will fall easily off a spoon. Hold on to the rest of the egg. Stir in the Gruyère, soppressata, and half of the blue cheese.

Dab a tiny bit of the batter into the four corners of a baking sheet to act as glue, and line the sheet with parchment. Spoon the batter onto the parchment and spread it out into an even rectangle that's about 9 by 13 inches (an offset spatula makes this easier to do). Tidy the edges. Scatter the remaining blue cheese over the top of the pizza. Beat a teaspoon or two of water into the remaining egg and brush the entire pizza with this egg wash. Now strew the minced rosemary over the top.

Slide the pan into the center of the oven and bake for 45 minutes, or until richly browned.

I slide the parchment off onto a big wooden board, cut the pizza into small squares, and serve it just like that. You could also pile the squares onto a platter. This is equally good hot and at room temperature.

little gougères and what to do with them

Flavored with cheese and a whiff of cayenne, the basic batter for *pâte à choux* is quick to pull together. This is one of those times in the kitchen when you ask yourself, Can this work? It does. You bring butter and water to a boil and dump in flour to make what looks like a sloppy mess. You stir it over heat, and within a minute or two, you have a tight, beautiful ball of dough. All you do then is beat eggs into the warm dough, one by one, until you've made a batter that is glossy and drops from a spoon. What with the eggs and all the beating, the batter rises high when you bake, crusty outside, cavernous in. The trick is to make sure you bake the puffs completely. They will appear done outside before the inside is completely dried. Take them out too soon, and they collapse. So be patient.

The pastry itself is versatile. Leave out the savory flavorings and you can use it to make profiteroles, filled with ice cream. It is the basis for Gâteau Paris-Brest, a ring meant to resemble a bicycle tire, studded with slivered almonds and filled with pastry cream. The batter can be fried as well, resulting in the delicate morsels known as *pets de nonne* (nun's farts).

But it's the cheesy ones I like best. Piled high on a plate, they get passed with cocktails. The tiniest might be floated on pea soup. If I feel like being fancy, I'll fill gougères with creamed ham (see opposite page).

✧ **Making individual gougères:** Heat the oven to 375 degrees. Cut 8 tablespoons (1 stick) unsalted butter into pieces and drop into a saucepan. Pour in 1 cup water, add a good pinch of coarse salt, a few gratings of nutmeg, and a pinch of cayenne, and bring to a boil over medium-high heat. When the butter is melted and the water bubbling, dump in 1 cup all-purpose flour and stir quickly with a wooden spoon, as directed on page 368. Then follow the procedure in the "pizza" recipe; you might not need all of the last egg. Stir in 1/4 pound of Gruyère, cut into tiny dice.

Drop the batter by spoonfuls—large or small, as you like—onto parchment-lined baking sheets, leaving plenty of room for the puffs to expand. Or fill a pastry bag fitted with a plain tip and pipe out the puffs; tamp the tails down with a wet finger. Medium puffs, made with heaped teaspoons of batter, will bake in 30 to 35 minutes. Larger will obviously take longer. The tiny ones, for soup, are made with a scant 1/2 teaspoon of batter apiece and should take 20 minutes. If you have any doubts about doneness, take a puff out and break it open. The inside should be fully dried, not damp looking.

Eat them hot or cool. They will keep for a few days in a sealed plastic bag, with all the air squeezed out, and you can reheat them in the oven.

✧ **Stuffing gougères:** Just about anything that's mayonnaisey can go into a gougère—I'm fond of Curried Chicken Salad (page 57). So can salmon mousse, and you might just want to set a few filled this way or with Chicken Hash (page 35) on a bed of Creamy Spinach (page 292) and call it dinner. If, come lunch, you have leftover larger gougères, make sandwiches with Piggy (page 221) and pickles. Or boiled ham, lettuce, and tomato.

✧ **Creamed Ham** Sweat a couple of minced shallots in a knob of butter in a skillet over medium-low heat. Pour in enough dry vermouth or dry white wine to cover the bottom of the pan, and cook until it's syrupy. Add about 2 cups minced leftover baked ham (if you want, you can substitute boiled ham) and season with salt, white pepper, and freshly grated nutmeg. Pour in a cup of heavy cream, bring it to a simmer, and cook until the cream has reduced and is pretty thick. Stir in a teaspoon or two of Dijon mustard, check the seasonings, and let cool for a minute or two before filling the gougères. If you're doing this for a party, you can fill the puffs well in advance and refrigerate them; reheat in a 350-degree oven for about 10 minutes.

goat cheese and red pepper turnovers

MAKES 18 TURNOVERS

Think spanakopita, with a twist.

1 large red bell pepper, roasted (see page 332) and cut into medium dice

5 ounces fresh goat cheese, at room temperature

2 tablespoons sour cream or plain yogurt

1 tablespoon chopped fresh basil

$^1/_2$ teaspoon ground cumin

Pinch of cayenne

Coarse salt

6 sheets phyllo

Olive oil, for brushing

1 tablespoon sesame seeds

Heat the oven to 375 degrees, and brush a baking sheet with olive oil.

Stir the bell pepper together with the goat cheese, sour cream, basil, cumin, cayenne, and salt to taste.

Lay 1 sheet of phyllo on a work surface, a long side facing you. Brush with olive oil, and cover with another sheet of phyllo. Slice the phyllo crosswise into 6 strips, each about 3 by 14 inches. Place 1 tablespoon of the filling at the bottom of each strip. Take a bottom corner of one strip and fold it up and across the filling, making a triangle. (Keep in mind that if you fold these too tight, chances are they will burst when you bake them, so keep them loose.) The bottom edge will now align with the side. Lift up the tip at the bottom of the strip and fold along the top straight edge, then fold across, at an angle. It's like folding a flag. Keep folding until you reach the top, and you'll have a triangular packet. Brush it with oil and put it on the baking sheet. Repeat with the rest of the ingredients.

Sprinkle the turnovers with the sesame seeds. You can make these in advance to this stage. Cover with plastic wrap and refrigerate for a few hours.

Bake for about 20 minutes, until crisp and browned. It'll take longer if you've chilled the turnovers. Let them cool for a few minutes before serving; the filling can be very, very hot.

tunisian spinach nibble SERVES 6

Soften bread in yogurt, add some eggs, some spinach, some feta, and harissa—the fiery spice paste from the Middle East—and bake it, and you have one of the most surprising and delicious things possible to nibble on.

In Tunisia, this would be called a tagine, after the vessel it is traditionally cooked in. I learned this dish from my friend Trudy Reswick, who spent many happy years in Tunisia before settling down on Calf Mountain in Virginia's Albemarle County. You don't need a clay tagine to make it; just pull out your cast-iron skillet. It's also a leftovers dish. Try substituting leftover Fennel à la Grecque (page 281) for the spinach. And for the bread, go for something dense and chewy. Multi-grain would be great.

2 packed cups cubed (the smaller the better) dense bread

1 cup plain yogurt

2 teaspoons vegetable or olive oil

10 ounces (or more) spinach

Coarse salt and freshly ground black pepper

4 large eggs

1 tablespoon harissa, homemade (page 376) or store-bought

1½ teaspoons ground fennel (or grind an equal amount of seeds to a powder in a spice grinder)

¼ pound feta, crumbled

Stir the bread and yogurt together in a mixing bowl and leave on the counter for about an hour for the bread to soften and absorb the yogurt.

Spoon the oil into a 9-inch cast-iron skillet and put the skillet into the oven. Turn the oven on to 375 degrees and let it heat up.

Meanwhile, rinse the spinach. Heat a large pot over high heat and add the spinach with whatever water is clinging to the leaves. Cook, stirring, until the spinach is completely wilted, the work of a matter of minutes. Drain the spinach and let it cool.

Squeeze the spinach dry, then chop it well. Add it to the mixing bowl with the bread and season with salt and pepper.

Beat the eggs with the harissa and fennel and add to the mixing bowl, along with the feta. Mix well.

When the oven's hot, take out the skillet and scrape in the batter. It will sizzle in the hot oil. Tamp it down evenly, then slide the skillet back into the oven for 45 minutes, or until the tagine is a rich brown.

Let the tagine cool for a few minutes, then invert it onto a platter. You can serve this hot or at room temperature, cut into diamonds for nibbling or wedges for plating.

harissa

This spicy paste is one of the staples of the North African kitchen, and my friend Trudy taught me to make this Tunisian version. You needn't be making a Tunisian dish to put it to use, though. Stir a little into some sautéed vegetables to liven them up, use it to marinate meats for grilling. Get the idea?

Baklouti chilies, the traditional Tunisian hot pepper for harissa, are available from Kalustyan's (www.kalustyans.com). You can substitute other dried chilies: guajillos, mulatos, pasillas—or even chipotles or moritas, if you want a fiery harissa.

Wipe 2 ounces of dried chilies clean, stem and seed them, and cover with simmering water. Let the chilies rehydrate for 15 to 20 minutes.

Meanwhile, put 4 teaspoons fennel seeds, 2 teaspoons coriander seeds, 1 teaspoon crushed red pepper, and 1 teaspoon coarse salt into a spice grinder. Grind to a fine powder, and pour into a food processor. Add 3 chopped garlic cloves.

Spoon 2 tablespoons of the soaking water into the processor, then drain the chilies and add them. Pulse a few times to make a very coarse paste. Scrape the paste down, then turn on the processor and pour in 6 tablespoons olive oil. Process until you have a thick paste; don't worry—it needn't be completely smooth.

Pack the harissa into a glass jar (you'll have about 2/3 cup), cover with oil, and refrigerate. It will keep for about a month.

raspberry vodka

This infusion is ideal to have on hand to use for summer drinks.

Put 1 pint of raspberries into a wide-mouthed glass jar, something that will hold at least 1 quart. Pour in 1 (750-ml) bottle of vodka, and close the jar. (Save the vodka bottle and take off the label if you want.) Leave the jar on the counter, out of the sun, for 3 weeks, giving it a shake when you remember. Strain the vodka into a pitcher, pressing down on the berries to get the last drops of vodka and juice out of them, and pour the now-pink vodka back into the bottle you saved or another one. I keep this in the freezer, where it could last forever.

You make the simplest cocktail by pouring some raspberry vodka over ice, adding a splash of seltzer, and squeezing in a small wedge of lime.

For a great summer highball, fill a glass with crushed ice and pour in a shot of raspberry vodka, then fill the glass with aranciata or limonata (Italian sodas that you can find in specialty stores) and garnish with a slice of orange or lemon.

You can also shake up some pretty terrific raspberry Martinis. Fill a shaker with ice, pour in 2½ ounces raspberry vodka and ½ ounce Grand Marnier, and shake vigorously for at least a minute. Strain into a cocktail glass and garnish with a long curl of orange zest.

condiments

condiments

Preserving things is a farm fantasy I've held on to since the days when I lived in Vermont.

On Saturdays or Sundays in the summer, I head to the farmers' market and see what's there that I can bring home and put into a jar. My friends make fun of me, but I don't see anyone laughing at what I do with the pickles and relishes and fruit filling my cabinets. Spicy mustard pickles get chopped up and give tang to a Smashed Potato Salad. Cherry Conserva may lend backbone to a rhubarb pie in spring or recapture that taste of spring in December as the filling for a crostata. As for Dilly Beans, they're great on a plate with mustardy oven-fried chicken, but more often than not they just go into a Martini.

Cookbook author Marion Cunningham says she "laments the loss of condiments from American tables," and I agree with her. They were once a part of every table setting. Fancy Victorians put them out in crystal bowls, with the proper fork for each, covering every available space. Ma Kettle, Betty MacDonald recounts in *The Egg and I*, just put out the jars. And that's what my friend Kelly does. Visit his apartment in New York City's East Village for dinner, and you will always have some kind of relish for your plate. I like that, the supper plate being a bit more than meat and potatoes and some veg or a salad.

Preserving doesn't have to take hours. You can make small batches in small periods of time. The recipes for Bread-and-Butter Pickles and Hot Mustard Pickles are more big-batch—since I love having these on hand—and that means a lot of slicing and chopping, but you can make half the amount. Dilly Beans and Pickled Cherry Peppers are kiss-simple. If you've never processed jars, invest in a book like *Pickled*, by Lucy Norris, or check online at sites like mrswages.com, and read up on canning basics.

You will find some recipes designed for life in the refrigerator—check out Quick Onion Pickles—that don't have to be processed and are a great place to start. Really, most of these recipes will be fine for at least 3 weeks in the refrigerator.

When you read the headnotes, you'll see I've given you some ideas of things to do with these preserves, but you'll find more ideas as you search through the book. Pickled Cherry Peppers are a great nibble, Honeyed Quince makes a truly fine crostata, and Sour Cherry Conserva makes a terrific addition to ice cream—on it or in it.

And here's a good thing to remember: when you go overboard with canning and your cabinets are filled to overflowing, you've got great house gifts on hand. Bring a jar of something when you're invited to dinner, instead of that bottle of wine.

tools for canning

Here are the pieces of equipment I can't do without.

- Very large stainless bowls
- Very large (10 quarts) pots—for cooking the pickles and for processing
- Canning funnel—with a big wide mouth
- Jar lifter—how else to get those jars out of a big pot of boiling water?
- Slotted spoon
- Lots of kitchen towels

refrigerator pickles MAKES 2 QUARTS

These are crisp and sweet and couldn't be easier. They're just the pickle for someone who doesn't want to venture into the world of processing jars but who does want the satisfaction of putting up a pickle.

Thanks to Mrs. P, my friend Tom Pearson's mom, for starting me off on this recipe.

6 (5-inch) Kirby cucumbers (about 1½ pounds), sliced thin

1 large (8 ounces) onion, sliced thin

1 tablespoon coarse salt

1½ cups rice or white vinegar

2 cups sugar

1 teaspoon celery seeds

4 big sprigs dill

Put the cucumbers, onion, and salt in a big bowl. Toss well, cover with ice cubes, and pop into the refrigerator for 2 hours.

Combine the vinegar, sugar, and celery seeds in a saucepan. Bring to a boil, then lower the heat and simmer for 5 minutes. Take off the heat and let the sugar brine cool.

Drain the cucumbers and onion and pack them and the dill into a half-gallon jar (or two 1-quart jars). Pour in most of the brine, poke around with a chopstick or the handle of a wooden spoon to release any air bubbles, then pour in the rest of the brine. Screw on the lid and refrigerate.

The pickles will be ready to eat after 24 hours. They will keep for about 6 weeks in the refrigerator.

dilly beans MAKES 6 PINTS

This is one of the simplest, and tastiest, pickles you can make. It's a recipe I've adapted from my buddy John Martin Taylor, a cook and writer who has the goods on Lowcountry cooking. These are great on any picnic table, and they also make one hell of an addition to a Martini.

2 1/2 pounds green beans

6 big sprigs dill, preferably with flowerheads

6 garlic cloves, peeled

6 small hot peppers (your choice) or 1 1/2 teaspoons crushed red pepper

3 1/2 cups white vinegar

3 1/2 cups water

6 tablespoons coarse salt

Wash the beans and trim them from the stem ends to a length 1/2 inch shorter than your jars. I use wide-mouthed jars for dilly beans, so the beans are about 4 inches long.

Have ready six impeccably clean pint jars. Put a sprig of dill into each, along with a garlic clove and a hot pepper (or 1/4 teaspoon crushed red pepper). Pack the beans into the jars, cut ends up.

Combine the vinegar, water, and salt in a saucepan and bring to a boil. Give it a stir to make sure the salt is dissolved. Fill the jars to within 1/4 inch of the rim with the brine. Poke with a chopstick to release air bubbles.

Screw on the caps, and process for 10 minutes. Allow to cool completely before moving them to the pantry, and let the beans cure for 2 weeks before eating.

These are best well chilled, so keep a jar in the fridge.

bread-and-butter pickles MAKES ABOUT 8 PINTS

I can't do without these pickles. I love having them around for lunch (on or next to a sandwich), and they are one of the best possible gifts.

You'll need a very, very big bowl, and a very big pot. A Japanese slicer or mandoline is invaluable for slicing the cucumbers.

Halve the recipe if you're short on prep time.

The photo is on page 277.

5 pounds Kirby cucumbers, scrubbed

3 large sweet onions (Vidalia, Walla Walla, etc.)

3 large red bell peppers

6 tablespoons coarse salt

6 cups sugar

6 cups cider vinegar

2 tablespoons yellow mustard seeds

1 tablespoon black mustard seeds (see headnote, page 388)

1 teaspoon celery seeds

½ teaspoon ground cloves

2½ teaspoons curry powder (I use a medium-hot Madras mix)

Slice the cucumbers about ⅙ inch thick. Halve the onions and slice into thin half-moons. Halve and seed the bell peppers, and cut into long thin slices, about ¼ inch wide. Layer all the vegetables in a huge bowl, sprinkling the salt between the layers as you go.

Cover the vegetables with ice cubes and let the bowl sit on the counter for 3 hours.

Take out your biggest pot—at least 10 quarts—and add the sugar, vinegar, mustard seeds, celery seeds, cloves, and curry powder. Set it over high heat, and stir to dissolve the sugar. Once the sugar is completely dissolved, pick out any unmelted ice cubes from the vegetables, and drain the vegetables. Add them to the pot and bring to a boil, stirring once in a while. This will take about 7 minutes. Remove from the heat.

Use a slotted spoon and a canning funnel to pack the vegetables into impeccably clean pint jars, filling them to within 1/2 inch of the top. Pour in enough brine to cover the pickles, then poke around with a chopstick or the handle of a wooden spoon to release any air bubbles. Pour in more brine if you need to, to come 1/4 inch below the rim. You'll have leftover brine.

Screw on the lids, and process for 10 minutes. Cool completely on kitchen towels.

kitchen wisdom

When I was growing up, I used to help my grandmother put up tomato sauce from bushels of tomatoes every September. We cooked the tomatoes, put them through a mill, and cooked down the sauce. We filled up the jars, processed them, and—here's the kitchen wisdom, or lore—turned the jars upside down to cool. I remember asking my grandmother about it, and her answer was, "That's how you do it."

Years later, I was working with Anne Willan, in the kitchen of her cooking school in Burgundy, helping her put up some preserve or other. I mentioned my grandmother's thing about cooling jars upside down, and Anne smiled, said she had never heard of it, and sat the jars upright. Then the two Portuguese women who cleaned for Anne came in, and Anne offered them each a jar. They smiled, thanked her, and walked away with their jars to the other end of the kitchen, where they stood the jars on their lids to cool.

So I keep up the tradition. I lift the jars out of the water bath, tighten the lids, and put them upside down on a kitchen towel. Is it science? Nope. But I've never had a problem with jars that haven't sealed either.

quick onion pickles MAKES ABOUT 1 QUART

My friend baking book author Carole Walter is a really good cook. She made these onions for me when I came to visit for lunch one autumn afternoon and served them on a bed of sliced oranges, with some black olives.

I use them for different salads: with shaved fennel, or with grated Roasted Beets (page 257). All these salads want is a drizzle of your best olive oil and some coarse salt and black pepper.

And I don't have to tell you how good these onions are on burgers, do I?

You can substitute a tablespoon of pickling spice for the spice mix if you want. And you can also tinker with the spice mix and make it your own.

The photo is on page 277.

FOR THE SPICE MIX (SEE HEADNOTE)

2 bay leaves

2 teaspoons coriander seeds

1 teaspoon mustard seeds

1/2 teaspoon white peppercorns

3 whole cloves

3 "petals" star anise

Pinch of crushed red pepper

FOR THE PICKLES

Coarse salt

2 pounds red onions, cut into thin half-moons

1/2 cup sugar

1/2 cup white vinegar

1/4 cup red wine vinegar

1/2 cup water

1 tablespoon coarse salt

FOR THE SPICE MIX

Crumble the bay leaves into a small bowl. Add the rest of the ingredients.

FOR THE PICKLES

Bring a large saucepan of water to a boil. Salt the water and add the onions. Bring back to a boil and blanch the onions for 1 minute. Drain well. Put the onions in an impeccably clean 1½-quart glass jar.

Combine the sugar, vinegars, water, salt, and spice mix in a small saucepan. Bring to a boil, stirring to dissolve the sugar. Once the brine is boiling, lower the heat and simmer for 5 minutes.

Bring the brine back to a full boil, and pour it over the onions. Poke around with a chopstick or the handle of a wooden spoon to release any air bubbles. Let the jar cool on the counter, then close it and refrigerate for at least 24 hours before serving.

These pickles will keep for about 6 weeks in the refrigerator.

hot mustard pickles MAKES ABOUT 9 PINTS

This is a good pickle to chop up and add to a potato salad. It's tangy and spicy—a wake-up call on your plate. Brown and black mustard seeds—traditional ingredients in curry—are more pungent than the common yellow seeds. You'll find them in specialty markets, and online from many sources.

You'll need a very large bowl and a 10-quart pot. Or you can halve this recipe.

1½ pounds green tomatoes, sliced about ⅛ inch thick

1 pound Romano beans or other flat beans (such as Dragon's Tongue), trimmed and cut into 1-inch lengths

2½ pounds Kirby cucumbers, ends trimmed and cut about ⅛ inch thick

3 large onions, sliced thin

2 green or purple bell peppers, cut into ¼-inch-wide slices

1 cauliflower (1½–2 pounds), cut into smallish florets

¾ cup coarse salt

About 4 quarts boiling water

2 quarts cider vinegar

2½ cups sugar

¼ cup dry mustard

2 tablespoons celery seeds

1 tablespoon whole allspice

1 tablespoon yellow mustard seeds

1 tablespoon brown or black mustard seeds

1 tablespoon ground turmeric

1 tablespoon black peppercorns

10 hot cherry peppers, cored and quartered

Toss the tomatoes, beans, cucumbers, onions, bell peppers, and cauliflower with the salt in a very large bowl. Pour in boiling water to cover, and let the vegetables sit on the counter for 3 hours.

Drain the vegetables, rinse them, and drain again. Repeat, giving the vegetables another rinse and drain.

Combine the vinegar, sugar, and spices in a very large pot and bring to a boil over medium-high heat. Give this a few stirs to dissolve the sugar completely. Add the vegetables and cherry peppers and bring back to a boil. Simmer for about 15 minutes, stirring occasionally, until the vegetables are crisp-tender.

Use a slotted spoon and a canning funnel to fill impeccably clean pint jars to within ½ inch of the rim. Try to make sure each jar gets some of the cherry peppers. Ladle in enough brine to come to ¼ inch below the rim. Poke around with a chopstick or the handle of a wooden spoon to release any air bubbles, and add more brine if you need it. You'll have leftover brine.

Seal the jars, and process for 15 minutes. Cool completely on kitchen towels before storing.

pickled cherry peppers MAKES 3 PINTS

These are so much better than the jars of cherry peppers you'll find in the grocery, and prettier too. This variety isn't the hottest in the market, but every once in a while you'll come across one that does pack some heat.

You can pickle them and stuff them and serve them the same day, if you want. See below, and see the box. But the season for these guys is short, and preserving means you can recapture summer in January.

The photo is on page 66.

2 1/2 pounds hot cherry peppers
2 1/2 cups white vinegar
2 cups water
1 tablespoon salt

Use a small sharp knife to cut out the stems of the peppers; take a bit of the flesh so you leave an opening. Take the tip of the knife and use it to tease out the seeds and veins. Just do the best job you can with this, not the most obsessive one. A few seeds aren't going to hurt anyone.

Bring the vinegar, water, and salt to a boil in a large saucepan. Add the peppers, bring back to a boil, and then turn off the heat.

If you plan on stuffing and filling them now, pull the peppers out with a slotted spoon and let them cool upside down on a few thicknesses of paper towels. Save some of the brine for serving.

If you're preserving the peppers, pack them into three impeccably clean pint jars. Pour in brine to come to within 1/2 inch of the rim, then poke around with a chopstick or the handle of a wooden spoon to make sure all the cavities of the peppers fill with brine. Pour in enough brine to come 1/4 inch below the rim.

Seal the jars and process for 15 minutes. Cool completely on kitchen towels before storing.

stuffed cherry peppers

You've probably seen the premade stuffed cherry peppers in Italian delis and salad bars, and maybe you've even served them. Forget about them. You won't believe how tasty they are when you make them yourself.

The classic is simple: break or cut the best provolone you can find into pieces that will fit into your peppers. Wrap each piece of cheese with a bit of sliced prosciutto, to cover it completely, and pack it into a pepper. Or get some sweet soppressata, sliced very, very thin, and use that instead of the ham.

Don't rein yourself in, though. Try different fillings. Chop up a quarter pound of aged Asiago into small pieces and mix it with 1/2 cup prepared olive salad (I like Alcaparrado from Goya), 8 chopped anchovy fillets, and 2 tablespoons chopped fresh flat-leaf parsley. If you can't find olive salad, chop up pimiento-stuffed olives and add 1 tablespoon capers. This should be enough for 10 to 15 peppers, depending on their size.

The tuna salad on page 56 is pretty good stuffed into the peppers too.

However you decide to stuff them, here's how to finish them for serving. Pack the peppers snugly into a bowl—single layer, please. Whisk together 1/3 cup olive oil and 2 tablespoons of the reserved brine, and pour this over the peppers. You're ready to go.

Stuffed, these will keep for about 5 days in the refrigerator. Serve them at room temperature. They're great as a nibble with drinks, as part of an antipasto platter, with some cheese and olives and sliced dried sausages; on a dinner plate with some fried fish; or next to a salad dressed with oil and vinegar.

tipsy onions MAKES 4 PINTS

I'll put these out with grilled cheese sandwiches, or slice them thin and add them to a steak sandwich. Or drop one into a glass of gin on the rocks and call it a Gibson.

1 cup coarse salt

2 cups boiling water

6 cups cold water

2 pounds small white onions—or small shallots—peeled

1 teaspoon crushed red pepper

4 bay leaves

½ cup gin

1 cup dry vermouth

About 2 cups white wine vinegar

Dissolve the salt in the boiling water in a large deep bowl. Chances are it won't all dissolve; not to worry—you're just getting the process going. Add the cold water, stir, and add the onions. Set a small plate on top of the onions to keep them submerged in the brine—they will want to rise to the surface and bob around—and leave in a corner of the kitchen for 2 days.

Once the onions have brined, drain them well. Divide them among four impeccably clean pint canning jars. To *each* jar, add ¼ teaspoon crushed red pepper, 1 bay leaf, 2 tablespoons gin, and ¼ cup dry vermouth. Fill the jars to within ½ inch of the rim with the vinegar, and screw on the tops.

Process the jars for 20 minutes. Cool completely on kitchen towels before storing.

honeyed quince MAKES ABOUT 4 PINTS

I keep jars of this tart, sweet, and delicious conserve in the pantry to make crostatas during the winter, but I have to say that I'll also warm some of this up and spread it on toasted crusty bread. Or pancakes.

I've adapted this from a recipe in Richard Sax's *From the Farmers' Market*, a delightful book from a great cook and writer.

4 1/2 pounds quinces, washed
2 cinnamon sticks
3 or 4 bay leaves
12 tablespoons (1 1/2 sticks) unsalted butter
Coarse salt
1 lemon, scrubbed
1 1/2 cups honey (use one with a lot of flavor)
2 1/2 cups dry vermouth or dry white wine

Peel the quinces, and tie the peels, cinnamon, and bay in a piece of cheesecloth, making a tight package.

Cut the quinces into quarters, cut out the cores and woody veins, and slice thin—thinner than 1/4 inch. Make things easy for yourself and use the slicing disk on a food processor.

Melt the butter in a large wide saucepan over medium heat. Add the quinces and a big pinch of salt and toss to coat the fruit with the butter. Cover and cook for 10 minutes. The quinces will start to get juicy.

Meanwhile, cut off the ends of the lemon and slice it lengthwise in half. Make a long V-shaped cut around the membrane in the center of each half and nudge out the seeds. Slice the lemon as thin as you can.

Stir the honey into the quinces, then add the vermouth and lemon and bury the cheesecloth package in the center. Bring to a simmer. Cover and cook at a lively simmer for 45 minutes, stirring once or twice.

Take the cover off, reduce to a gentle simmer, and cook for another 25 to 30 minutes, stirring often, until the quinces are very tender. The mixture will have turned a dusty rose color and thickened but will still be on the saucy side. Lift the packet of peels out and into a small strainer. Hold the strainer over the pot and press down on the packet with a spoon to get all the juice out and back into the quinces.

Pack into impeccably clean pint jars, seal, and process for 10 minutes. Cool completely before storing.

Warm the conserve before serving.

quinces

It's unlikely that you'll find quinces in the grocery; they're more a farmers' market thing. But when you do find them, buy extra and set them out in a bowl. They'll perfume the room for a week.

sour cherry conserva MAKES 4 PINTS

I love tart cherries and had despaired that their season was so short until I found this recipe in my friend Nick Malgieri's wonderful *Great Italian Desserts*. These are now a staple in my pantry, and I find that I end up making more than one batch a season. You should too.

It helps when you have a friend around to pit the cherries with you. The yield will vary, depending on the juiciness of the cherries.

6 pounds sour cherries
6 cups sugar
1 cinnamon stick
3 star anise
4 tablespoons golden rum

Stem the cherries, then wash and pit them. Put them in a large heavy pot with the sugar, stir well to dissolve the sugar, and turn the heat to high. Tie the cinnamon and star anise in a piece of cheesecloth and bury it in the cherries.

Bring the cherries to a boil, skimming any froth as it rises. This gets very juicy. Once you've got a full boil, pull out the cherries with a slotted spoon or spider and put them in a bowl by the stove. Boil the syrup, skimming diligently, until it reaches 220 degrees. Return the cherries to the syrup (if there's juice in the bowl, toss it), and boil until the temperature comes back to 220 degrees.

Spoon 1 tablespoon rum each into four impeccably clean pint jars. Fill the jars to within 3/4 inch of the top with cherries, then add enough syrup to come 1/2 inch below the rim. Poke with a chopstick or the handle of a wooden spoon to release air bubbles. Add more liquid if necessary.

Screw on the lids and process for 15 minutes. Cool completely on kitchen towels.

sour cherry ratafia MAKES ABOUT 1 1/2 QUARTS

Ratafia is an old-time cordial. You will have come across it if you read Regency novels; some matron has an attack of vapors and will be revived on her fainting couch by sipping ratafia.

I don't faint often, but I do find this fruit-infused cordial handy. Sip it after dinner if you want, or use it to make Kirs.

2 pounds sour cherries, pitted

1 (750-ml) bottle fruity red wine, like a Merlot

1 cup superfine sugar

1 cup brandy

Combine the cherries and red wine in a large glass jar with a tight lid, and leave in a sunny spot for 6 weeks.

When the cherries have macerated, strain the wine into a bowl, pressing on the cherries to get out all the juice.

Put the sugar and brandy in a jar, screw on the lid, and shake to dissolve the sugar completely. The best way to make sure it's completely dissolved is to shake, then let the jar sit for a bit—if any sugar settles on the bottom, shake it up again.

Stir the sugared brandy into the wine, and decant into bottles. This will keep for ages in the refrigerator, and it's best served chilled.

fruit and ratafia

Spoon macerated fruit into fancy bowls or wineglasses, and you have an elegant dessert that takes moments to prepare.

The photo is on page 411.

Slice up a pineapple and some nectarines or peaches, and place in a shallow bowl. Pour in enough ratafia to come about halfway up the fruit, and refrigerate for at least 2 hours, stirring once or twice, to make sure the fruit is well chilled. Add a sliced banana to the macerated pineapple when you serve it.

dessert

dessert

No matter what you've done for dinner—planned and cooked for hours, thrown something together quickly, ordered in, or freshened up leftovers—it is not a meal unless there's dessert.

This is, I believe, a law, and if it's not, it should be. Something sweet signals your mouth that its job is done, the cycle complete.

This isn't to say that the only time for eating something sweet is after dinner. There are those of us addicted to afternoon treats. A cookie and a cup of tea in the middle of the morning or afternoon (yes, sure, it's just one cookie—I know). Or that sliver of tart at 11:00. Company for lunch? Make a buckle. Lunch alone—well, maybe an apple. It's raining, so you have to have pudding. Or maybe you just find the process of making dessert therapeutic.

That last case is me. Working flour into butter and adding a few drops of water and having it turn into a dough satisfies me, and then rolling that dough out makes me smile. I'm hoping you share these pleasures, because there are some pretty good tarts in the following pages. Some are just about as simple as possible, like the Free-Form Italian Plum Tart, which you can adapt to just about any fruit in season and is so quick that you can and should add it to your weekday repertoire when you're making a simple supper. It's something I do often, when I have friends over for dinner after work. The first thing I do when I get home is to make the pastry and put it in the refrigerator to rest while I cut up the fruit and heat the oven. The tart is in the oven when guests arrive, and I have to tell you, there's no more welcoming smell. And you've got that safety net of knowing you'll end the meal on a high note. The crostatas—which are made with an Italian sweet pastry—are pretty easy too. And once you master that pastry, you can make all sorts of quick and easy jam and marmalade tarts.

I do know, though, that some of you are pastry-phobic. So there's cake. An angel cake for a birthday, shortcake for the 4th of July, chocolate cakes for the chocolate lovers. Plum Cake and Blueberry Buckle are delightfully old-fashioned. They fill the house with the aroma of butter and bubbling fruit. That scent is even more intense and enticing when you roast fruit.

I think of ice cream as an investment, kind of like money in the stock market. Yes, you can serve it alone, but it's also ideal for dressing up something purchased. Toast slices of pound cake from the grocery and top them with a scoop of Crème Fraîche Ice Cream, and you're up a rung or two on the ladder of tasty. Break up some shortbread cookies and layer them in a pretty glass with softened Strawberry Ice Cream, plop a berry on top, and the kids will go wild. I like making Ice Cream Sandwiches with toasted brioche, but you can also bring home some big, soft cookies from the bakery and use those to make your sandwiches.

And listen, saying you don't bake is no excuse for not making dessert. That pound cake from the grocery is usually pretty good, and just because it's sold without icing doesn't mean that you can't take a second to mix some confectioners' sugar and lemon juice to make a glaze for it. Berries and cream take no time. You could bring home some fresh apricots, slice them, and pour Prosecco over them. At the very least, you can cut up some oranges into wedges and pretend you're in a Chinese restaurant.

roasted pears SERVES 4 TO 6

Desserts should be pretty, and this dish of glistening roasted pears garnished with jewel-like pomegranate seeds fits the bill.

2 tablespoons unsalted butter

4 pears, peeled, quartered lengthwise, and cored

3 tablespoons sugar

3 tablespoons marmalade or jam (your choice)

1 tablespoon cognac or other brandy

Seeds of 1 pomegranate (see the box)

Heat the oven to 350 degrees.

Melt the butter over medium-high heat in an ovenproof skillet large enough to hold the pears in one layer. When the foaming slows down, add the pears and sprinkle them with the sugar. Brown the pears quickly, shaking the pan and flipping them (turn up the heat if the pears start releasing a lot of juices rather than browning).

Slide the skillet into the oven and bake for 15 minutes, until the pears are tender.

Meanwhile, melt the marmalade in a little saucepan. Stir in the cognac.

Pour the marmalade over the pears and turn the pears around in it—gently, so you don't break them. Spoon the pears out onto a platter, and make sure to scrape all the glaze and juices over them. Strew the pomegranate seeds over the pears.

You can serve this hot or let it sit for an hour or so.

seeding a pomegranate

You don't have to end up with stained hands.

Fill a good-sized bowl with water. Cut through the rind of the pomegranate and, holding it in the water so it doesn't stain your fingers, twist and break it into big pieces. Still working underwater, nudge out all the seeds. Any bits of the whitish connective tissue will rise to the top and can be captured and discarded. Drain the seeds.

honey baked apples SERVES 6

This is comfort at its best, and a nice twist on the garden-variety baked apple. Two different apples are used here: sweet apples are grated to make a filling that almost melts into the Golden Delicious base. These are delicious hot or warm.

Use a flavorful honey—tupelo, if you have it.

3 Golden Delicious apples

1 tablespoon unsalted butter

1/4 cup dry vermouth

3 small sweet apples (Rome or McIntosh; about 3/4 pound total)

1/2 cup heavy cream

1 large egg yolk

3 tablespoons honey

Grated zest of 1 lemon

Coarse salt

Honey Crème Anglaise (page 406), for serving (optional)

Position an oven rack in the upper third of the oven and heat the oven to 350 degrees.

Cut the Golden Delicious apples in half through the equator and scoop out the core with a melon baller. Leave a bit of the core at the base of each half to keep the apple cups intact.

Put the apple halves in a baking dish, cut side up, and dot with the butter. Pour the vermouth into the dish, and bake the apples for 10 minutes.

Meanwhile, peel and core the sweet apples and grate them on a box grater onto a clean kitchen towel. Catch up the ends of the towel and squeeze over the sink, getting some of the juice out of the apples. Drop the apples into a bowl, and add the cream, yolk, honey, lemon zest, and a pinch of salt. Mix well—no bits of visible yolk.

Mound the sweet-apple filling onto the Golden Delicious apples. Slide the dish back into the oven and bake for 1 hour, basting three or four times. The Golden Delicious apples should be very tender, just to the point of splitting, and the filling should be richly browned.

Let cool for 5 minutes or so before serving. Or make the apples in advance and serve them slightly warm or at room temperature.

Serve in dessert bowls, with or without a puddle of honey crème anglaise.

honey crème anglaise MAKES ABOUT 1 1/2 CUPS

I love this classic dessert sauce with honey as the sweetener.

1/2 cup heavy cream
1/2 cup milk
2 large egg yolks
1/4 cup honey

Have ready a bowl filled with ice and some water. Set a smaller bowl and a strainer on the ice.

Rinse a saucepan with cold water (so it will be easier to clean later), and pour in the cream and milk. Bring to a simmer.

Meanwhile, whisk the yolks and honey in a mixing bowl until light. When the cream is simmering, pour it in a steady stream into the yolks, whisking while you pour. Whisk for about 30 seconds, then return the mixture to the saucepan. Cook, stirring constantly, over medium-high heat, until the cream thickens and coats the back of the spoon. Strain the sauce into the bowl set over ice. Let it cool completely over the ice, whisking every once in a while.

Serve right away, or refrigerate for a day.

coating the spoon

It sounds so simple, doesn't it? And it really is, as long as you know what it means.

First of all, since I'm telling you to cook this sauce at a pretty high heat, be sure to take the pan off the stove when you're doing this test. That way you won't end up with cream filled with little scraps of curdled egg yolk.

When you first start cooking the sauce, lift the spoon out and see how thin the sauce looks on the spoon and how lightly coated the spoon is as a reference for later (no need to take the pan off the heat for this). As the sauce starts to thicken—and you'll see it happen as you stir—lift the spoon again. If the coating is thicker, take the pan off the heat and run your finger across the spoon horizontally. You'll leave a valley. If the sauce on the top half of the spoon starts to make individual drips into the valley right away, you haven't cooked the sauce long enough. Return it to the heat. When you test and the top half holds for a second or two, then starts easing down in a line, you're done.

baked nectarines SERVES 6

Juicy summer nectarines are baked with heavy cream, which forms a sauce. Peaches work here as well. No need to peel them; just wash well to get rid of the fuzz.

6 ripe nectarines

$^1/_2$ cup heavy cream

1 tablespoon all-purpose flour

2 tablespoons sugar

2 tablespoons brandy or amaretto

Heat the oven to 350 degrees, and butter an 11-inch gratin or similar dish.

Halve the nectarines along the seam and pull out the pits. Pack the halves cut side up in the gratin dish. This will be a very snug fit, with some of the nectarines almost on their sides. That is what you want.

Whip the cream to soft peaks in a small bowl. Add the flour and sugar and whip to firm peaks. Whip in the brandy. Spoon the cream over the nectarines.

Slip the dish into the oven and roast for about 40 minutes. The nectarines should be soft but still holding their shape, the cream should be lightly browned, and the juices in the bottom of the dish should be thick and bubbling.

Let cool for 10 minutes before serving. The nectarines can sit on the counter for 30 minutes or so, but they really are at their best when served very warm.

Place 2 halves in each dessert bowl and spoon the juices over.

pork roast with fruit stuffing (page 218)

blueberry buckle (page 424)

fruit and ratafia (page 397)

applesauce apple tart
(page 434)

coriander shortbread fans

(page 444)

chocolate whipped cream cake
(page 436)

five-spice angel food cake
(page 440)

raspberry buttermilk sherbet (page 461)

pink applesauce MAKES ABOUT 4 1/2 CUPS

The color comes from the skins—Rome apples are best—and from cranberry juice.

Just because you'll be putting this sauce through a food mill doesn't mean you don't have to core the apples. The seeds make the sauce bitter.

I don't sweeten this, so I can use it as a side dish for dinner. But I will add some sugar when I add it to a tart (see page 434).

3 pounds Rome or Ida Red apples (about 7)

3/4 cup cranberry juice

Quarter the apples and cut out the cores. Cut the apples into chunks and put them in a saucepan with the cranberry juice. Bring to a boil over high heat, then reduce the heat to medium, cover partway, and cook the apples for 20 minutes.

Turn off the heat, cover the pan completely, and let the apples sit for 20 minutes or so. They should be completely tender.

Put the apples through a food mill fitted with the medium disk.

LEFTOVERS

Stir some into leftover rice pudding, or even into leftover rice, for breakfast. Or use it on (or in) pancakes.

shortcake MAKES ONE 8-INCH LAYER CAKE

I've been baking this tender cake—almost cake, almost biscuit—for thirty years now. When I lived in Vermont, I'd make it for breakfast, putting slabs of the cake into bowls, topping it with fresh-picked raspberries from the yard, and ladling in top milk, which we got from the dairy farmer down the road.

Now I don't have a yard or a dairy farm nearby, so I have to make do with store-bought cream and fruit. But it's still the best shortcake ever.

FOR THE CAKE

2 cups all-purpose flour

4 teaspoons baking powder

1/3 teaspoon salt

2/3 cup unsalted butter, softened

2/3 cup sugar

2 large eggs

2/3 cup milk

FOR SERVING

Strawberries for Shortcake (see below)

1 cup heavy cream, whipped

or

Roasted Rhubarb (see below)

1 cup heavy cream, whipped

2 tablespoons chopped candied ginger

FOR THE CAKE

Heat the oven to 350 degrees. Butter and flour two 8-inch round cake pans.

Whisk the flour, baking powder, and salt together in a bowl.

Beat the butter in a large bowl with an electric mixer until it starts to lighten. Gradually pour in the sugar, beating while you pour, and continue beating until very light. Beat in the eggs.

Now switch to a wooden spoon and stir in the dry ingredients and milk in batches: half the dry, all the milk, and the rest of the dry. Beat for a moment or two with the spoon until the batter is smooth. It will be stiff.

Divide the batter between the pans, and pat it out into the pans with floured fingers. Give the pans a rap on the countertop to release any air bubbles, then slip them into the oven. Bake the cakes for about 25 minutes, until risen and browned in spots.

Let the cakes cool on racks for about 5 minutes, then turn them out of the pans and let cool completely on the racks.

FOR SERVING

Set 1 layer on a cake plate. Spoon some of the juices or syrup from whichever fruit you're using over the cake and then spoon on half the fruit. Spread about half the whipped cream over the fruit and set the second layer on top. Repeat, spooning juice or syrup, then fruit, then cream. If you're serving the rhubarb, scatter the ginger on top of the cream.

Serve the shortcake right away, or refrigerate for later.

strawberries for shortcake

Hull and slice 1 pint strawberries. Toss with 1 packed tablespoon brown sugar, 1 teaspoon balsamic vinegar, and a grind or two of black pepper. Refrigerate for at least an hour.

roasted rhubarb

Trim 1½ pounds rhubarb and cut into ⅓-inch dice. Toss in a large baking dish with 1 cup sugar, ½ teaspoon ground ginger, and a pinch of salt. Roast in a 350-degree oven for 30 minutes. Let cool completely.

plum cake MAKES ONE 10-INCH CAKE

A German-style home dessert, this cake is as old-fashioned as they come.

It's a dense batter, so it's easiest to make this in a standing mixer with the paddle. But it certainly works with a hand mixer; you might just switch to a sturdy wooden spoon when you add the flour.

1 3/4 cups all-purpose flour
2 teaspoons baking powder
1/2 teaspoon salt
8 tablespoons (1 stick) unsalted butter, softened
1 1/3 cups sugar
2 large eggs
1 teaspoon vanilla extract
1/4 teaspoon almond extract
2–3 tablespoons almond paste
20 Italian plums, halved vertically and pitted

Heat the oven to 375 degrees, and butter a 10-inch springform pan.

Sift the flour, baking powder, and salt into a bowl and give it a stir or two with a fork.

Cut the butter into a few pieces, and beat it (in a mixer bowl or other large bowl) with an electric mixer until smooth. Still beating, pour in 1 cup sugar and beat until the butter and sugar are very light. This will take a few minutes. Add 1 egg and beat for 30 seconds or so. Scrape the bowl, add the other egg, and beat for at least 1 minute. Add both extracts and mix. Pour in the flour, mixing it in on low so you don't have flour flying all over the kitchen, then up the speed of the mixer and beat the batter for about 30 seconds.

Scrape the batter into the springform pan and spread it out evenly. Crumble the almond paste and scatter it as evenly as you can over the top. Arrange the plums on top in concentric circles—you will likely end up with two circles and a space in the middle to cram the rest of the plums into—pushing them into the batter and alternating skin up, skin down.

Bake the cake for about 40 minutes, until the juices from the plums are bubbling. Take it out of the oven and immediately sprinkle with the remaining 1/3 cup sugar. Let the cake cool for 10 minutes on a rack before releasing the sides of the springform, then let it cool completely before slicing.

variation

I first learned to make this cake with peaches. You'll want about 6, quartered (no need to peel them), and you may want to up the sugar coating at the end to 1/2 cup.

rhubarb sour cherry crisp SERVES 6 OR SO

Crisps are such good, simple desserts: easy to make, and fun to experiment with. If you haven't made the conserva, you can substitute sour cherries in syrup, which you can find in some groceries and specialty stores.

FOR THE FRUIT

2 pounds rhubarb

2/3 cup bitter orange marmalade

1/2 pint Sour Cherry Conserva (page 395) or 1 cup store-bought sour cherries in light syrup

3 tablespoons cornstarch

Pinch of ground cloves

Pinch of salt

FOR THE CRUMBLE

1/2 cup sugar

3/4 cup all-purpose flour

1/2 cup oats (not the quick ones)

Pinch of salt

8 tablespoons (1 stick) unsalted butter, softened

1/2 cup sliced almonds

Heavy cream or vanilla ice cream, for serving

Heat the oven to 350 degrees, and butter a 2 1/2-quart casserole (something about 7 by 12 inches, with low sides).

FOR THE FRUIT

Wash the rhubarb and cut away any remnants of leaves. Cut into 3/4-inch lengths and drop into a mixing bowl. Chop the marmalade, so there aren't long bits of rind, and add to the bowl. Pour in the conserva, with the juice, and add the cornstarch, cloves, and salt. Toss well to get the cornstarch dissolved. Scrape the fruit into the casserole.

FOR THE CRUMBLE

Stir the sugar, flour, oats, and salt together in a bowl. Add the butter and work it with your fingers, pinching and rubbing, until it is completely incorporated and the crumble holds together when you pick up a handful and squeeze it. Toss in the almonds.

Pick up a handful of the crumble and squeeze it, then break it into larger and smaller bits over the fruit. Continue until you've used up all the crumble and covered the fruit completely.

Bake for about 45 minutes, until the fruit is bubbling merrily and the crumble is lightly browned. Best served warm, with cream or ice cream.

blueberry buckle MAKES ONE 8-INCH CAKE

Buckle is a good word, isn't it? And what this is, is a giant and tender muffin, bursting with blueberries and topped with gently spiced crumbs. If you can find tiny wild blueberries, by all means use them.

The photo is on page 410.

FOR THE CRUMBS

3/4 cup all-purpose flour

1/3 cup sugar

1/2 teaspoon ground cinnamon

1/4 teaspoon ground ginger

Pinch of salt

6 tablespoons (3/4 stick) unsalted butter, softened

FOR THE CAKE

8 tablespoons (1 stick) unsalted butter, softened

1 cup sugar

2 large eggs

2 cups plus 2 tablespoons all-purpose flour

1 teaspoon baking powder

1 teaspoon baking soda

1/2 teaspoon salt

1/2 cup sour cream

1 teaspoon vanilla extract

1 pint blueberries, picked over, washed, and dried on paper towels

Heat the oven to 350 degrees. Butter an 8-inch springform pan and line the bottom with parchment (blueberries stain).

FOR THE CRUMBS

Stir the flour, sugar, spices, and salt together in a bowl. Add the butter and work it with your fingers, pinching and rubbing, until it is completely incorporated and the crumbs hold together when you pick up a handful and squeeze it.

FOR THE CAKE

Cut the butter into pieces and drop them into a large bowl. Beat with an electric mixer for a minute or two, until light. With the mixer running, pour in the sugar and continue to beat until very light and fluffy. Add the eggs and beat well.

Combine the 2 cups flour, baking powder and soda, and salt in a bowl. Whisk well to distribute the leavenings. With the mixer on low, mix in a third of the flour, then half of the sour cream, then another third of the flour and the rest of the sour cream. Mix in the remaining flour and the vanilla, turn the mixer to medium-high, and beat for about 30 seconds.

Toss the blueberries with the remaining 2 tablespoons flour and fold into the batter. Scrape into the springform pan and smooth out the top.

Pick up a handful of the crumbs and squeeze, then break them into larger and smaller bits over the cake. Continue until you've used up all the crumbs and covered the cake.

Slip the cake into the oven and bake for about 1 hour and 10 minutes. The tips of the crumbs and any exposed crust should be golden brown, and a cake tester should come out clean, though a crumb or two is fine.

Let cool on a rack. When the buckle is cool enough to handle, release the sides of the springform. Lift the buckle up off the base and peel off the parchment. You need to balance the cake in your hand and juggle it a bit, but that should not be a problem. Serve warm or at room temperature.

blueberries and cream SERVES 4

Sure, you can just pour some cream over blueberries and call it dessert. But macerating the berries for a while turns it into something special. If you can find tiny wild blueberries, buy them.

1 pint blueberries

2 tablespoons sugar

1 teaspoon chopped fresh lemon thyme (or regular thyme and a pinch of grated lemon zest)

Freshly ground white pepper

Heavy cream or strawberry ice cream, homemade (page 452) or store-bought

Toss the blueberries, sugar, and thyme with a few grinds of white pepper. Refrigerate for at least 2 hours.

When dessert time rolls around, divide the berries among four bowls and serve with a pitcher of cream. Or spoon the berries over scoops of ice cream.

free-form italian plum tart MAKES ONE 12-INCH TART

Free-form tarts are the easiest of all pastries: no trying to fit the dough into a pie plate, seeing it break, and patching it together, and no worrying about making a top crust and crimping it or, if you dare—gasp—attempting a lattice. You roll the dough out into something that more or less resembles a circle, slide it onto a baking sheet, add fruit and sugar and some butter, and fold back the edges of the dough. Then you bake it. It happens fast, so you could even think about making one of these for a weeknight dinner.

Since this tart is eminently adaptable to what might be in season, I've given a couple of variations.

FOR THE PASTRY

1 cup all-purpose flour

2 tablespoons sugar

Grated zest of 1 small lemon

Salt

8 tablespoons (1 stick) cold unsalted butter

1–2 tablespoons ice water

FOR THE FRUIT

20 or so Italian plums

Scant 1/2 cup sugar—Vanilla Sugar (page 22) if you have it

2 tablespoons unsalted butter

FOR THE PASTRY

Toss the flour, sugar, zest, and a pinch of salt together in a bowl, or stir with a fork. Unwrap the butter and drop it into the flour to coat it, then pick it up and cut it into bits. Work the flour into the butter with your fingers, two knives, or a pastry cutter until it looks like coarse oatmeal, with a few bigger bits of butter still left. Stir in the cold water with a fork until the pastry comes together.

Form the dough into a disk (or an oval or a rectangle—this is a free-form tart, remember), keeping in mind that it will be easier to roll out a circle if you start with a circle. Pat the ragged edges of the dough in with your palms, since you've got a better chance of ending up with a smooth edge if you start with one. Wrap the disk in plastic wrap or wax paper and pop it into the refrigerator for about 30 minutes.

Halve and pit the plums while the pastry rests. Heat the oven to 350 degrees, and line a baking sheet with parchment paper.

Roll the dough out on a floured counter to a circle that's about 14 inches in diameter—or an equivalent oval or rectangle. Slide the pastry onto the baking sheet. Arrange the plums cut side down on the pastry, leaving a margin of a couple of inches. Sprinkle with the ½ cup sugar and dot with the butter. Fold the pastry edge back over the fruit as neatly as you care to.

Bake for about 40 minutes, until the fruit is bubbling and the pastry is golden. Serve it warm.

variations

apple tart

Peel, core, and slice 3 Granny Smith apples very thin. Arrange them neatly, following the shape of your pastry. Use the same amount of sugar and butter. If you want, glaze the fruit with warmed apricot jelly when the tart comes out of the oven.

peach tart

Peel 4 peaches and cut them into chunks. If you have very juicy, really ripe peaches, toss three-quarters of them with 1 tablespoon instant tapioca. Use the other chunks for the top of the tart. Pile the fruit onto the pastry, leaving a bigger margin, 4 inches this time. Use the same amount of sugar and butter, but you might want a pinch of ground cloves in the sugar. Let this tart sit for a couple of hours before cutting, because the fruit is so juicy and you want the juices to be reabsorbed.

pear tart

Peel and core 4 Bosc pears. Cut them into chunks and sauté them in 2 tablespoons butter over medium-high heat. Stir in 1/4 cup sugar or vanilla sugar (page 00). If the pears are truly ripe, they will start giving up their juices pretty quickly. They are ready when they have started to brown and the juices have thickened a bit. Let the pears cool for a few minutes before you pile them onto the pastry. Squeeze 1/2 a lemon over the fruit and sprinkle with another 1/4 cup sugar. You can brush the baked tart with warmed apricot jelly if you want.

marmalade crostata MAKES ONE 9-INCH TART

The pasta frolla for this Italian tart is a cookie-type pastry that is very easy to work with—yes, you *can* make a lattice. A crostata is never overfilled, so you have a good balance of fruit and pastry. And this is the kind of tart you can make with what you have around the house. Marmalade is traditional (pink grapefruit marmalade, which you can get from Stonewall Kitchen, is terrific), but I also make it with Sour Cherry Conserva or Honeyed Quince (see the variations).

FOR THE PASTA FROLLA

2 cups all-purpose flour

1/2 cup sugar

Salt

14 tablespoons (1 3/4 sticks) cold unsalted butter, cut into pieces

1 large egg

1 teaspoon vanilla extract

FOR THE FILLING

1 (12- or 13-ounce) jar Seville orange marmalade

1 large egg, beaten with 1 tablespoon water for an egg wash

FOR THE PASTA FROLLA

Put the flour, sugar, a pinch of salt, and the butter in a food processor. Pulse 6 or 7 times, then process for about 10 seconds. The mixture should be sandy, the texture of cornmeal. Add the egg and vanilla, pulse a few times, and then process until the dough forms a ball. You may need to alternate between processing and pulsing, but keep going: let the machine do its work.

Dump the dough out on a lightly floured counter, and knead in any stray bits. Divide into 2 pieces, one slightly larger than the other. Roll the larger piece into a 10- to 11-inch circle and fit it into a

9-inch tart pan with a removable bottom. Roll the second piece of pastry into a 10-inch circle, and cut into 10 strips. If you have problems rolling the pastry, wrap in plastic wrap or cover it and refrigerate it for 20 minutes or so.

Heat the oven to 350 degrees.

FOR THE FILLING

Spoon the marmalade out onto a cutting board and chop up the long pieces of rind. Scrape it into the tart shell and spread out evenly. Make a simple lattice top, arranging 5 strips running top to bottom across the filling and the other 5 strips running side to side. Pinch off all the bits of pastry that are straying over the edge of the tart pan. Brush the pastry with the egg wash.

Bake for 40 to 45 minutes. The crostata should be a deep golden brown, and the fruit should be bubbling. Don't wimp out and take it out of the oven too soon. Let the crostata sit for an hour before serving.

variations

Use a pint of Honeyed Quince (page 393), a pint of Sour Cherry Conserva (page 395), or a 16-ounce jar of sour cherries in light sugar syrup in place of the marmalade. If using the sour cherries, drain the cherries first, reserving the syrup, and then spoon 3 tablespoons of the syrup into the tart with the cherries.

With any of these, it's nice to strew the lattice with 1/3 cup sliced almonds before you bake.

lemon tart with almond pastry

MAKES ONE 9-INCH TART

The almonds in this pastry add a tasty crunch. If you can find them, use Meyer lemons for the curd, because they're so aromatic and sweet—for a lemon, that is. But don't fret if you can't; the curd will just be a bit more tart with regular lemons. And tart is good.

FOR THE LEMON CURD

- 2 large eggs
- 3 large egg yolks
- 1/3 cup sugar
- Pinch of salt
- Grated zest of 2 lemons
- 1/2 cup fresh lemon juice (from about 3 lemons)
- 6 tablespoons (3/4 stick) unsalted butter, cut into pieces

FOR THE PASTRY

- 1 cup all-purpose flour
- 2 tablespoons sugar
- Pinch of salt
- 8 tablespoons (1 stick) cold unsalted butter
- 1/3 cup sliced almonds
- 1 large egg yolk
- 1–2 tablespoons ice water

FOR THE LEMON CURD

Have ready a bowl set in a larger bowl filled with ice. Whisk the eggs, yolks, sugar, and salt in a saucepan. Stir in the lemon zest and juice and the butter. The mixture may look curdled right now; not to worry. Stir the curd constantly over medium heat. The butter will melt; the curd will start looking much prettier, and it will soon thicken and coat the back of the spoon (see page 407; take the pan off the heat when you check for this). Scrape the curd into the bowl set on ice to stop the cooking. It can sit there while you make the pastry.

FOR THE PASTRY

Whisk the flour, sugar, and salt together in a bowl. Drop the butter into the flour to coat it, then pick it up and cut it into small pieces. Cut the butter into the flour with your fingers or a pastry blender until the mixture resembles coarse oatmeal. Toss in the almonds, then toss in the yolk and stir with a fork, making sure to distribute the yolk throughout the pastry. Add the ice water by the tablespoon until the pastry comes together (it will clean the sides of the bowl). Gather the pastry into a ball (firmly, so you crush some of the almond slices in the process), then put it on a floured work surface and form it into a disk with neat sides.

Roll the pastry out into a 12-inch circle and fit it into a 9-inch tart pan with a removable bottom. Trim the overhang. Line the pastry with heavy-duty foil and put it in the refrigerator for 20 minutes or so.

Heat the oven to 350 degrees.

Bake the pastry, still lined with foil, for 15 minutes. Remove the foil and continue to bake the pastry until it is a rich, toasty brown and fully cooked. This should take 15 to 18 minutes.

Let the pastry cool on a rack for 10 minutes (leave the oven on), then fill it with the curd. Slide it back into the oven for 20 minutes, or until the curd is glossy and set. Let the tart cool completely on a rack before taking it out of the pan and serving.

Some people might serve this with whipped cream. I don't.

applesauce apple tart MAKES ONE 9-INCH TART

I first came across a tart like this when I was working with Martha on her *Martha Stewart Cookbook*. I fell in love with the idea: applesauce and very thinly sliced apples in buttery pastry—a combination of creamy and crisp. It's so beautiful.

The photo is on page 412.

FOR THE PASTRY

- 1 cup all-purpose flour
- 2 tablespoons sugar
- Grated zest of 1 small lemon
- Salt
- 8 tablespoons (1 stick) cold unsalted butter
- 1–2 tablespoons ice water

FOR THE FILLING AND GLAZE

- 1 tablespoon unsalted butter
- 3 tablespoons sugar
- 2 tablespoons Calvados or cognac
- 1 cup Pink Applesauce (page 417)
- 1/4 cup red currant jelly (or black currant or seedless raspberry)
- 1 tablespoon water
- 2 Rome apples (or Cortland or Ida Red)

FOR THE PASTRY

Whisk the flour, sugar, zest, and a pinch of salt together in a bowl, or stir with a fork. Unwrap the butter and drop it into the flour to coat it, then pick it up and cut it into bits. Work the flour into the butter with your fingers, two knives, or a pastry cutter until it looks like coarse oatmeal, with a few bigger bits of butter still left. Stir in the ice water with a fork until the pastry comes together.

Form the dough into a flat disk with very neat sides. (Remember when you form the disk that it will be easier to roll out a circle if you start with a circle.)Wrap it in plastic wrap or wax paper, and pop it into the refrigerator for about 30 minutes.

Meanwhile, heat the oven to 350 degrees and start the filling.

FOR THE FILLING AND GLAZE

Melt the butter in a small saucepan or skillet over medium-high heat. Stir in the sugar. When the sugar has melted and bubbled up, pour in the Calvados. Stir in the applesauce and take the pan off the heat.

In another small pan, heat the jelly and water, stirring until the jelly is melted and smooth, for a glaze.

Roll the dough out on a floured counter to a circle that's about 12 inches in diameter. Fit the pastry into a 9-inch tart pan with a removable bottom. Run your rolling pin over the tart pan to cut off the excess pastry. Press a piece of heavy-duty foil into the pan, tight against the pastry. If you want, add some pie weights, but I have to tell you that I've never needed them with this pastry. Bake for 15 minutes.

Remove the foil and slide the pastry back into the oven. Bake for another 15 minutes or so, until the pastry is fully cooked and toasty brown. Let cool on a rack.

You can finish the tart now and serve it at room temperature, or wait until the last minute and then serve it hot.

Heat the oven to 400 degrees.

Cut the apples in half, through the stem. Cut out the cores neatly—a melon baller is useful. Slice the apples impossibly thin on a mandoline so each half-moon has a rim of peel.

Spread the applesauce over the bottom of the pastry. Arrange the apple slices on top in concentric circles. Slide the tart into the oven and bake for 10 to 12 minutes—just to warm the apples through.

Brush the red currant glaze over the apples (you may not need all of it) and run the tart under the broiler for 1 minute. It's best eaten the day it is made.

chocolate whipped cream cake MAKES ONE 8-INCH LAYER CAKE

Imagine the best Yankee Doodle possible. Imagine one of the easiest cakes possible. No creaming butter and sugar: just whip cream, add eggs and the dry ingredients, and you've got cake!

The photo is on page 414.

$1\frac{1}{4}$ cups cake flour

$\frac{1}{3}$ cup Dutch-processed cocoa

2 teaspoons baking soda

$\frac{1}{4}$ teaspoon salt

2 cups heavy cream

$\frac{1}{2}$ teaspoon instant espresso powder

2 large eggs

1 cup sugar

2 tablespoons honey

1 teaspoon vanilla extract

Heat the oven to 375 degrees. Butter two 8-inch round cake pans and line the bottoms with parchment.

Whisk the flour, cocoa, baking soda, and salt in a small bowl.

Pour 1 cup of the cream into a mixing bowl, add the espresso powder, and beat to stiff peaks with an electric mixer. Beat in the eggs one at a time. Beat in the sugar and honey. Whisk in the dry ingredients until just combined and smooth. Stir in the vanilla.

Divide the batter between the baking pans, and give the pans a rap on the counter to release any air bubbles. Bake the cakes for 20 to 25 minutes, until a cake tester comes out with just a crumb or two.

Let the cakes cool in the pans on racks for 10 minutes or so; they'll fall a little (don't worry about it). Then turn the cakes out of the pans, peel off the parchment, and let cool completely on the racks.

Whip the remaining 1 cup cream to stiff peaks. Put one of the cake layers on a serving plate. Spread with half the whipped cream. Top with the other layer and the rest of the whipped cream. Refrigerate until you're ready to serve the cake. I think this cake is best eaten within a day.

Note: If you've got some cherries preserved in brandy hanging around, spoon some of the brandy over the cake before you spread on the whipped cream, and top each layer with some of the cherries.

grandma's chocolate cake MAKES ONE 9-INCH LAYER CAKE

This is the chocolate cake I grew up with, and woe to me if I turn up at any family gathering without it.

My mother contributed the recipe (which came from her mom, Anne Gorman) to a community cookbook. Her headnote said, simply, "Sweet and moist."

FOR THE CAKE

8 tablespoons (1 stick) unsalted butter

4 ounces unsweetened chocolate

2 cups all-purpose flour

1/4 teaspoon salt

1 1/2 teaspoons baking soda

1 2/3 cups milk, at room temperature

2 large eggs, at room temperature

1 3/4 cups sugar

2 teaspoons vanilla extract

FOR THE FROSTING

8 tablespoons (1 stick) unsalted butter, very soft but not at all oily

3 cups confectioners' sugar

1/2 cup unsweetened cocoa

Pinch of salt

3/4–1 cup heavy cream

FOR THE CAKE

Heat the oven to 350 degrees. Butter two 9-inch round cake pans and dust them with cocoa.

Put the butter and chocolate in a heatproof bowl over a pot of just-simmering water to melt.

Stir the flour and salt together. Dissolve the baking soda in the milk.

Crack the eggs into a large bowl and beat them with an electric mixer until they lighten in color. Pour in the sugar gradually, beating all the while, and beat until very light and fluffy. Stir the butter and chocolate together, and pour into the eggs. Yes, the chocolate should still be warm. Beat, and scrape the bowl to make sure you've mixed the chocolate in evenly.

Whisk in about one third of the flour, and then half the milk; then another third of the flour and the rest of the milk. Finish with the remaining flour and the vanilla. Don't beat the batter, just whisk to get rid of any lumps. The batter will be pretty thin.

Pour the batter into the pans, and give the pans a whack on the counter to release any air bubbles. Bake for 25 to 30 minutes, until a tester comes out clean, or with just a crumb or two. Let cool for 5 minutes on racks, then turn the layers out of the pans and let cool completely on the racks.

FOR THE FROSTING

Put the butter in a large bowl and beat it with the mixer until it's lightened. Put the confectioners' sugar, cocoa, and salt in a strainer over the bowl and beat the sugar in. Here's the drill: First the sugar flies out of the bowl, then as you beat, the frosting will start to darken. Keep beating, and you will end up with a dark chocolate mass. And that's what you want. Scrape the bowl and pour in about ¼ cup of the cream. Beat well on high speed. Another ¼ cup cream, and beat again. Repeat with another ¼ cup cream. Beat in enough of the remaining cream to make the frosting creamy and spreadable.

Frost the cake and make some swirls in the frosting so the cake looks pretty.

five-spice angel food cake MAKES ONE 10-INCH CAKE

Time was when my nephew David Finamore Rossler craved chocolate cake. He's moved on and now requests angel food cake for his birthday. To tell the truth, he asks for this cake for everyone's birthday.

The photo is on page 415.

FOR THE CAKE

1 cup cake flour

1 1/2 cups superfine sugar

1 teaspoon Chinese five-spice powder

A few gratings of nutmeg

1 1/2 cups egg whites (from 11–12 large eggs), at room temperature

1/4 teaspoon salt

1 1/2 teaspoons cream of tartar

1/2 teaspoon vanilla extract

FOR THE GLAZE

1 cup confectioners' sugar

1/3 cup maple syrup

1 teaspoon vanilla extract

Pinch of salt

FOR THE CAKE

Heat the oven to 350 degrees.

Sift the flour together with 1/2 cup of the sugar, the five-spice powder, and nutmeg, then repeat—sift a total of 4 times to aerate the flour.

Beat the egg whites in a large bowl with an electric mixer at medium-low speed until frothy. Add the salt and cream of tartar and beat at medium-high until soft peaks form. While beating, gradually add the remaining 1 cup sugar, in a slow, steady stream. Once you have all the sugar in, increase the speed to high and beat until the whites are glossy and form stiff peaks. Whisk in the vanilla.

If you've been using a standing mixer, transfer the whites to a larger bowl. Sift half the flour mixture over the whites and fold it in gently. Sift the rest of the flour on top and fold it in gently but thoroughly.

Spoon the batter into an ungreased 10-inch tube pan and jiggle the pan to settle the batter. Smooth the top and slip the pan into the oven. Bake for 30 to 35 minutes, until the top is lightly browned.

Invert the pan (onto a bottle, if your pan doesn't have legs), and let cool completely.

Run a knife around the edge of the pan and along the tube and pull the insert out. Carefully release the cake from the bottom of the insert and slide it off. Set the cake, bottom side up, on a pedestal stand if you've got one.

FOR THE GLAZE

Put all the ingredients into a bowl. Beat with a fork until smooth.

Spoon the glaze onto the top of the cake and spread it to the edges with a knife or a small offset spatula. If it hasn't started to drip down the sides on its own, nudge the glaze in a few places with the knife.

Angel cakes should be cut with serrated knives, with a sawing motion. Otherwise, they get smooshed.

variation

Lemon is another fine flavoring for angel cake. Replace the five-spice and nutmeg with the grated zest of 1 lemon and add 1/4 teaspoon lemon extract along with the vanilla. Make a glaze with 1 cup confectioners' sugar and the grated zest and juice of 1 lemon.

walnutty torte with mocha cream

MAKES ONE 8-INCH LAYER CAKE

You'll notice that there's no sugar in the cream topping. But the torte is sweet, and the combination of cake and cream is hard to beat.

You'll need to plan ahead when you make this cake. It's best when it has sat in the refrigerator for at least 12 hours.

FOR THE CAKE

1/2 pound (2 cups) walnuts

1 cup sugar

6 large eggs, separated

1/2 teaspoon salt

FOR THE CREAM

1 cup heavy cream

1 tablespoon instant espresso powder

2 teaspoons unsweetened cocoa

FOR THE CAKE

Heat the oven to 350 degrees. Butter and flour two 8-by-2-inch round cake pans.

Spread the walnuts out on a baking sheet and toast them in the oven for 10 to 15 minutes, shaking the pan once or twice, until fragrant. Pour the nuts out onto a plate and let them cool completely. (Leave the oven on.)

Drop the nuts into a food processor and pour in 1/4 cup of the sugar. Pulse and process the nuts until you have a fine meal.

Beat the egg yolks and the remaining 3/4 cup sugar in a large bowl with an electric mixer until very light and tripled in volume. When you lift the beaters from the yolks, the yolks should make a ribbon as they drizzle from the beaters. Fold in the nuts.

Beat the whites in another large bowl (with clean beaters) at medium-low speed until frothy. Add the salt and continue beating at medium-high speed until stiff peaks form. Fold about one third of the whites into the batter to loosen it up, then fold in the rest of the whites gently but thoroughly.

Scrape the batter out into the two pans. Give the pans a gentle rap on the counter to release any air pockets. Bake for 20 minutes, or until the tops are an even light brown and the layers spring back when you tap them gently in the center.

Let the cakes cool completely on racks. They'll collapse some as they cool.

FOR THE CREAM

Pour the cream into a chilled bowl and add the espresso powder and cocoa. Beat the cream to stiff peaks.

Place one torte layer on a cake plate and spoon half the cream on the top—not the sides. Cover with the second layer and top with the rest of the cream. Cover loosely with foil and refrigerate for 12 to 24 hours before serving.

coriander shortbread fans MAKES 24 COOKIES

This tender, buttery shortbread is gently perfumed with coriander and caraway. Wrap a fan in a piece of wax paper and bring it to work for an 11 o'clock treat.

The photo is on page 413.

1¾ cups all-purpose flour

½ cup cornstarch

½ cup sugar

1 teaspoon ground coriander

¾ teaspoon caraway seeds, crushed

Coarse salt

½ pound (2 sticks) unsalted butter

Line a baking sheet with parchment. Whisk the flour, cornstarch, sugar, coriander, caraway, and a pinch of salt together in a mixing bowl.

Cut each stick of butter into 4 pieces. Smash each piece on your counter or a big cutting board with the heel of your hand, flattening it out. Gather it up with a dough scraper and smash it again. Your goal is to make the butter pliable and smooth, so you can work it into the flour quickly and evenly, but leave it still cool and not greasy. As you finish smashing each piece of butter, scrape it up and drop it into the mixing bowl.

Use your fingers to work the flour and butter together, pinching and tossing until you've distributed the flour through the butter, then knead the dough in the bowl until it comes together and cleans the sides of the bowl. Don't overdo it with the kneading—you'll end up with tough cookies. Work the dough just enough for it to come together.

Form the dough into 3 balls. Flatten each ball into a 5-inch round on a piece of parchment. Use the knife edge of your hand (under the pinkie) to push in the edges of the round to tidy them up, and flatten the round with your palm. Then lift up the parchment, flip the round into your palm, peel off the parchment, and set the round on the baking sheet. Use a fork to make a decorative pattern around the edges of the rounds. If the dough cracks under the fork, pat it back in and mark it again with the fork.

Slide the baking sheet into the refrigerator—no need to cover—and chill the dough for 30 minutes

Heat the oven to 300 degrees.

Bake the shortbread until it's the palest gold, 40 to 45 minutes. Set the baking sheet on a cooling rack and immediately cut each round into 8 wedges. Let cool completely, still on the baking sheet, on the rack.

Store the cookies in an airtight container.

chocolate pudding SERVES 6

Just what pudding should be: creamy, cool, and chocolatey.

3 cups milk

1 cup heavy cream

4 large egg yolks

1/4 cup cornstarch

2 tablespoons unsweetened cocoa

Fine sea salt

6 ounces Lindt bittersweet chocolate, chopped fine, or 6 ounces (1 cup) of the best chocolate chips

2 tablespoons unsalted butter, softened

1 teaspoon vanilla extract

Pour the milk and cream into a saucepan and bring to a simmer over medium heat.

While the milk heats, whisk the yolks in a large bowl until they're light. Add the cornstarch, cocoa, and a pinch of salt, and whisk. This will be pretty stiff.

Once the milk is simmering, pour about a cup of it into the yolks, whisking constantly. Pour in the rest of the milk, whisk, then pour it all back into the saucepan. Whisk constantly until the mixture thickens and comes just to a boil—one or two big bubbles. Turn off the heat and add the chocolate. Whisk to melt the chocolate, then get out a rubber scraper and get into the corners of the pan, making sure you don't have any streaks of white left. Whisk in the butter and vanilla until the butter melts.

Pour the pudding into a large bowl, or into six small ones—custard cups, footed dessert bowls, that kind of thing. Chill for at least an hour before serving. If you have some aversion to skin, press plastic wrap on the surface of the pudding before chilling.

rice pudding SERVES 6

Little rivers of preserves make this very creamy pudding look almost like stained glass. Choose a preserve that has pieces of fruit in it, something like sour cherry or fig.

3/4 cup Arborio rice

1 quart milk

1 vanilla bean

1/2 cup sugar

3 large egg yolks

About 1/2 cup preserves (see headnote)

Wash the rice until the water runs clear (see page 300).

Pour the milk into a large heavy saucepan. Cut the vanilla bean lengthwise in half with a paring knife and scrape the sticky seeds out with the back of the knife. Add the seeds and the bean to the milk (don't worry that the seeds are clumped; they'll break up as you cook), along with the rice and sugar.

Bring the milk to a boil, then reduce the heat to as low as possible, cover the pan, and simmer the rice until it's very tender, say 25 minutes. The rice should be pretty soupy. Remove from the heat and pull out the vanilla bean.

Beat the yolks in a small bowl, then add them to the rice, stirring until the pudding thickens a little.

Spoon the pudding into six dessert bowls and add a very generous tablespoon of preserves to each bowl. Swirl the preserves through the pudding with the spoon handle or a chopstick. Cover the bowls with plastic wrap and let them cool down.

Serve the pudding at room temperature or chilled.

vanilla ice cream MAKES ABOUT 1 QUART

Fancy ice creams are all well and good, but sometimes I've got a craving for plain old vanilla. Simple pleasures are the best.

By the way, if you have stainless steel metal bowls, use them here. They are particularly good when you want to chill something down quickly, as you do with this technique.

2 1/2 cups heavy cream

1 cup milk

2/3 cup sugar—Vanilla Sugar (page 22) if you have it

1 vanilla bean

6 large egg yolks

Coarse salt

Combine the cream, milk, and sugar in a saucepan. Slit the vanilla bean in half the long way and scrape out the sticky seeds. Add the seeds and bean to the saucepan and turn the heat to high. Bring to a simmer, then turn off the heat. Let this infuse for 15 minutes.

Meanwhile, whisk the yolks in a large bowl. Fill another large bowl with ice and nestle a smaller bowl in it. And take out a strainer.

Once the cream has infused, take out the bean and bring the cream to a full, rolling boil. Pour the boiling cream into the yolks, whisking vigorously for at least 1 minute, then pour the custard through the strainer into the bowl set over the ice. Stir in a pinch of salt, and leave the custard to cool completely, stirring occasionally.

Freeze according to the instructions for your ice cream maker, then transfer to a plastic container and let the ice cream cure in the freezer for 2 hours before serving.

Note: Don't throw that vanilla bean away. Rinse it, let it dry completely, and use it for vanilla sugar. Or add it to your bottle of homemade extract, if you have one going.

variations

This ice cream adapts itself very happily to the flavors of other spices. Go on, experiment.

cardamom ice cream

Crush 1/4 cup cardamom pods in a mortar. Don't obsess: you just want to crack the pods open to release the tiny seeds. Add the pods and seeds to the cream, milk, and sugar, and infuse the cream with them instead of the vanilla bean. Strain out the seeds and pods, bring the cream to a full, rolling boil, and proceed with the recipe. Stir in 1/2 teaspoon vanilla extract with the salt.

white pepper ice cream

Add 1 to 1 1/2 teaspoons white pepper—freshly and finely ground—to the cream, milk, and sugar along with the vanilla bean for infusing. Or, if you don't have a vanilla bean, just bring the cream, milk, sugar, and pepper to a rolling boil and proceed with the recipe. Stir in 1 teaspoon vanilla extract with the salt.

ginger ice cream

Cut a 4-inch piece of ginger into coins and smash them with the flat of a chef's knife. Add the ginger to the cream and milk and bring to a simmer, then turn off the heat, cover, and let infuse for 30 minutes. Remove the ginger, squeezing it over the milk to get out all the juices, then add the sugar and proceed with the recipe. Stir in 1 teaspoon vanilla extract and 1/4 cup chopped crystallized ginger before freezing.

crème fraîche ice cream MAKES ABOUT 1 QUART

I learned this incredibly easy technique for making an ice cream base from Karen De Masco, the talented and delightful pastry chef at Craft restaurant in New York City. You can substitute sour cream for the crème fraîche.

This is a great foil for the flavors of Sour Cherry Conserva (page 395). I'll serve it alongside a cherry crostata. Or, if I've saved some syrup from the cherries, I'll certainly spoon some on. But it's very easy to turn this into a pretty classy fruit ice cream; see the variation.

2 cups milk

1 cup heavy cream

$^{2}/_{3}$ cup Vanilla Sugar (page 22) or regular sugar

Pinch of coarse salt

6 large egg yolks

1 cup crème fraîche (see headnote)

1 teaspoon vanilla extract

Have ready a bowl nestled in a larger bowl filled with ice. You'll need to have a strainer at hand as well.

Rinse out a saucepan with cold water (for easy cleanup) and add the milk, cream, and sugar. Bring to a full, rolling boil over medium-high heat, stirring early on to dissolve the sugar. Meanwhile, whisk the yolks in a large bowl.

Once the milk is boiling, pour it in a stream into the yolks, whisking constantly. Continue to whisk for at least 1 minute. Strain the base into the bowl nestled in ice. Whisk in the crème fraîche and vanilla extract and let this cool completely, whisking once in a while.

Freeze following the instructions for your ice cream maker. When the ice cream is finished, transfer it to a plastic container and put it in the freezer for a few hours to cure before serving.

variation

sour cherry ice cream

Drain a pint of Sour Cherry Conserva (page 395)—save the syrup for drizzling—and chill the cherries while you make and chill the base. Fold the cherries into the ice cream after it comes out of the ice cream maker and freeze for at least 3 hours before serving.

strawberry ice cream MAKES ABOUT 1½ PINTS

Philadelphia-style ice cream, which has no eggs, is clean and fresh tasting, and it highlights the flavors of berries. If you can find heavy cream that hasn't been ultrapasteurized, use it here. It has the best flavor.

1 pint strawberries

⅔ cup sugar

1 teaspoon molasses

½ teaspoon balsamic vinegar

Freshly ground black pepper

2 cups heavy cream

1 teaspoon vanilla extract

Coarse salt

Hull the strawberries and cut them in half. Drop them in a food processor, along with the sugar, molasses, vinegar, and a few grinds of black pepper. Process, stopping to scrape down the sides once or twice, until you have a completely smooth puree.

Scrape the puree into a large pitcher and add the cream, vanilla, and a pinch of salt. Stir well, cover with plastic wrap, and refrigerate for at least 2 hours. You can make the ice cream base a day or two ahead.

Freeze in an ice cream maker according to the manufacturer's instructions. Pack into a plastic tub and freeze for at least 2 hours before serving.

variations

blackberry ice cream

Replace the strawberries with 2 (6-ounce) baskets of blackberries. Process the berries with 2/3 cup sugar, 1/2 teaspoon vanilla extract, a pinch of salt, and a few grinds of black pepper.

raspberry ice cream

Replace the strawberries with 2 (6-ounce) baskets of raspberries. Process them with 2/3 cup sugar, 1/2 teaspoon balsamic vinegar, and a pinch of salt.

ice cream sandwiches

I fell in love with Sicily the day I found out about ice cream sandwiches for breakfast. Street vendors in Palermo split open a small brioche, fill it with the gelato of your choice, wrap it in a small piece of wax paper, and send you on your way. You stroll and eat, or sit and eat, and then stop someplace for a coffee.

From that point on, I became a fan of a sandwichy ice cream sandwich, one made with bread instead of cookies.

You need brioche baked as a loaf, but you could easily use challah instead. Cut thickish slices and toast them lightly. Spread one slice with butter, another slice with jam, and then fill with slightly softened ice cream (barely soft enough to spread, or it will leak out of your sandwich), about 1/2 cup per sandwich. Have fun mixing and matching flavors of jam and ice cream. Red currant jelly and peach ice cream. Raspberry jam and Crème Fraîche Ice Cream. You might even want to drizzle Ginger Ice Cream with chocolate sauce for that sandwich.

Wrap the sandwiches snugly in plastic and freeze for a few hours. When you're ready to serve them, unwrap and cut each sandwich in half on the bias.

strawberry rhubarb syrup MAKES 3 CUPS

Pour this syrup over ice cream or slices of pound cake. Or serve it with pancakes, along with a plop of sour cream.

- 1 pound rhubarb, trimmed and cut into $^1/_2$- to 1-inch pieces
- 1 pint strawberries, hulled and halved
- 1$^1/_2$ cups sugar
- 1 tablespoon molasses
- 1$^1/_2$ cups fruity red wine, like a Merlot
- Pinch of coarse salt

Put all the ingredients into a saucepan and bring to a boil. Reduce the heat to low, cover partway, and simmer until the fruit is very tender, about 30 minutes.

Run the fruit and all the juices through a food mill fitted with a coarse disk.

Wipe out the saucepan and pour in the syrup. Bring to a boil and cook at an active simmer, skimming and stirring, for 5 minutes to thicken and reduce it slightly.

Let cool, then store in the refrigerator in glass jars for up to a month.

mango ice cream with caramelized mango

MAKES ABOUT 1 QUART

You could make this creamy eggless Philadelphia-style ice cream without the caramelized mango, but it's so much better with.

FOR THE ICE CREAM

2 ripe mangoes, peeled, pitted, and chopped coarse

Grated zest and juice of 1 lime

1/2 cup sugar

1 tablespoon molasses

Pinch of coarse salt

2 cups heavy cream

FOR THE CARAMELIZED MANGO

1/3 cup sugar

1 mango, peeled, pitted, and cut into large dice

FOR THE ICE CREAM

Process the mangoes in a food processor until you've made a smooth puree. Add the lime zest and juice, the sugar, molasses, and salt. Process for a minute or so to dissolve the sugar. Scrape the puree out into a pitcher or bowl, whisk in the cream, cover, and refrigerate for at least 8 hours.

FOR THE CARAMELIZED MANGO

Pour the sugar into a heavy medium skillet. Cook over medium heat, swirling the sugar around in the pan often, until it is dark amber. Add the diced mango. The caramel will sputter and seize up. Don't worry. Cook, stirring, just until the caramel dissolves. Scrape the mango into a bowl, cover, and chill thoroughly.

Freeze the ice cream base according to the instructions for your ice cream maker. When it's just about frozen, stir in the caramelized mango. Chances are the ice cream will melt some; just keep freezing it until it's firm again. Transfer to a plastic container, and let the ice cream cure in the freezer for at least 2 hours before serving.

pineapple orange sherbet with pan-roasted pineapple

SERVES 6

Sherbets are very easy to make. And serving a hybrid—sorbet mellowed by a hint of cream—hits all the right buttons.

1 large (5 pounds) pineapple

Grated zest and juice of 1 orange

1 cup plain yogurt

1 cup Simple Syrup (page 460)

Coarse salt

3 tablespoons unsalted butter

2 tablespoons honey

Cut the top and bottom off the pineapple. Slice off the peel, and cut out the eyes. Cut the pineapple lengthwise into quarters and cut out the core. Cut 1½ of the wedges into chunks. Reserve the rest of the pineapple for pan-roasting.

Puree the chunks in batches in a food processor. Work the puree through a coarse sieve into a large measuring cup or bowl; you need 2 cups of puree. Whisk in the orange zest and juice, the yogurt, and simple syrup. Add a pinch of salt. Cover and put in the refrigerator to chill for an hour or so.

Freeze the sherbet according to the instructions that came with your ice cream maker. Transfer the sherbet to a plastic container and put it in the freezer for at least 2 hours before serving.

Cut the remaining pineapple into long slices about ⅓ inch thick. Cut across the slices to make wedges or batons about ⅓ inch wide.

Heat a large skillet over high heat. Add the butter, and when it stops sizzling, add the pineapple. The pineapple will get very juicy as it cooks. Stir often, and when the juices thicken, add the honey. Continue cooking and stirring until the pineapple starts to brown. This entire process will take about 10 minutes.

Let the pineapple cool for about 15 minutes, so it's not piping hot when you serve it. You can also make it in advance and serve it at room temperature.

Serve the sherbet in bowls, with the pan-roasted pineapple spooned on top.

grape sorbet MAKES 1 QUART

Think of the best grape Popsicle you've ever had.

Karen De Masco, the extraordinary pastry chef at Craft restaurant, taught me how to make this.

FOR THE GRAPES

3 pounds Concord grapes

¼ cup sugar

FOR THE SIMPLE SYRUP

1 cup sugar

1 cup water

FOR THE GRAPES

Wash the grapes and pull them off the stems. Toss in a bowl with the sugar, cover with plastic wrap, and let the grapes macerate for 8 hours or so.

FOR THE SIMPLE SYRUP

Combine the sugar with the water in a saucepan. Bring to a boil over medium-high heat, stirring to dissolve the sugar. Boil for a minute or so, then let the syrup cool completely (makes 1¼ cups).

Puree the grapes in 4 batches in a food processor until juicy. (If you do this in larger batches, you'll make a mess.) Don't worry about the seeds: you're processing to release them from the flesh and to chop up the skins.

Pour the grape puree into a sieve set over a bowl and work it through with a wooden spoon or rubber scraper. You will end up with about 3 cups of grape juice.

Whisk in the simple syrup and chill well.

Freeze in your ice cream maker. (It will be soft when it comes out.) Pack the sorbet into a plastic container and let it cure in the freezer for at least 2 hours to firm up before serving.

raspberry buttermilk sherbet MAKES ABOUT 1 QUART

When I was growing up, a Good Humor truck drove through our neighborhood, ringing a bell, every summer afternoon. Ice cream truck music drives me nuts now, but it certainly didn't then. My favorite was raspberry sherbet on a stick. Here's my tribute.

The photo is on page 416.

4 (6-ounce) baskets raspberries
1¼ cups buttermilk
1¼ cups Simple Syrup (page 460)
1 teaspoon fresh lemon juice
Pinch of salt

Whir the raspberries in a food processor until you have a loose slush. Pass the slush through a strainer set over a bowl, working with a wooden spoon or rubber scraper to get all the pulp. Discard the seeds.

Whisk the buttermilk, simple syrup, lemon juice, and salt into the pulp. Chill for an hour or so.

Follow the instructions that came with your ice cream maker to freeze the sherbet. Scrape it out into a plastic container and pop it into the freezer for at least 2 hours before serving.

credits

The author is grateful for permission to reprint the following recipes:

"Lemonade" and "Dilly Beans" by John Martin Taylor. First published in *Hoppin' John's Charleston, Beaufort & Savannah*, Clarkson Potter/Publishers. Copyright © 1997 by John Taylor. Reprinted by permission of the author.

"Roast Pork" ("Piggy") by Chris Schlesinger and John Willoughby. First published in *Saveur*, July/August 2000, issue 44. Copyright © 2000 by Chris Schlesinger and John Willoughby. Reprinted by permission of the authors.

"Sour Cherry Conserva" by Nick Malgieri. First published in *Great Italian Desserts*, Little, Brown. Copyright © 1990 by Nicholas Malgieri. Reprinted by permission of the author.

"Grape Sorbet." From *Craft of Cooking* by Tom Colicchio, copyright © 2003 by TC Enterprises. Photographs copyright © 2003 by Bill Bettencourt. Used by permission of Clarkson Potter/Publishers, a division of Random House, Inc.

index

Note: Page numbers in **bold** refer to recipe photographs.

C

D

H

M

V

W

Y

Z